THE EFTA COURT IN ACTION

THE EFTA COURT IN ACTION

Five lectures

by

PROF. DR. CARL BAUDENBACHER
President of the EFTA Court
Director of the Institute of European and International
Business Law at the University of St. Gallen
Visiting Professor at the University of Iceland

GLP
German Law Publishers
www.germanlawpublishers.com
International Law Edition

ISBN 978-3-941389-04-5

The Deutsche Nationalbibliothek lists this publication in the Deutsche Nationalbibliografie; detailed bibliographic data are available on the Internet at http://dnb.d-nb.de.

Typesetting: GreenTomato GmbH, Stuttgart
Printing and binding: Kessler Druck + Medien GmbH & Co. KG,
Michael-Schäffer-Straße 1, 86399 Bobingen

Foreword

In international legal theory, it is widely consented that the establishment of the EFTA Court is an important example of judicialisation of international law. Diplomacy was replaced by adjudication as a dispute resolution mechanism. The EEA Agreement is the only association agreement ever concluded by the European Union which allows the associated States to have their own court. It is no exaggeration to state that without the Court the EEA Agreement could not function.

The present publication is based on a series of lectures the author gave at the University of Iceland School of Law in the spring and winter of 2009. The style of delivery has been maintained as far as possible. "Law in action" is meant to be juxtaposed to the "law on the books". This is a distinction that has been introduced by the **legal realists,** a famous American school of thought from the 1920's and the 1930's. It is said that the concept of "law in action" has first been used by *Roscoe Pound*, the Dean of Harvard Law School, in a 1910 article (see Law in Action: The Dean's View – University of Wisconsin Law School, <http://www.law.wisc.edu/law-in-action/davislawinactionessay.html>, last visited on 26 September 2009; concerning Legal Realism see, e.g., *Brian Leitner*, American Legal Realism, The University of Texas School of Law, Public Law and Legal Theory Research Paper No. 042, October 2002).

"Law on the books" means: You must look at what is written in the EEA Agreement, what is written in the ESA Court Agreement and in other relevant instruments. However, what counts at the end of the day is how this is dealt with in reality ("in action") and it may well happen that in reality things take a turn which was not foreseen by the drafters of an agreement or, if we think of domestic law, by the drafters of a national statute or a constitution. But the focus of law in action goes further. It includes the institutional framework of an international agreement, in particular the governments, and in case of the European integration treaties the surveillance agencies. Under the EEA Agreement, the case law of the Court of Justice of the European Union, as it is called now, is of paramount importance. At any rate, law in action looks **beyond the cases**. From that perspective, it may, e.g., count whether a judge is a liberal or a leftist or if a judge is a conservative or a right winger. In European law it may be important whether a judge is favourable vis-à-vis integration or whether he or she is a sovereigntist and a eurosceptic. It may make a difference whether an European judge has in his previous life been a judge in his or her country of origin or a practicing lawyer or a professor or whether a judge has been a politician or a civil servant or a career diplomat throughout his or her life. It may make a difference whether a judge is appointed for lifetime or only for a certain term, probably with the possibility of reappointment.

Like all the other EFTA Court Judges, I have taken an oath to keep the secrecy of the deliberations which, according to common understanding, also covers the secrecy of the vote. In other words, no dissenting opinions can be made public. I do not intend to break that oath. However, I am confident that I will be able to give you some **insight** into the working of the EFTA Court which you hardly get when reading one of the usual textbooks. Of course, this will be the insight of one who has been and is being involved.

I am indebted to Judge *Thorgeir Örlygsson* and Registrar *Skúli Magnússon* from the EFTA Court as well as to my legal secretary *Moritz Am Ende* for having reviewed the manuscript. My administrative assistant *Kerstin Schwiesow* has typed and corrected the text. It goes without saying that I bear sole responsibility for the content of this publication and for any possible mistakes it may contain.[1]

Luxemburg / St. Gallen, January 2010
Carl Baudenbacher

1 Around the time when the manuscript was finalized, the Lisbon Treaty entered into force. This may have a certain impact on the terminology.

Table of Contents

Introduction

The EEA Agreement, which was concluded on 2 May 1992 between the EC and its Member States on the one hand and the EFTA States on the other, provides in Article 108 that the EFTA States shall establish an independent EFTA Surveillance Authority and an EFTA Court of Justice. The Agreement on the Establishment of a Surveillance Authority and a Court of Justice (Surveillance and Court Agreement or ESA/Court Agreement, SCA) was signed on the same day, together with the EEA Agreement.

When going through your class materials, I noticed that you deal with EEA law in **Iceland** and in **Norway**. It is clear that you cannot cover everything, and it is understandable that you look to Norway for many reasons. But there is a third country in the EFTA pillar. It is also important to have a look at what is going on in **Liechtenstein** and it is furthermore crucial to look at what is going on in the EU. The EEA Agreement, as you know, is based on a two pillar model with the EFTA pillar on the one side – thin, but still functional – and the EU pillar on the other side. It is not only based on the principle of homogeneity, but also on the notion of **reciprocity**. There are reciprocity expectations on both sides. Reciprocity as a principle is even laid down in the recitals of the preamble to the EEA Agreement. That means that the EFTA pillar has to live up to the legitimate expectations of the other side, e.g. as regards the effect of EEA law in the legal orders of the EEA/EFTA States and State liability, with respect to the methods of interpretation, with regard to the access to the EFTA Court: is there an equally open access to the EFTA Court as there is to the ECJ in the EC pillar? Nevertheless, I notice that in all the capitals of the EFTA States, in Oslo, in Reykjavík and in Vaduz, there has always been a tendency of looking just at your own situation. That is inappropriate and short-sighted, as it does not cover the whole truth. You have to look to the **other** EEA/EFTA **States**, and you have to look to the **other pillar**. You have to see what is going on in EU law, not only in substantive law but also in procedural law, and I will also talk a bit about the latter.

Lecture 1
The EFTA Court as part of the governance structure of the EEA

A. Overview over the institutions

Observers of EEA law in action have so far mainly focused on the Court and on ESA. The first President of the EFTA Surveillance Authority *Knut Almestad* called the EFTA Court and the EFTA Surveillance Authority "perhaps a bit daringly ... the quintessence of the EEA Agreement"[2]. He was right on that. But there are other players in the game. One must in particular not overlook the role of the governments.

There are three types of institutions under the EEA Agreement: (1) **Community institutions** (in particular the European Commission and the Court of Justice of the European Union), (2) EFTA **institutions** (EFTA Surveillance Authority [ESA]; EFTA Court; Standing Committee of the EFTA States, ESA/Court Committee, EFTA Board of Auditors); (3) EEA **institutions** (EEA Council, EEA Joint Committee, EEA Joint Parliamentary Committee, EEA Consultative Committee). The European Commission, the ECJ, ESA and the EFTA Court will be dealt with extensively in this publication. A word will also be said on the EFTA Board of Auditors.

The highest EEA decision making body is the EEA **Council** which comprises representatives of the EC Commission, the EC Member States and the EEA/EFTA States. It is the main political forum for the EEA conceived by the EEA Agreement. Meeting at the ministerial level, it has the overall political responsibility for the Agreement. Decisions are taken by unanimity (Article 90 EEA). The EEA Council convenes twice a year or whenever the circumstances require so (Article 91 EEA). The Joint Parliamentary Committee is another forum for political dialogue in the EEA, established by Article 95 EEA. It consists of 66 members, half from the European Parliament and half from their colleagues in the EEA/EFTA States' national parliaments, and may express its views in the form of reports or resolutions. Explicitly, it has the task to examine the annual report of the EEA Joint Committee on the functioning and the development of the EEA Agreement, Article 95(4) EEA. Lastly, the EEA Consultative Committee is a consultative body representing the social partners in the EEA States (see Article 96 EEA).

2 [1994–1995] EFTA Court Report 177.

In order to preserve the homogeneity with the EC legal order, the EEA legal order is continuously updated. New Community legislation is incorporated into the EEA Agreement by the EEA **Joint Committee**. The EEA Joint Committee is therefore a "quasi-legislative" link between the Community and the EEA legal order. It is made up of representatives of the Contracting Parties (Article 93[1] EEA, i.e. the EEA/EFTA States, the EC States and the European Commission). Depending on whether the subject at issue concerns a competence of the Community or the Member States within the EU, either the Commission or the EU Member States will speak for the Community. In most cases the ambassadors of the EEA/EFTA States to the Community and representatives of the Commission meet, as most issues relate to the Community as such.

Decisions to incorporate new Community legislation into the EEA Agreement are taken "by agreement" between the Community side, on the one hand, and the EFTA States **speaking with one voice**, on the other (Article 93[2] EEA). The EFTA States coordinate their positions in the Standing Committee of the EFTA States. The decisions of the Standing Committee are made by unanimous vote (Article 6[2] of the Agreement on a Standing Committee of the EFTA States). Thus, in all relevant cases each EEA/EFTA State has a veto right as it may prevent the EFTA side from taking a common position, and thus inhibit the Community and the EFTA side to make a decision "**by agreement**". The EFTA Court held in Case E-6/01 *CIBA v Norwegian State* that such a decision "may constitute a simplified form of an international agreement between the Community and its Member States on the one hand, and the EFTA States party to the EEA Agreement on the other ...". The Court added that "the competence of the EEA Joint Committee is not unlimited. It must, in particular, be exercised within the boundaries of the EEA Agreement and with due respect for essential procedural requirements"[3]. The Court had already given interpretation to two Joint Statements of the EEA Joint Committee in Case E-2/00 *Allied Colloids*[4]. It is quite remarkable that the EFTA Court has the competence to interpret decisions of the EEA Joint Committee since the latter consists not only of the representatives of the EEA/EFTA States, but also of those of the Community and of the EU Member States. As modern **hermeneutics** have revealed, an interpreter will necessarily add something to the text he or she interprets. The EEA Joint Committee has no competence to change the main part of the EEA Agreement no matter whether the TFEU, the text of reference for the EEA Agreement, has been amended. The only institution which may – by way of rendering judgments and thereby establishing case law – "amend" the main part of the EEA Agreement are the EEA Courts: The ECJ, the CFI and the EFTA Court (see infra, lecture 4).

Disagreement relating to the amendment of the Agreement may ultimately lead to the suspension of the affected part of the Agreement (Article 102[5] EEA). This threat

3 [2002] EFTA Court Report 283, at paragraph 33.

4 [2002] EFTA Court Report 35.

has been sufficient to deter all parties from engaging in any conflict concerning the implementation of new *acquis communautaire*.

Another task of the EEA Joint Committee is to **solve disputes** between the Contracting Parties. If the EEA Joint Committee in such a dispute has not reached an agreement on a solution within six months, a Contracting Party may, in order to remedy possible imbalances, either take a safeguard measure or apply Article 102 EEA *mutatis mutandis*. The latter means that the affected part of the Agreement is regarded as provisionally suspended. Pursuant to Article 105 EEA, the EEA Joint Committee shall finally review the case law of the ECJ and of the EFTA Court. In case of a **judicial conflict**, the dispute settlement provisions of the EEA Agreement may ultimately apply. The EFTA Court has always been aware of this threat. However, the EEA Joint Committee can neither incorporate ECJ case law into the EEA Agreement, nor overrule judgments of the EFTA Court.

B. EFTA Court

1. General

As I mentioned, Article 108(2) EEA provides that the EFTA States shall establish a court of justice, the EFTA Court. In order to meet their respective obligation, the EFTA States concluded the Surveillance and Court Agreement.

2. Nomination and appointment of judges

According to Article 30(1) SCA the judges of the EFTA Court shall be appointed by common accord of the governments of the EFTA States. Nomination is done by the individual governments; each government has the right to nominate one judge. In Iceland and in Norway the Ministry of Foreign Affairs takes the respective decision, in Liechtenstein it is the whole government. In practice this system means that the individual governments have in principle the right to decide who will be their judge. After the expiry of their **six year** term, judges may be reappointed. Again, the decision is taken by the governments acting by common accord. Reappointment has normally been a formality once a judge has been renominated by his government. But in one case, reappointment only took place two weeks before the term of office of the judge expired. Since the judge in question had been renominated months before, one can safely assume that his reappointment was blocked by another government.

Article 30(1) SCA further states that the judges shall be chosen from persons whose independence is beyond doubt and who possess the qualifications required for appointment to the **highest judicial offices** in their respective countries **or** who are **jurisconsults** of recognised competence. That provision has been taken over from the ECJ's

Statute. But in substance it essentially follows the Statute of the International Court of Justice whose Article 2 provides that the Court "shall be composed of a body of independent judges, elected regardless of their nationality from among persons of high moral character, who possess the qualifications required in their respective countries for appointment to the highest judicial offices, or are jurisconsults of recognised competence in international law". The first requirement is clear, but the second is not. In the context of the ICJ, the expression "jurisconsult of recognised competence" has been construed as meaning, in particular, that a candidate must be a person who is competent in international law, i.e. who has a **recognised reputation**. This reputation can be the result of academic activity, in particular scholarly writings, or of practice. In the context of the ECJ, the term "jurisconsult" is understood as referring to the holders of a University chair[5]. This must also be deemed as relevant in the EEA context. It is clear that competence in international law does not suffice. EEA law is different from public international law, it comprises both public and private law. That is also why, unlike at the ICJ, diplomatic experience does not confer recognised competence in EEA law[6].

3. Composition

The **five members** of the Court which took office on 1 January 1994, when the EEA Agreement entered into force, were *Leif Sevón* from Finland, *Bjørn Haug* from Norway, *Kurt Herndl* from Austria, *Sven Norberg* from Sweden and *Thór Vilhjálmsson* from Iceland. *Leif Sevón* was elected the Court's first President. He had been a high civil servant in the Finnish administration, a university professor and a judge on the Supreme Court of Finland as well as an EEA negotiator for his country. *Leif Sevón* later became a judge of the Court of Justice of the European Communities and the Chief Justice of Finland. After his appointment to the ECJ, he was replaced by *Gustav Bygglin*, a legal secretary in the Finnish cabinet and a former senior judicial secretary of the Supreme Court of Finland. *Bjørn Haug* had, after a career in an industrial group, been the Regjeringsadvokat of Norway. *Kurt Herndl* had been a high civil servant in the Austrian administration, and an Ambassador as well as an Assistant Secretary-General of the UN Secretariat in Geneva. *Sven Norberg* had, *inter alia*, served as a judge of the Svea Court of Appeal, a director of legal affairs in the EFTA Secretariat and had been a key player in the EEA project being involved in the preparatory works, but also acting as a negotiator and facilitator. *Thór Vilhjálmsson* had been professor of law, Chief Justice of his country and a judge on the European Court of Human Rights. On 30 June 1995, judges Bygglin, Herndl, and Norberg had to resign as a consequence of their countries' accession to the EU on 1 January 1995.

5 See, e.g., L. Neville Brown/Tom Kennedy, The Court of Justice of the European Communities, 5th ed., [2000] London, 49.

6 See with regard to the ICJ Chittharanjan F. Amerasinghe, Judges of the International Court of Justice – Election and Qualifications, [2001] 14 Leiden Journal of International Law, 335 et seq.; Mariano J. Aznar-Gómez, Article 2, in: Andreas Zimmermann/Christian Tomuschat/Karin Oellers-Frahm (eds.), The Statute of the International Court of Justice. A Commentary, [2006] Oxford.

Since 6 September 1995, the Court has consisted of **three judges**. At the time, those were *Bjørn Haug*, *Thór Vilhjálmsson*, and myself. I was nominated by Liechtenstein, although I am a Swiss citizen, but there is no nationality requirement for EFTA Court judges. In my previous professional life, I was an university professor, an arbitrator, the main advisor to the Liechtenstein government during the EEA negotiations and a member of the Liechtenstein Supreme Court. In 1997, *Thór Vilhjálmsson* who had only been appointed for a three years term in 1994[7] was reappointed for another six years. At the end of 1999, *Bjørn Haug*'s term expired, and he was replaced by *Per Tresselt* who had been a civil servant and a diplomat for his country, namely a Deputy Under-Secretary of State in the Ministry of Foreign Affairs, Ambassador to the German Democratic Republic, Consul-General in the united Berlin and Ambassador to Russia. *Thór Vilhjálmsson* was elected President. At the end of 2002, he retired and was replaced by *Thorgeir Örlygsson*, a former law professor at the University of Iceland, judge and Secretary General of the Ministry of Trade and Industry. Judge *Örlygsson's* term was renewed in 2008. I was reappointed in 2001 and in 2007. In 2003, I was elected President and re-elected in 2006 and in 2009. When *Per Tresselt* retired at the end of 2005, *Henrik Bull* took the oath as the new Norwegian judge. He had served as an official in his country's Ministry of Justice and as a negotiator in Norway's EEA and EC accession negotiations before becoming a professor at the University of Oslo.

4. Secrecy of the vote

Like at the ECJ, **no dissenting opinions** can be made public at the EFTA Court. Article 2 of the Court's Statute provides:

"Before taking up his duties each Judge shall, in open court, take an oath to perform his duties impartially and conscientiously and to preserve the secrecy of the deliberations of the Court."

Although this provision only speaks of the secrecy of the deliberations, it is common understanding that it also covers the vote. Dissenting opinions are oppressed, they cannot be made known. This is a system which fundamentally differs from your domestic system. The official explanation is that it **protects** the individual judges from government pressure. In my view, the system is outdated and should be changed[8]. Moreover, in a three members court, it may be difficult at times to keep the secrecy. However, as long as the system of dissenting opinions being oppressed exists, the judges must respect their duty not to speak about the vote. At the end of the day, they have taken an oath to that extent.

---

7 When the Five Members Court took office, three judges were appointed for a six years term and two for a three years term. Who would get six years and who three was decided by lot. The judges of the Three Members Court are all appointed for a six years term.

8 See Vlad Perju, Reason and Authority in the European Court of Justice, [2009] 49 Va. J. Int'l L., 307 et seq.

C. EFTA Surveillance Authority

According to Articles 4 and 7 SCA, an independent EFTA Surveillance Authority consisting of three members who shall be chosen on the grounds of their general competence and whose **independence** is beyond doubt shall be established.

According to Article 9 SCA, the members of the ESA College are appointed by common accord of the governments for a renewable term of office of **four years**. Unlike most members of the European Commission, the members of ESA are not former ministers. The ESA College by majority has always consisted of civil servants and diplomats of the EEA / EFTA States. This is only different in the case of Liechtenstein. Both gentlemen from that country who have so far served as College Members, Dr. *Bernd Hammermann* and *Kurt Jäger*, had previously worked for private corporations. Many of the College Members from Iceland and from Norway served as their country's ambassadors to the European Union before being appointed to the ESA College. In that capacity, they had also been members of the ESA / Court Committee.

Unlike the president of the Court, the **president** of ESA is being appointed by the governments (Article 12 SCA). Except for a short period of time from January 2004 to 7 August 2005 when *Hannes Hafstein* from Iceland served as president, ESA has always been headed by its Norwegian member. *Hafstein* had been the chief negotiator of Iceland during the EEA negotiations and had served as an ambassador of his country to the European Communities (and was as such a member of the ESA / Court Committee). He died in office on 7 August 2005[9]. The Norwegian government, which bears 89 % of the costs of the EEA, has apparently found it appropriate to have one of its own heading the EFTA Surveillance Authority during all these years. Just as a side remark: According to Article 30 SCA, the president of the Court is elected by the judges. This does not, however, mean that governments have not tried to influence the Court's presidential elections. I could further elaborate on that, but will limit myself to saying that such attempts did not succeed.

ESA plays an important role in the Court's life. According to Articles 108(2) EEA and 31 SCA, it may **bring lawsuits** against EEA/EFTA States for non-compliance with their obligations under the EEA Agreement. ESA may also be a defendant in **nullity actions** brought by EEA / EFTA States or natural or legal persons under Articles 108(2) EEA and 36 SCA. If it is not a party, ESA participates in all the Court's cases by submitting **written and oral observations** under Articles 20 of the Court's Statute and 97(1) of the Rules of Procedure.

9 The Icelandic government had, however, decided not to re-nominate him before, so that his term would have expired by the end of that year.

D. European Commission

The European Commission is an influential player in the governance structure of the EEA. In addition to representing the Community in the EEA Joint Committee (in most cases), it has submitted **written and oral observations** in every case dealt with by the EFTA Court under Articles 20 of the Court's Statute and 97(1) of the Rules of Procedure. It is to be noted in this context that the EFTA Court does not have an Advocate General. The Commission has from the beginning seen its role in the court proceedings as some sort of a replacement for an Advocate General. It is in fact of utmost importance that the Commission shows up in every case. It thereby makes a contribution to securing homogeneity of the case law in the EEA and on certain occasions it constitutes a counterweight to governments. But one must not overlook that the Commission often pursues its own agenda. In some major cases, the Court has not followed the suggestions of the Commission. Finally, it appears that ESA would, before bringing a major case to the Court, in one form or the other seek the advice of the Commission.

E. ESA/Court Committee

The ESA/Court Committee is the body within which the EEA/EFTA States exercise their functions under the SCA. It consists of the EU **ambassadors** of the three EEA/EFTA States. The Committee has no legal basis in the SCA and you should not think of it as some sort of independent international body. The Committee fulfills the tasks assigned to the governments under the SCA, its members act upon instruction from the Member States. It is in particular responsible for the approval of the budget and the financial statement of ESA and of the Court. It also deals, e.g., with amendments to the Staff rules and regulations, the Court's Statute and its Rules of Procedure in as far as the States have a say. The chairmanship in the Committee is rotating every six months.

F. EFTA Board of Auditors (EBOA)

Unlike in the EU, there is no independent Court of Auditors in EFTA. An EFTA Board of Auditors was established in May 1992. In the EEA context, it is responsible for the performance of the annual financial audit of ESA and of the Court. The audit itself has, however, been outsourced to a private auditing firm. Every EEA/EFTA State is represented by one of its nationals on the EBOA. The members are civil servants of the EEA/EFTA **governments** and each of them is on the payroll of the government which has appointed him or her. In 1994, EBOA was chaired by a Norwegian, from 1995 to 2002 by an Icelander, and since 2003 again by a Norwegian.

The **Mandate** of EBOA is as follows: The Board shall act as the supreme authority for the auditing of ESA and the Court as required by and in accordance with the Financial Regulations of each institution. The scope of EBOA's activities shall be, in the context of "good governance", to verify the legality, regularity, economy, efficiency and effectiveness of financial management of each institution's activities. In doing so, EBOA shall observe the independent position and mandate of ESA and the Court vis-à-vis the EFTA States, as well as the mandate of the ESA/Court Committee itself[10].

EBOA has had difficulties to stay within its mandate and to comply with its rules of procedure. Occasionally, the temptation to deal with issues that had nothing to do with financial management became too strong for EBOA to resist. In fact, when dealing with the auditors, I have sometimes been reminded of the Roman poet *Juvenal's* phrase "*Quis custodiet ipsos custodes?*"[11] which could be translated into English as "Who will guard the guards themselves?" Be that as it may. But what makes the situation unacceptable is the fact that unlike the EU Court of Auditors, EBOA is not a truly independent body. Although ESA/Court Committee Decision No 5/2002 on the Mandate of EBOA (at three) prescribes in Article 6 that EBOA "shall establish its own annual budget for the audits of the EFTA Surveillance Authority and the EFTA Court", this was never done. There is **no transparency** with regard to the costs of the auditing mechanism and to the origin of the means that are put at EBOA's disposal. Some two years ago, EBOA decided to create its own "resource group" consisting of an Icelander and a Norwegian. It is neither known on what legal basis this was done, nor who bears the costs of this new group. It is also unclear what the group's tasks are. Finally, one member of EBOA who was appointed to the Board by the ESA/Court Committee in 2002 has since that year been a Director and since 2005 the Chairman of the Financial Market Authority of his country. The Financial Market Authority in question is, *inter alia*, responsible for the preparation of the implementation of EEA secondary law in the country concerned. It also acts as administrative authority interpreting and applying EEA law. The other EBOA members as well as the governments knew about this ongoing conflict of interest. In autumn of 2009, the Court heard two cases in which the Financial Market Authority of the country in question was involved in its capacity as the body that prepares the implementation of secondary EEA law and applies implemented secondary EEA law by way of decision on applications of financial market operators. The Court considered whether it ought to recuse itself *en banc*, but after having received a declaration by the government concerned that the gentleman in question would step down from his position in EBOA, it decided not to do that[12].

10 See Decision of the ESA/Court Committee No 5/2002 of 23 October 2002 on the Mandate of the EFTA Board of Auditors ("at three").

11 Juvenal, Satire 6, 346 et seq.

12 E-1/09 ESA v Liechtenstein, judgement of 6 January 2010, nyr.; E-4/09 Inconsult Anstalt v Finanzmarktaufsicht, judgement of 27 January 2010, nyr.

Lecture 2
Access to the EFTA Court

A. Overview

Article 108(2) EEA provides:

> *"The EFTA States shall establish a court of justice (EFTA Court). The EFTA Court shall, in accordance with a separate agreement between the EFTA States, with regard to the application of this Agreement be competent, in particular, for: (a) actions concerning the surveillance procedure regarding the EFTA States; (b) appeals concerning decisions in the field of competition taken by the EFTA Surveillance Authority; (c) the settlement of disputes between two or more EFTA States."*

These types of action have been further elaborated on in the SCA. Moreover, the SCA contains provisions on a preliminary reference procedure and a procedure for failure to act. For the sake of order, I must mention that so far there has not been a case under Article 108 (2) (c) EEA.

The three most important types of procedure of the EFTA Court are the infringement procedure (ESA vs. an EEA/EFTA State), the preliminary reference procedure, and the nullity procedure. They are essentially taken from EC law, but there are certain differences.

B. The infringement procedure (ESA vs. an EEA/EFTA State)

1. General

The provisions regarding the infringement procedure are laid down in the EEA Agreement itself, Article 108 (2) (a) and, in more concrete terms, in Article 31 of the Surveillance and Court Agreement. This provision states:

> *"If the EFTA Surveillance Authority considers that an EFTA State has failed to fulfil an obligation under the EEA Agreement or of this Agreement, it shall, un-*

> *less otherwise provided for in this Agreement, deliver a reasoned opinion on the matter after giving the State concerned the opportunity to submit its observations. If the State concerned does not comply with the opinion within the period laid down by the EFTA Surveillance Authority, the latter may bring the matter before the EFTA Court."*

The provision is essentially identical in substance to Article 258 TFEU (ex Article 226 EC). There is, however, no article in EEA law mirroring Article 260 TFEU (ex Article 228 [2] EC). A non-complying EEA/EFTA State cannot be imposed a penalty payment.

2. ESA's policy

Five questions are of particular importance when dealing with ESA's record in the application of Article 31 SCA.

(1) What is ESA's general policy in bringing cases? Is ESA active or passive? Is ESA giving governments a lot of leeway?

(2) What is ESA's policy if it has opened a case and a court of an EEA/EFTA State makes a reference on the same legal question? Will ESA then pursue the case or drop it?

(3) What is ESA's policy if it has opened a case and learns that the legal question which is at stake will be dealt with by the ECJ in a case involving EU law which is identical in substance to EEA law?

(4) What is ESA's policy if it has opened a case and a court of last resort of an EEA/EFTA State subsequently finds that there is no infringement? Will ESA then pursue the case or drop it?

(5) What is ESA's policy in cases in which a national court of last resort has refused to make a reference although the EEA law situation is not clear? Would ESA then say "something is rotten in the State of Denmark"?

The following **propositions** may be considered:

(1) The answer to question 1 is rather clear. ESA is openly **less active** than the European Commission in bringing cases. In total, ESA brought 33 cases to the Court since 1994. If we subtract the 19 cases of non-contested failure of timely implementation of secondary law, the number drops to 14. That is less than one case a year. To put these numbers into perspective: Until the end of 2008, the Commission brought in total 206 infringement actions against the three countries having left EFTA for the EC shortly after the establishment of the EEA, i.e. Austria (114), Finland (47) and Sweden

(45)[13]. The ratio between "substantial" and non-contested infringement cases seems to be comparable in the EU. ESA admits that it is not eager to bring cases. It is following a **moral suasion approach** trying to convince the governments that they ought to comply with their obligations under the EEA Agreement. In ESA's own words: "To the extent possible, the Authority endeavours to solve all matters by informal means, through contacts with the national administrations concerned. Formal infringement proceedings are opened only where an informal exchange of views fails to solve the problem at hand."[14]

European Voice, the weekly magazine which is much read in Brussels had an article on this in October 2008 under the heading "Are national interests weakening the EFTA Court?" It suggested that there may be another explanation, namely that ESA College Members, unlike the EC Commissioners, are former civil servants from the Member States who often **go back** to the Member States or to a new post in the Member States' diplomatic service after having finished their term in Brussels[15]. In fact, even some of the College Presidents have returned to government service in the country they came from after their time at ESA. To give an example, *Bjørn T. Grydeland*, a political scientist by training, was Permanent Under-Secretary of State before being appointed Norwegian ambassador to the European Union in 2001. In this capacity, he also served as a member of the ESA/Court Committee. From the beginning of 2006 to August of 2007, he was the President of ESA before being appointed Secretary General in the Foreign Ministry of his country. The Secretary General is the highest ranking civil servant in the Foreign Ministry. His appointment to the post in Oslo was publicly announced more than half a year before his term as President of ESA expired. I will not further comment, but you are free to draw your own conclusions.

(2) If ESA has opened a case and a national court in the EEA/EFTA State concerned makes a reference to the Court, ESA will normally stay the proceedings and submit observations in these reference proceedings. An example of this is the Liechtenstein **Single Practice Rule** case. On 10 April 2000, ESA delivered a reasoned opinion in accordance with Article 31 SCA to the Government of the Principality of Liechtenstein concluding that "by preventing nationals having a practice in another EEA State from establishing themselves as doctors or dentists in Liechtenstein, Liechtenstein has failed to fulfil its obligations under Article 31 of the EEA Agreement on freedom of establishment". Liechtenstein was given two months to comply with the reasoned opinion[16]. On 13 June 2000, the Liechtenstein Administrative Court referred three cases to the

13 Cf. Annual Report of the ECJ 2008, 113, available online at http://curia.europa.eu/jcms/jcms/Jo2_7000/ (last visited on 28 July 2009).

14 EEA/EFTA States Internal Market Scoreboard February 2009, 12 (The EEA/EFTA Internal Market Scoreboards are available online at http://www.eftasurv.int/information/internalmarket/, last visited on 19 November 2009).

15 European Voice of 16 October 2008, 20. Available online at <http://www.europeanvoice.com/article/imported/are-national-interests-weakening-the-efta-court-/62709.aspx> (last visited on 27 November 2009).

16 Dec. No. 73/00/COL.

EFTA Court in which it asked whether the Single Practice Rule was compatible with Article 31 EEA[17]. ESA then submitted observations in all three cases, but did not bring an action against Liechtenstein.

(3) The policy in question is, however, not limited to preliminary reference proceedings before the EFTA Court. If ESA has opened infringement proceedings and becomes aware that the legal question at stake will be dealt with by the ECJ in a case involving EU law which is identical in substance to EEA law, it may, as experience shows, stay its own proceedings and submit observations under Articles 20(3) or 40(3) of the ECJ's Statute. In other words ESA and the Contracting Party concerned may decide to resolve their dispute by means of taking a "free-ride" on the ECJ's preliminary ruling procedure. This may be seen as a particularly bold case of ESA's general low-profile strategy of avoiding open confrontation with the EEA / EFTA States' governments. To give some examples: The Governments of Norway and Iceland as well as ESA pleaded in Case C-341/05 *Laval*, a matter which involved the question of whether EU law could restrict labour unions from taking industrial action[18]. Of course, in this particular case the reason may also just have been that the proceedings involved issues of general interest: *Laval* was probably the most important case decided in 2007, and 15 governments of EU-Member States pleaded as well. But things were definitely different in C-170/04 *Rosengren and Others*[19], a case on the legality of the Swedish prohibition of import of alcoholic beverages by private individuals, where both ESA and the Norwegian government pleaded. Indeed, a similar rule existed in Norway, and ESA had issues with it[20]. With respect to C-42/02 *Lindman*[21], a case on the taxation of winnings from games of chance which had been referred by a Finnish court, one wonders finally what other reason than "silent conflict settlement" might have induced both ESA and the Government of Norway to plead before the ECJ. Norway had comparable legislation in force before the Lindman ruling which had been the object of discussions with ESA [22]. Similar considerations are likely to have been decisive in C-223/01 *AstraZeneca v Lægemiddelstyrelsen*[23], a case relating to marketing authorisations of generic medicinal products. It even seems that ESA is prepared to procrastinate bringing a lawsuit upon the request of a government which argues that a parallel case is pending before the ECJ.

As a result, one may conclude that ESA indeed prefers the "indirect" method of participating in preliminary reference proceedings before the EFTA Court or before the European Court of Justice over bringing infringement actions on its own.

---

17 Cases E-4/00 Dr Johann Brändle, E-5/00 Dr Josef Mangold, E-6/00 Dr Jürgen Tschanett, [2000–2001] EFTA Court Report 123, 163 and 203; see also infra, lecture 3.

18 Case C-341/05 Laval un Partneri Ltd v Svenska Byggnadsarbetareförbundet and Others [2007] ECR I-11767.

19 Case C-170/04 Klas Rosengren and Others v Riksåklagaren [2007] ECR I-4071.

20 Cf. ESA Annual Report 2004, p. 26.

21 Case C-42/02 Diana Elisabeth Lindman [2003] ECR I-13519.

22 Cf. ESA Annual Report 2006, p. 22.

23 Case C-223/01 AstraZeneca A/S v Lægemiddelstyrelsen [2003] ECR I-11809.

(4) If a court of last resort of an EEA/EFTA State finds that there is no infringement, ESA may drop the case. An important example is the Liechtenstein **Security for Costs** saga. On 4 July 2001, ESA delivered a reasoned opinion in accordance with Article 31 SCA to the Government of the Principality of Liechtenstein stating that "by maintaining the rule provided in Article 57, paragraph 1, of the Law on Civil Proceedings [...] according to which natural plaintiffs not resident in Liechtenstein and having no chargeable assets in that country may be asked to furnish security for costs in court proceedings if the defendant so requests, where no such requirement can be imposed on natural plaintiffs residing in that State in the same circumstances, Liechtenstein has failed to fulfil its obligations under Articles 3 and 4 of the EEA Agreement". Liechtenstein was given three months to comply with the reasoned opinion[24]. On 17 January 2003, the Liechtenstein State Court confirmed its case law according to which the rules in question of Liechtenstein law were compatible with the EEA Agreement[25]. After this, ESA did not pursue the case although it was quite clear to most observers that the legal situation in Liechtenstein was untenable. I will come back to that case later.

With the Liechtenstein *Helplessness Allowance* case, there is an important exception to the policy just described. But the circumstances were somewhat special, as I will explain.

(5) If a court of last resort of an EFTA State has **refused to make a reference**, this will, as a rule, not have any consequences. Exceptionally, ESA may bring a direct action if the case in its view is important enough. There are two examples for that:

One is the *Gaming Machines* case E-1/06 which concerned the compatibility of the newly introduced Norwegian state monopoly for the operation of one-armed bandits, so-called gaming machines[26]. ESA had opened an investigation upon complaints from private operators and at the same time the case was tried through the Norwegian judiciary. In October 2004, ESA issued a reasoned opinion; some days later, the Oslo City Court found the monopoly to be contrary to EEA law. In August 2005, this judgment was overruled by the Court of Appeal, and the matter was brought before the Norwegian Supreme Court. The Norwegian government urged the Supreme Court not to refer the case, but to keep it in the country. Who reads the Norwegian language? Few people do. Keeping the case in the country means to a certain extent keeping it **out of the lime light**. If the case goes to Luxembourg, the European Commission will appear and Member States from the EFTA side and from the EU side may participate. The fact that the case has been referred to the EFTA Court will be made public in the Official Journal of the European Union.

24 Dec. No. 239/01/COL.
25 Judgment of the State Court of 17 February 2003, StGH 2002/37 (LES 2005, 145).
26 Case E-1/06 Gaming Machines [2007] EFTA Court Report 7.

Allow me a side remark: Unfortunately, this has not been the only case in which government officials have tried to convince a national court to **refrain from making a reference** to the Court. What a commentator wrote in 1985 in a general international law context has therefore some truth when it comes to the functioning of the EFTA pillar: "The nature of decisions which can be referred by national courts to international jurisdictions are commonly delicate and sensitive ones … and thus states may be tempted to put pressure on local national courts to avoid such references. This, in turn, would logically neutralize the effectiveness of international courts by starving them of work …"[27].

Back to the *Gaming Machines* case. At the end, when even the Norwegian Supreme Court refused to make a reference, ESA stepped in and brought an infringement action. The Appeals Committee of the Supreme Court which had decided against the reference then decided by two votes against one to **postpone** the case until the Court had ruled on it. The Committee had discussed the case in a meeting with other justices of the Supreme Court, and there had been divided opinions amongst the justices[28].

On closer inspection, one must, however, conclude that ESA's attitude in *Gaming Machines* was not that different from other cases. It seems quite clear that ESA had hoped that one of the three courts involved would bring the matter to the EFTA Court by way of a **preliminary reference**. In that regard, I may mention once more that ESA so far has not brought an infringement action to the EFTA Court in a case where, after it had opened an infringement procedure, a court of last resort had stated that EEA law is not infringed.

The second example is the Liechtenstein *Helplessness Allowance* case E-5/06[29]. That is one of the most important matters the Court has ever decided. I am rather sure you never heard about it because your focus is on Iceland and Norway which, as I said, is understandable at first sight, but I am here to correct that a bit. All the wealthy countries in the European Economic Area, whether on the EC side or on the EFTA side, provide such allowances. That is a payment made to people who are helpless, it is – at least in Liechtenstein – not dependent on them having paid in (i.e. **non-contributory**) and it comes in addition to sickness and old age benefits. If someone is unable to dress without assistance, to go to the bathroom without assistance and the like, then he or she is entitled to receive this helplessness allowance. All the countries made payment dependent on **residence**, also Liechtenstein. In Liechtenstein there are thousands of commuters from Austria crossing the border every day. And at the end of their active life they spend their old age in Austria. The Liechtenstein government **denied** them payment of helplessness allowance. One of these Austrians brought a case and took it to the Supreme

27 Louis-Edmond Pettiti, Independence of International Judges, in: Shimon Shetreet and Jules Dechênes (eds.), Judicial Independence, Dordrecht/Boston/Lancaster 1985, 496.

28 Order of the Appeals Committee of the Høyesterett of 5 December 2005 in HR-2005-01895-U (Case Number 2005/1320).

29 Case E-5/06 Helplessness Allowance [2007] EFTA Court Report 295.

Administrative Court. The Supreme Administrative Court claimed that the provision at stake constituted *acte clair*, i.e. that the legal situation was clear and unambiguous[30]. It **refused to make a reference** to the EFTA Court although the Austrian applicant had asked for it and on 12 February 2003, it ruled against the applicant[31]. The Court was therefore prevented from ruling on the case. In November 2003, ESA received a complaint and subsequently started infringement proceedings. In April 2005, it issued a letter of formal notice and delivered a reasoned opinion in March 2006. In November 2006, ESA brought the matter before the Court. The Court found in favour of ESA.

This case has a peculiar background. Rumour has it that ESA did not only act on its own initiative when it decided to sue Liechtenstein. There are indications that the Commission told ESA to go after that country. Not so much because tiny Liechtenstein was so important to the Commission, but because the same provisions which are part of EEA law (and which have been taken from EC law), namely Regulation 1408/71, are also part of the bilateral **Free Movement of Persons Agreement** concluded between Switzerland and the European Union in 1999. In other words, Regulation 1408/71 is valid in three different contexts, in supranational EC law, in EEA law and in classic international law. What the Commission wanted was ESA to obtain a victory against Liechtenstein, but what it probably really sought was to have a precedent und thereby an argument to go after **Switzerland**. The Swiss Supreme Court had, like the Liechtenstein Supreme Administrative Court, held in a judgment of 24 July 2006 that helplessness allowances need not be exported. Under the bilateral Free Movement of Persons Agreement, the Supreme Court is bound to follow old ECJ case law. The Court argued that there was no old ECJ case law[32]. The Commission may one day take the judgment of the EFTA Court and ask for an amendment of the Free Movement of Persons Agreement with the consequence that the Swiss too will have to pay the helplessness allowance to all the Italians, the French and the Austrians who spent their working life in the country as commuters and now live in their countries of origin.

3. Some remarks

ESA's policy has led to certain successes. However, whether it puts enough pressure on the governments of the EEA/EFTA States to comply with their obligations under the Agreement in a timely manner is debatable.

---

30 In its 1982 judgment in C-283/81 CILFIT v Italian Ministry of Health [1982] ECR 3415, 3430, the ECJ has qualified the obligation of EC courts of last resort to refer matters for preliminary rulings by recognising the acte clair doctrine. Under this approach, national courts or tribunals in the sense of the third paragraph of Article 267 TFEU (ex Article 234 EC) need not refer a case where the question of Community law is relevant to the outcome of the case and there is no previous judgment of the ECJ on the point of law if "the correct application of Community law is so obvious as to leave no scope for any reasonable doubt as to the manner in which the question raised is to be resolved" (paragraph 21).

31 See the reference in Case E-5/06 ESA v Liechtenstein [2007] EFTA Court Report 295, at paragraph 3.

32 ATF 132 V 423.

Firstly, there have been cases in which ESA's attempts to find a solution *à l'amiable* **have taken years**. This can come at the expense of the main beneficiaries of the EEA Agreement: **individuals and economic operators**. In the early days, ESA seems to have been inclined to wait patiently as long as governments maintained that the necessary implementation measures were imminent. In Case E-5/01 *ESA v Liechtenstein*, the Principality of Liechtenstein should have had informed ESA about the implementation of Council Directive 87/344/EEC on the coordination of laws, regulations and administrative provisions relating to legal expenses insurance by 1 May 1995. ESA finally lodged an application with the Court on 27 April 2001[33]. In recent years, the following cases may be mentioned: In the *Finnmark* case (E-3/05), ESA had received a complaint in April 1999, sent a letter of formal notice in October 2000, a supplementary letter of formal notice in December 2003, issued a reasoned opinion in July 2004 and brought Norway before the Court in April 2005. ESA finally lost the case[34]. In E-1/05 *Life insurances*, ESA opened proceedings on its own initiative in December 2000, sent a letter of formal notice in April 2003, a reasoned opinion in July 2003 and brought the application to the Court in January 2005[35]. In E-1/03 *Flight taxation*, proceedings were opened on ESA's initiative in April 1998, a letter of formal notice was sent in December 1998 and a reasoned opinion in September 1999. Iceland then promised to put a new bill to Parliament in October 2002, 3 years later. ESA sued only in January 2003, after not having received any new information[36]. In E-2/06, the *Norwegian Waterfalls* case, again infringement proceedings were opened on ESA's own initiative in March 2001, a letter of formal notice was sent in June 2001 and a reasoned opinion was issued in February 2002. No application to the Court was made because the Norwegian government signaled its willingness to amend the legislation. After a change of government in April 2006, ESA brought the case before the Court in the same month[37].

Secondly, it is doubtful whether ESA's approach is able to provide sufficient guidance for the EEA/EFTA States and for private operators. Deals cut behind closed doors do not produce any effect beyond the case at hand. This is bad for **legal certainty** and **predictability**.

Thirdly, the question arises whether the policy at issue takes sufficient account of the fact that the courts of the EEA/EFTA States, and in particular the supreme courts, are **less active** in referring cases to Luxembourg than their counterparts in most EU countries.

Fourthly, the Court may be prevented from answering legal questions also in cases in which the well-understood interests of individuals and economic operators require such clarification. The EEA Agreement is an important example of what in legal theory

33 [2000–2001] EFTA Court Report 287.
34 [2006] EFTA Court Report 101.
35 [2005] EFTA Court Report 234.
36 [2003] EFTA Court Report 143.
37 [2007] EFTA Court Report 163.

has been called the judicialisation of international law. Diplomacy is thereby largely replaced as a dispute resolution mechanism by adjudication[38]. ESA's policy gives preference to diplomacy and weakens adjudication. This may go against the very **essence of the Agreement**.

Fifthly: The Court's own experience shows that its contributions to the development of the case law of the Union Courts are highly appreciated **in the Union**. The same could be true in the case of ESA.

Finally: ESA's policy to drop its own proceedings once there is a case pending before the ECJ involving EC law which is identical in substance to the EEA law in question calls for (at least) one additional comment: To my best knowledge there are **no judges from the EEA / EFTA** countries sitting on the ECJ.

C. The preliminary reference procedure

1. General

The preliminary reference procedure is not mentioned in the EEA Agreement. Article 34 SCA provides:

> *"The EFTA Court shall have jurisdiction to give advisory opinions on the interpretation of the EEA Agreement. Where such a question is raised before any court or tribunal in an EFTA State, that court or tribunal may, if it considers it necessary to enable it to give judgment, request the EFTA Court to give such an opinion. An EFTA State may in its internal legislation limit the right to request such an advisory opinion to courts or tribunals against whose decisions there is no judicial remedy under national law."*

The provision has to a large part been modelled on the template of Article 267 TFEU (ex Article 234 EC).

Similarly to the ECJ, the Court has dealt with **important cases** under the preliminary reference procedure. I may just mention the judgments concerning effect, State liability and fundamental rights[39], but also rulings on the four fundamental freedoms, on competition law and on important questions of secondary law[40]. The question is, however, whether the right cases have come before the Court.

---

38 See, e.g., Cesare P. Romano, The Proliferation of International Judicial Bodies: The Pieces of the Puzzle, [1999] 31 N.Y.U. J. Int'l L. & Pol. 709 et seq.

39 With regard to fundamental rights, see infra, lecture 4.

40 See Carl Baudenbacher, EFTA Court – Legal framework and case law, 3rd ed., 2008, http://www.efta-court.int/images/uploads/Legal_Framework_Finalweb.pdf (last visited on 16 November 2009).

2. Notion of court or tribunal

Under the six-factor test usually applied by the ECJ when interpreting Article 267 TFEU (ex Article 234 EC), to constitute a "court or tribunal" within the meaning of that provision, the referring body must (1) be established by law, (2) be permanent, (3) have compulsory jurisdiction, (4) conduct inter-partes procedures, (5) apply rules of law and evidence, and (6) be independent[41]. The Court gave a broad interpretation of what qualifies as a court or tribunal in E-1/94 *Restamark*, where the *Tullilautakunta*, an appeal body that appeared to be linked closely to the Finnish customs administration, was held to constitute a court despite the fact that **no adversarial procedure** takes place before that authority[42].

It is quite obvious that with the *Restamark* judgment the Court wanted to give individuals and economic operators **broad access to justice**. As I said before, it was the Court's very first case, and it was a beautiful case. In fact the EFTA Court was more liberal than the ECJ at the time, but the ECJ adopted the same approach in its later judgments in C-54/96 *Dorsch Consult*[43] and in Joined Cases C-110/98 to C-147/98 *Gabalfrisa*[44]. The Court confirmed its approach in two judgments with regard to the *Norwegian Marketsradet*, Joined Cases E-8/94 and E-9/94 *Mattel/Lego*[45] and Case E-4/04 *Pedicel*[46] as well as in a case with regard to the *Liechtenstein Appeals Commission of the Financial Market Authority*[47].

3. Admissibility of a request for a preliminary ruling and of the questions of a national court

The Court also was quite liberal when giving judgment on the admissibility of a request for a preliminary ruling and of questions by national courts. In the early years, governments frequently argued that certain questions should be deemed not admissible. The Court held repeatedly that the national court, which alone has direct knowledge of the facts of the case, is in the best position to appreciate, with full knowledge of the matter before it, the necessity for a preliminary ruling to enable it to give a judgment[48]. But it is not for the Court to give opinions on general or hypothetical questions[49]. Again, let me add a remark from the perspective of Legal Realism, as a marginal note so to speak:

41 See, e.g., Case C-393/92 Municipality of Almelo and Others v. Energiebedrijf IJsselmij NV [1994] ECR I-1477, at paragraph 21.

42 Case E-1/94 Restamark [1994-1995] EFTA Court Report 15.

43 Case C-54/96 Dorsch Consult [1997] ECR I-4961.

44 Joined Cases C-110/98 to C-147/98 Gabalfrisa [2000] ECR I-1577.

45 Joined Cases E-8/94 and E-9/94 Mattel/Lego [1994–1995] EFTA Court Report 113.

46 Case E-4/04 Pedicel [2005] EFTA Court Report 1.

47 Case E-4/09 Inconsult Anstalt, judgement of 27 January 2010, nyr

48 See, e.g., Cases E-1/95 Samuelsson [1994-1995] EFTA Court Report 145, and E-5/96 Nille, 1997 EFTA Court Report, 30, at paragraph 12.

49 See, e.g., Case E-6/96 Wilhelmsen [1997] EFTA Court Report 53.

If you are not overloaded, and we are not, then why should we throw out cases if the situation is not crystal clear?

4. Special elements of Article 34 SCA

There are three major differences between Articles 267 TFEU (ex Article 234 EC) and 34 SCA. (1) The wording of Article 34 SCA does not indicate that any court is legally obliged to make a reference to the Court. (2) The rulings of the Court are, according to the wording of Article 34 SCA, not legally binding. (3) The right to make a reference may be limited by the national legislature.

Legal situation of the courts of last resort

The supreme and constitutional courts of the EEE / EFTA states are of the view that they are **completely free** in deciding whether to make a reference or not. To be sure, we have received references from Supreme Courts, two from Iceland, three from Norway, five from the Liechtenstein Supreme Administrative Court, and one reference in the early days from the Swedish Supreme Court. However, not a single reference was made by the Liechtenstein Supreme Court and by the Liechtenstein State Court. And we hear of cases decided by courts of last resort in other countries which would have deserved to be referred.

The interpretation given to Article 34 SCA by the supreme courts has two consequences: (1) Cases which should have been referred have not been referred. (2) Since the highest courts are not setting a good example, the lower courts are not eager to refer either. Certain lower courts tend to say the supreme court can refer at the end of the day. They thus shift the responsibility to the supreme court and in small countries, as you easily imagine, supreme court judges and members of government are sometimes rather close to each other. This is unsatisfactory. The judicial system in the EFTA pillar as a whole must be able to deliver the **same results** with regard to the protection of individuals and economic operators as the judicial system in the EC. This is clearly set out in the recitals of the preamble to the EEA Agreement and in the recitals to the ESA Court Agreement. I would also use the famous "as long as" way of argument with which you are familiar from many cases. As long as ESA is not able to guarantee these results by making more frequent use of the infringement procedure, one will have to assume that the courts of last resort should refer. We have seen that ESA is rather passive. And the supreme courts are not very active either. Therefore, how on earth should the cases come to the Court that deserve to come to the Court? *Skúli Magnússon*, an assistant professor at this University and the Registrar of the EFTA Court, has argued that it follows from the principle of loyalty laid down in article 3 EEA that **someone in the system** must refer, even if Article 34 SCA does not impose that obligation on any specific court[50]. Since Article 34 SCA does not distinguish between courts of last resort and lower courts, one could even say that all courts of the EEA/EFTA States should refer. Whether you assume the existence of a direct legal obligation or an *obligation de résultat* is not decisive.

Not only the supreme courts, but also **most commentators** have concluded from the wording of Article 34 SCA, that the supreme courts are free to decide whether to refer or not to refer[51]. This is a mistake, and I admit that I made this mistake as well. We were all too much focused on the ESA/Court Agreement and did not take into account the EEA Agreement when interpreting the types of action which exist in EEA law. It was *Skúli Magnússon* who came up with a new approach. In a lecture given in the Spring 2009 in Reykjavík he took the view that that the types of action as regulated in the ESA/Court Agreement must be interpreted **in light of the** EEA **Agreement**. That the preliminary reference procedure is not explicitly mentioned in the EEA Agreement does not mean that it must not be interpreted that way.

Legal nature of the EFTA Court's rulings

The fact that, strictly speaking, the rulings of the Court are not legally binding has no negative consequences on homogeneity and reciprocity. A national court which makes a reference to the Court will tend to follow the latter's ruling. If it were to refuse to do so, it would bring the EEA/EFTA State concerned into a situation of breach of the EEA Agreement[52]. Supreme courts of the EEA/EFTA States have rendered important judgments concerning the value of the Court's opinions for the decision of the case before them. The Supreme Courts of Norway and of Iceland have made it clear that, inspite of the lack of a formally binding nature of the Court's rulings rendered under Article 34 SCA, they will **not normally depart** from them. A leading commentator said that the Supreme Court of Norway "has set the requirements to diverge from these opinions so strictly, that it in practice amounts to an obligation to follow them"[53]. In Iceland, the situation appears to be comparable[54]. The Supreme Administrative Court of Liechtenstein has in every case strictly followed the EFTA Court's opinion[55]. One

---

50 Skúli Magnússon, Málskot ákvarðana um að leita ráðgefandi álits EFTA-dómstólsins frá sjónarhóli EES-réttar, Úlfljótur, 1. ed. [2009], 5, 14-15.

51 See, e.g., Stefán Már Stefánsson, State Liability in Community Law and EEA Law, in: Carl Baudenbacher/Per Tresselt/Thorgeir Örlygsson (eds.), The EFTA Court Ten Years On, [2005] Oxford and Portland, Oregon, 145, 155.

52 See Henrik Bull, The EEA Agreement and Norwegian Law, [1994] E.B.L.Rev., 291, 296.

53 Hans Petter Graver, EEA, Supremacy and the Liquidity of Law – does EU Law Trump the Norwegian Constitution?, ARENA Working Papers, 2005, 5 <http://www.arena.uio.no/news/news2005/Arena%20Conference%20Nov05/Graver.pdf> (last visited on 20 November 2009).

54 See Thorgeir Örlygsson, Iceland and the EFTA Court, Twelve Years of Experience, in: Mario Monti, Prinz Nikolaus von und zu Liechtenstein, Bo Vesterdorf, Jay Westbrook (eds.), Economic Law and Justice in Times of Globalisation, Festschrift for Carl Baudenbacher, [2007] Baden-Baden/Berne/Vienna, 225, 234/

55 See the article by the Court's President, Andreas Batliner, Die Anwendung des EWR-Rechts durch liechtensteinische Gerichte – Erfahrungen eines Richters, Liechtensteinische Juristen-Zeitung 4/04, 139, 140.

must finally not overlook that judgments of the EFTA Court rendered under Article 34 SCA are being regarded as a source of inspiration by the Union courts in no other way than judgments rendered in direct actions (see infra, lecture 5).

That means that the rulings of the EFTA Court under Article 34 SCA are **not just advisory**. They are of a *sui generis* nature like the whole EEA Agreement, as the Court has stated for the first time in *Sveinbjörnsdóttir*[56]. That poses difficulties for conservative jurists. Conservatives tend to say it's either black or white, *tertium non datur*. But the EEA Agreement is a *tertium*, it's a bastard, or a hybrid, a mixed breed. We cannot tackle the questions posed by EEA law just by relying on old fashioned distinctions between black and white.

The possibility to limit the right to make a reference to the supreme courts

Of all the six EFTA States that were parties to the EEA Agreement only **Austria** made use of the possibility to limit the right to make a reference to the supreme courts, and that was strange enough[57]. Iceland has not limited this right, but under Act No. 21/94 a decision of a district court to make a request may be appealed to the Supreme Court. There we have seen a development which at times was rather surprising. However, first of all, I must mention that the Court has received many important cases from **Icelandic courts**. The references concerning State liability and primacy came from the Reykjavík District Court. The case concerning direct effect was referred by a Finnish court. Norwegian courts did not refer such sensitive questions. Still *de facto* they are bound by our respective rulings. Coming back to Iceland: At one stage, I think after our *Sveinbjörnsdóttir* judgment, the **Icelandic State Attorney General** started to challenge every single reference by a district court before the Supreme Court. The Supreme Court threw out cases and questions. It rendered some judgments which have been criticised, *inter alia*, by Professor *Davíð Þór Björgvinsson*, the Icelandic judge at the European Court of Human Rights[58]. In its more recent case law the Supreme Court of Iceland has taken account of this criticism and has become more open minded again with regard to the question of whether to admit references to the EFTA Court from lower courts.

As I said several times, you cannot deal with EEA law by just focussing on your own country. You have to look at what others are doing. In **Norway**, there is free access to the EFTA Court. If a lower court decides to make a reference you cannot challenge that before a higher court. The same situation exists in **Liechtenstein**.

---

56 Case E-9/97 Sveinbjörnsdóttir, [1998] EFTA Court Report, 95, at paragraph 59.

57 See the critical remarks by the former Austrian EFTA Court Judge Kurt Herndl, Der EFTA-Gerichtshof und Österreich – ein Beispiel für nützliche Zusammenarbeit?, Afmælisrit Thor Vilhjálmsson, [2000] Reykjavík, 247, 252 et seq.

58 Davíð Þór Björgvinsson, EES-réttur og landsréttur [2006], Reykjavík, Bókaútgáfan Codex, 363 et seq.

I mentioned that supreme court judges are sometimes rather close to their country's government. It may happen that they refuse to make a preliminary reference because they know or suspect that the EFTA Court will rule against what they perceive as the interest of their country. In other words, the refusal to refer is in such cases based on **political** or **economic considerations** or on both. It is exactly in these situations that European law must offer an effective remedy. You may have seen that in the Union it occurs quite frequently that a judge from a lower court goes against his country's highest court's case law by making a reference to the ECJ. Once the ECJ has answered the questions referred in a different way than the supreme court concerned, the first instance court judge must rule accordingly, i.e., against the case law of the highest court. In football, you would speak of **a wall pass via Luxembourg**, the national judge plays the ball, the ball comes back and then the goal is scored.

The same happened in the Liechtenstein Security for Costs saga. **Liechtenstein** (like many countries in earlier times) had a provision in its Code of Civil Procedure which stated that a foreign plaintiff must **pay security** for the potential costs of an action under certain circumstances. It was rather obvious to any independent observer that this constituted a breach of the free movement of capital which is guaranteed in the EEA Main Agreement. ESA opened an infringement case against Liechtenstein, but then the State Court found the Liechtenstein regulation to be compatible with EEA law[59]. ESA took its hands off and did not pursue the case[60]. A single judge from a **first instance court** eventually made a reference concerning the matter[61]. He did not refer the main question, namely whether a provision according to which natural plaintiffs not resident in Liechtenstein and having no chargeable assets in that country may be asked to furnish security for costs in court proceedings if the defendant so requests, but a **side issue,** namely whether a provision such as that contained in Article 56(2) of the Civil Procedure Code was compatible with EEA law. Article 56(2) stated:

> "*At its discretion, the court may permit, inter alia, deposit books from a domestic savings bank or a domestic agricultural or other lending institution for the purpose of posting security. The judge may permit security to be provided by means of a mortgage on a plot of land in Liechtenstein providing a legal security or a guarantee issued by solvent guarantors resident in Liechtenstein, where the person required to provide security is unable to procure a different kind of security or can do so only with great difficulty.*"

The **European Commission** submitted observations and suggested that the Court go beyond the question of the national court which would have meant that the whole chapter on the obligation of foreign plaintiffs to pay security of cost would have been at stake. The Court limited itself to answering the question referred and held that Article 56(2) of the Civil Procedure Act was incompatible with the free movement of capital.

59 State Court of 17 February 2003, StGH 2002/37 (LES 2005, 145).

60 See supra, B.2.

61 Case E-10/04 Piazza [2005] EFTA Court Report 76.

But we pointed to the pleading of the Commission[62]. This was in 2005. In 2008, the State Court, referring to the Court's *Piazza* judgment and the Commission's pleadings in that case, held that the legal situation was now clear and **annulled the whole chapter** in the Liechtenstein Civil Procedure Act. The government was given a certain period of time to come up with a new solution[63]. The judge from the first instance court had meanwhile referred the main question to the Court, but withdrew the reference when he learned about the State Court's ruling[64].

The **situation in Iceland** is unsatisfactory. Unequal access to the Court in Norway and Liechtenstein on the one hand and in Iceland on the other hand is a problem. I would suggest that the Supreme Court of Iceland, as a matter of principle, should give the lower courts the freedom to do what they feel is their obligation. There is an interesting development with regard to this question in the EC pillar. On 16 December 2008, the ECJ gave a judgment in a case referred by a Hungarian court, *Cartesio*, where it basically stated that a rule of national law, which restricts the right of a lower court to decide freely on whether to make a reference or not, is not legal[65]. And this, ladies and gentlemen, is also important for the situation in the EFTA pillar from a point of view of **equal access** to the European courts. We have not ruled on it, but at first sight I cannot see a reason why this should not be relevant. The Court held in many cases that although it is not required by Article 3(1) SCA to follow the case law of the ECJ when interpreting the main part of the Surveillance and Court Agreement which deals, *inter alia*, with the types of procedure, that case law is relevant when the expressions used in Community law are identical in substance to those of the SCA[66]. The ECJ's *Cartesio* ruling should contribute to opening the eyes of the Supreme Court judges who ought to leave it to the judges of the lower courts to decide whether they want to refer or not.

I know that Mr *Magnússon* also discussed another matter when giving his recent lecture. He asked the rhetorical question what would happen if a lower Icelandic court would just make the reference without asking the Supreme Court for permission and the case arrived on the desk of the EFTA Court. Obviously, I cannot answer, but he said that the EFTA Court would certainly deal with this **under** EEA **law** and not under Icelandic law. The EFTA Court is not allowed to interpret Icelandic law but we would have to look at the point from an EEA law perspective.

62 Loc. cit., Report for the Hearing, at paragraphs 84 et seq.
63 Judgment of the State Court of 30 June 2008, StGH 2006/94.
64 Case E-4/08 Sebjaniv c Peters [2008] EFTA Court Report, 299.
65 Case C-210/06 Cartesio, judgment of 16 December 2008, nyr.
66 See, e.g., E-1/94 Restamark, loc. cit., at paragraph 24.

D. The nullity procedure

1. Legislation

The nullity procedure is mentioned in Article 108(2)(a) of the EEA Agreement. Moreover, Article 36 SCA provides:

> *"The EFTA Court shall have jurisdiction in actions brought by an EFTA State against a decision of the EFTA Surveillance Authority on grounds of lack of competence, infringement of an essential procedural requirement, or infringement of this Agreement, of the EEA Agreement or of any rule of law relating to their application, or misuse of powers. Any natural or legal person may, under the same conditions, institute proceedings before the EFTA Court against a decision of the EFTA Surveillance Authority addressed to that person or against a decision addressed to another person, if it is of direct and individual concern to the former.(…)"*

Article 36(1) SCA essentially corresponds to Article 263 TFEU (ex Article 230[1] EC). Article 36(2) SCA is narrower than the EU law rule insofar as decisions in the form of a regulation are not mentioned. Accordingly, EEA law does not contain a provision mirroring Article 277 TFEU (ex Article 241 EC). The Court has no jurisdiction to declare decisions of the EEA Joint Committee on the incorporation of new Community legal acts into the EEA Agreement null and void. EFTA individuals and economic operators must therefore rely on their EC counterparts in that respect with regard to the legal act in question as part of Community law. The Court does, however, have the competence to interpret decisions of the EEA **Joint Committee**, the body that decides on the adoption of EC law into the EFTA pillar of the EEA[67]. Moreover, there are good reasons for arguing that if a legal act had a serious flaw, the Court would not apply it, no matter whether it had already been declared void by the ECJ and repealed by the EEA Joint Committee[68].

2. No two tier-system in the EFTA pillar

In the EFTA pillar there is only one court that has jurisdiction to hear actions for nullity. This corresponds to the situation as it existed in the Union before the establishment of the Court of First Instance. The Court has from early on followed the practice of also taking into account the relevant case law of the CFI[69].

---

67 Cases E-6/01 CIBA, [2002] EFTA Court Report 281; E-2/00 Allied Colloids [2002] EFTA Court Report 35. See supra, lecture 1.

68 See Carl Baudenbacher, Between Homogeneity and Independence: The Legal Position of the EFTA Court in the European Economic Area, [1997] 3 CJEL, 169, 184.

69 See Cases E-2/94 Scottish Salmon Growers Association [1994-1995] EFTA Court Report 59, at paragraph 13; E-2/02 Bellona [2003] EFTA Court Report 52, at paragraphs 39 and 40.

3. Locus standi of operators who are not the addressees of a decision

Under the *Plaumann* formula adopted by the ECJ in 1963, persons other than those to whom a decision is addressed may only claim to be individually concerned if that decision affects them by reason of certain attributes that are peculiar to them, or by reason of circumstances in which they are differentiated from all other persons, and by virtue of these factors, distinguishes them individually just as in the case of the person addressed[70]. That means that certain claimants are **excluded** from having *locus standi*. In T-177/01 *Jégo Quéré*[71] the CFI, inspired by Advocate General *Jacobs'* opinion in C-50/00 *Pequeños Agricultores*[72], departed from the ECJ's *Plaumann* formula and adopted a new definition of individual concern, according to which a provision of EC law must affect the individual's legal position in a way which is both definite and immediate, by restricting his rights or imposing obligations on him. The ECJ stuck to its ancestral case law and annulled the CFI's judgment. In *Pequeños Agricultores*, the ECJ had ruled accordingly. These judgments concerned regulations, but the restrictive interpretation of *locus standi* applies also to decisions.

The Court dealt with the issue of *locus standi* of persons other than the addressee to bring an action for nullity of a decision of the EFTA Surveillance Authority in a number of cases. The starting point was always that although it is not required by Article 3(1) SCA to follow the reasoning of the ECJ when interpreting the main part of that Agreement, the reasoning which led that Court to its interpretations of expressions of Community law is **relevant** when those expressions are identical in substance to those which are to be interpreted by the Court[73].

In some instances the Court has nevertheless shown a tendency toward being **liberal** in cases of doubt when it comes to granting other persons than the addressees of a decision locus standi. The reasoning was often characterized by pragmatism and result-orientation. In *Bellona*, the Court even noted that things in Community law appeared to be in flux[74]. However, in a recent case, we essentially aligned ourselves with the ECJ's case law[75].

E. Conclusions

All in all, there seems to be room for improvement with regard to access of individuals and economic operators to the EFTA Court. That ESA is less active in bringing cases

70 Case 25/62 Plaumann [1963] ECR (English special edition) 95, at paragraph 54.

71 Case T-177/01 Jégo Quéré [2002] ECR II-2365; and Case C-263/02 P Jégo Quéré [2004] ECR I-3425.

72 Case C-50/00 P Pequeños Agricultores [2002] ECR, I-6677.

73 See Cases E-2/94 Scottish Salmon Growers, [1994-1995] EFTA Court Report 59; E-2/02 Bellona [2003] EFTA Court Report 52, at paragraphs 38-40; Joined Cases E-5/04, E-6/04 and E-7-04 Fesil and Finnfjord [2005] EFTA Court Report 117, at paragraph 53.

74 Loc. cit., at paragraph 37.

75 Case E-5/07 Private Barnehagers, [2008] EFTA Court Report 62, at paragraphs 45–53.

than the Commission has been demonstrated. Together with the reluctance of national supreme courts to make use of the preliminary reference procedure, this may contribute to a situation which would not be in accordance with the principle of **reciprocity** which is underlying the EEA Agreement and has been explicitly mentioned in Recital 4 of its preamble. What is frequently overlooked in the capitals of the EEA/EFTA States is the fact that individuals and businesses from the EFTA pillar who operate in EC countries enjoy **broad access to the ECJ** under the Article 267 TFEU (ex Article 234 EC) preliminary ruling procedure. In Case 452/01 the Liechtenstein citizen *Margarethe Ospelt* who owned agricultural land in Austria successfully petitioned the Austrian Supreme Administrative Court to make a reference to the ECJ[76]. In Case C-92/02, the Norwegian migrant worker *Nina Kristiansen* obtained access to the ECJ through the Tongeren District Labour Court (Belgium)[77]. In Case C-286/02 *Bellio Fratelli*, the Prefettura di Treviso (Italy) referred a case to the ECJ involving a Norwegian exporter of fish flour from Norway to Italy[78].

The reciprocity argument has only been discussed by few authors in the context of the effect and supremacy debate. In 1999, editorial comments in CMLRev stated that "since EFTA operators benefit from the characteristics of direct effect and supremacy of the EC legal order to enforce their EEA rights within the EC national Courts, their EC counterparts should be in a similar position to obtain a comparable level of legal redress in the EFTA national Courts"[79]. *Leif Sevón* and *Martin Johansson* emphasised that if individuals and economic operators from the Community would not enjoy the same possibility of invoking the Agreement as their EFTA counterparts, there would be an imbalance. "While individuals and economic operators from the EFTA States would be in a position to invoke the Agreement before courts and administrative authorities in the E.C. Member States, this would not be the case for individuals and economic operators from the E.C. Member States in the EFTA States."[80] *Sven Norberg* concurred with that view[81].

Whether EC actors have the same kind of access to the EFTA Court (and consequently also EFTA actors) is an open question. I may mention the policy of the supreme courts in all three EEA/EFTA States in general and the Austrian doctors' State liability case specifically. Austrian doctors have been refused access to the Court because the Liechtenstein Supreme Court did not make a reference although the Austrian plaintiff had

76 [2003] ECR, I-9743.

77 [2003] ECR, I-14597.

78 [2004] ECR, I-3465; see regarding the merits of that case infra, lecture 5.

79 Editorial comments: European Economic Area and European Community: Homogeneity of legal orders?, CMLRev 1999, 697, 698; see also Carl Baudenbacher, Staatshaftung im gesamten Europäischen Wirtschaftsraum: EuGH und EFTA-Gerichtshof im Doppelpass, EWS 2000, 425.

80 The protection of the rights of individuals under the EEA Agreement, 24 European Law Review, 373, 384 (1999).

81 Afmælisrit Thór Vilhjálmsson, Perspectives on the Future Development of the EEA Agreement, 2002, 367 ff., 374.

asked the court to do so[82] (see infra, lecture 3). However, there have also been cases in which EC operators convinced a national court in an EEA/EFTA State to make a reference to the EFTA Court. An example is the Greek citizen *Athanasios Tsomakas* and his colleagues who had been employed as sailors on a Norwegian vessel[83].

The ECJ found in C-50/00 *Pequeños Agricultores* that the nullity procedure must be seen as part of an overall system of means of protection[84]. You could ask the question whether our system is in fact equally effective as the EC system. But then – if we take homogeneity seriously also in matters of procedure – the correct solution is not to deviate from *Pequeños Agricultores*. Rather, the situation in the field of preliminary rulings must be remedied and others should think whether their policy in bringing infringement actions is good enough.

82 Judgment CO.2004.2-38 (5 June 2008).

83 Case E-3/04 Tsomakas Athanasios and Others v The Norwegian State [2004] EFTA Court Report 95.

84 Case C-50/00 Unión de Pequeños Agricultores [2002] ECR I-6677, at paragraph 40.

Lecture 3
Effect of EEA law and State liability

A. Prehistory

There has been a prehistory of the EEA Agreement which you must know if you want to understand the provisions and the case law dealing with effect and State liability in EEA law[85]. If you are not familiar with that, you cannot apprehend why certain mechanisms have been designed under the EEA Agreement the way they have. In 1972, EFTA took a major hit when the United Kingdom joined the European Community. Together with the UK Ireland and the EFTA State Denmark acceded to the Community. As a consequence, the remaining EFTA States were prompted to conclude **bilateral Free Trade Agreements** with the EU. However, under these agreements there was no common EFTA Court. That means that on the Community side the ECJ had jurisdiction to deal with cases concerning the FTA's whereas on the side of the EFTA countries the individual supreme courts were competent. An important question was whether citizens and economic operators would have access to the courts under the FTA's. In that respect, the EFTA states closed the door quickly. In the dualistic Nordic countries it was out of the question that provisions of the FTA's would have direct effect because they had not been implemented into the national legal orders. That means that only governments were deemed to be bound by those agreements and only governments could derive rights from them. There were no court rulings at the time. I give you a quotation of Professor *Ulf Bernitz* from the University of Stockholm who is probably the most famous European law professor in Sweden. He characterized the Swedish attitude as "a kind of legal protectionism"[86].

A bit surprising, in Austria and in Switzerland, countries that have the reputation of being monist, the Supreme Courts ruled in the same way. Let me first talk about the *Stanley Adams* judgment of the **Swiss Supreme Court**[87]. The Free Trade Agree-

---

85 See in that respect also the background paper of the EFTA Secretariat on the case law in the Community and the EFTA countries on the application and interpretation of the Free Trade Agreements (FTA's) and other agreements: Group of Legal Experts on the Application and Interpretation of the Free Trade Agreements Between the EFTA Countries and the European Communities. A Case Study, Note by the Secretariat, EFTA/GLE 1/87, 18 September 1987, Introduction (vii).

86 Ulf Bernitz, European Law in Sweden, [2002] Stockholm, 25, see also Ulf Bernitz, The EEC-EFTA Free Trade Agreements with Special Reference to the Position of Sweden and the other Scandinavian EFTA Countries, [1986] CML Rev., 567 et seq.

87 ATF 104 IV 175 Stanley Adams.

ment concluded between Switzerland and the EEC, as all the FTA's, contains a rule stating that an **abuse of a dominant position** is incompatible with its good functioning. *Stanley Adams*, a British national born in Malta, was a manager of *Hoffmann-La Roche*, the large pharmaceutical company headquartered in Basle, Switzerland. He had noticed that his undertaking was engaged in anti-competitive behaviour, to be concrete, in abuses of a dominant position on the EC territory. He reported this behaviour to the European Commission, in modern terminology you would call him a "whistle blower". Following this, unbelievable things happened. It appears to be established that the Director General, the highest ranking civil servant of DG Competition, revealed Mr *Adam's* identity to the lawyer of *Hoffmann-La Roche* who by the way was a member of the Swiss Parliament. *Hoffmann-La Roche* called a prosecutor in Switzerland who opened criminal proceedings. *Stanley Adams* had left his post at *Hoffmann-La Roche* and lived in Italy where he planned to start a new career as a pig farmer. When he wanted to visit relatives in Switzerland, he was arrested and finally sentenced to one year in prison on probation for economic espionage by the courts in Basle. His Swiss wife who had also been arrested committed suicide after having been questioned by federal agents. Mr *Adams* took his case before the Swiss Supreme Court and invoked the Free Trade Agreement between the EEC and Switzerland. He argued that the kind of behaviour which he had reported was incompatible with the good functioning of the Free Trade Agreement. How on earth could he have committed espionage in favour of a foreign power if the country was bound by way of a public international law agreement with this foreign power to oppress the kind of behaviour he had reported? In its judgment of 3 May 1978 the Supreme Court simply said that the invoked provision of the FTA did **not have direct effect** and could therefore not be relied on by a private citizen. The FTA in the court's view was only binding on governments. Rumor has it that the EC Commissioner in charge of competition and the said Director General did not dare to travel to Switzerland anymore out of fear to be arrested, too. For the sake of completeness, I may add that after having faced a lot of difficulties, Mr *Adams* successfully claimed a relative modest amount of damages suffered as a consequence of the Commission's breach of confidentiality concerning his identity[88].

The Swiss Supreme Court was given a **second chance** to show more openness in the *Omo* case[89]. *Omo* is the name of a well-known detergent on the continent for the laundry in washing machines. *Omo* was produced by a group of companies, and, as usual, the prices in Switzerland were much higher than the ones in Germany. A parallel importer bought the powder in Germany and imported it into Switzerland without the consent of the trade mark owner and sold it at a lower price. The trade mark owner brought an action for alleged violation of his mark and the parallel importer invoked the provisions of the Free Trade Agreement concerning free movement of goods. In its judgment of 25 January 1979, the Supreme Court again found that a private party

88 Case C-145/83 Adams v Commission, [1985] ECR, 3539.
89 ATF 105 II 49 Bosshard Partners Intertrading AG v Sunlight ('OMO').

could **not rely** on those provisions. The Supreme Court looked for material differences between the German powder and the Swiss powder, because under trade mark law the import could only be blocked if the trade mark owner could show a relevant **material difference**. Only then would a deception of the consumers be established in that the consumer who bought the German product was deceived about the quality of the powder. The question arises, how can there be a material difference between two detergents stemming from the same holding, the same concern, whether it is produced in Germany or in Switzerland? The Supreme Court found that the German powder did not contain blue needles, whereas the Swiss powder did, and that the Swiss powder was milder on the cloth. The Supreme Court added that this was a quality difference Swiss housewives cared about. That was in 1979! I do not know where the judges, all male, acquired this important knowledge, but they wrote it into the judgment. The Austrian Supreme Court in 1980 reached the same conclusion in a case involving parallel imports of copyrighted gramophone records. But the Austrian judges used much more cautious language than their Swiss colleagues[90].

The narrow-mindedness of the EFTA actors did not prevent the ECJ from being generous. On 26 October 1982 it held in its famous *Kupferberg* judgment which concerned the FTA concluded with Portugal[91] that provisions of the Free Trade Agreements were able to produce **direct effect** in the EC legal order. In this landmark ruling the ECJ found, *inter alia*, that according to international law, every agreement must be performed bona fide. That the courts of one of the parties consider that "certain of the stipulations in the agreement are of direct application whereas the courts of the other party do not recognise such direct application is not in itself such as to constitute a lack of reciprocity in the implementation of the agreement"[92]. It must be noted that the governments of Denmark, Germany, France and the United Kingdom had urged the ECJ to deny direct application, *inter alia*, because of lack of reciprocity[93].

The result of all this was free access to the courts of the EC Member States and (by way of the preliminary ruling procedure) to the ECJ under the Free Trade Agreements, but no access to the courts of the EFTA States. Swiss professor *Olivier Jacot-Guillarmod*, who later was an EEA negotiator and would have become the Swiss judge of the EFTA Court had Switzerland ratified the EEA Agreement, called this a **judicial restraint of trade**[94]. And Dutch international law professor *Henry Schermers* observed: "There is no discrepancy in the treaty obligations; the law is the same for all treaty parties, but there is discrepancy in the actual possibility to get away with breaches of the law."[95]

90 Judgment of the Austrian Supreme Court of 10 July 1979, Austro-Mechana, published in [1980] GRUR Int., 185 et seq.

91 Case 104/81 Kupferberg [1982] ECR 3641.

92 Loc. cit., at paragraph 18.

93 Loc. cit., at paragraphs 10, 15, 16.

94 Olivier Jacot-Guillarmod, Federal Tribunal (Switzerland) Decision of 25 January 1979, Bosshard Partners Intertrading AG v Sunlight AG, ATF 105 II 49, [1981] CML Rev., 427 et seq.

95 Henry G. Schermers, The Direct Application of Treaties with Third States: Note Concerning the Polydor and Pabst Cases, [1982] CML Rev., 563, 567.

B. Starting points

1. Homogeneity rules

When negotiating the EEA Agreement, the representatives of the European Commission did not want to have a situation of unequal access to the courts anymore. That we have to bear in mind when talking about effect and State liability.

EEA law and EC law constitute separate legal orders. But EEA law is essentially **identical in substance** to EC law. In order to create a level playing field for individuals and economic operators in the whole EEA, the fathers and mothers of the EEA Agreement created special homogeneity rules. The most important ones are laid down in Articles 6 EEA and 3(2) SCA.

> *Article 6 EEA*
> *"Without prejudice to future developments of case law, the provisions of this Agreement, in so far as they are identical in substance to corresponding rules of the Treaty establishing the European Economic Community and the Treaty establishing the European Coal and Steel Community and to acts adopted in application of these two Treaties, shall, in their implementation and application, be interpreted in conformity with the relevant rulings of the Court of Justice of the European Communities given prior to the date of signature of this Agreement."*

> *Article 3(2) SCA*
> *"In the interpretation and application of the EEA Agreement and this Agreement, the EFTA Surveillance Authority and the EFTA Court shall pay due account to the principles laid down by the relevant rulings by the Court of Justice of the European Communities given after the date of signature of the EEA Agreement and which concern the interpretation of that Agreement or of such rules of the Treaty establishing the European Economic Community and the Treaty establishing the European Coal and Steel Community in so far as they are identical in substance to the provisions of the EEA Agreement or to the provisions of Protocols 1 to 4 and the provisions of the acts corresponding to those listed in Annexes I and II to the present Agreement."*

2. Protocol 35

In Protocol 35, the EEA Contracting Parties agreed that for cases of possible conflicts between implemented EEA rules and other statutory provisions, the EFTA States undertake to introduce, if necessary, a statutory provision to the effect that EEA rules **prevail** in these cases.

3. ECJ Opinion 1/91

The issue of homogeneity has been one of the main subjects of the famous, and some say infamous, Opinion 1/91 of the ECJ.[96] Others call it a fundamental opinion and yet others a fundamentalist opinion. The ECJ did not trust the EFTA States. It obviously had the feeling that they had manoeuvred before, the Nordic EFTA States by not implementing the FTA's into their domestic law, the Swiss Supreme Court in *Stanley Adams* and in *Omo* by refusing to accept direct effect and the Austrian Supreme Court in *Austro-Mechana* by doing the same[97]. The ECJ compared the goals and the contexts of the EC Treaty on the one hand and of the EEA Agreement on the other and concluded that even if the wording of the law was identical, there was **no real guarantee** that direct effect and primacy were safeguarded under the EEA Agreement. This was not so much a normative statement, but rather an expression of distrust on behalf of the ECJ. Moreover, the ECJ used the opportunity to underline the uniqueness of Community law. But once the EEA Agreement had entered into force, the governments of the Nordic countries tried to make the opposite out of the ECJ's concerns. They argued in every case that the ECJ had **authoritatively excluded** direct effect and primacy (and, consequently, State liability) in EEA law. The Icelandic government reiterated this two years ago, although the battle over EEA State liability is long over[98]. The EEA/EFTA State governments tried to turn this expression of fear or of doubt by the ECJ into an allegedly normative sentence.

4. Academic literature

Academic literature was **split** over the issue of effect and State liability in EEA law. Writers from EU countries tended to assume that these general principles were, possibly in a slightly different form, also present in EEA law. The influential former Advocate General *Walter van Gerven* wrote in 1992 that these general principles quite clearly were to be deemed to be part of EEA law because a legal system that would not encompass them would not at all be homogeneous with Community law: "[S]tripping Community law of its general principles amounts to taking its heart. An EEA legal system that would not encompass such general principles would therefore be a legal system that is not at all homogeneous with Community law."[99] Professor *Thomas Bruha*, a German advisor to the Liechtenstein government in the EEA negotiations, argued in 1999 that the principle of direct effect applied also in EEA law[100]. Observers from the Nordic countries were, however, of the opposite view. *Leif Sevón*, one of the most outstanding lawyers in the

96 Opinion 1/91 [1994] ECR I-5267.

97 See supra, A.

98 Case E-1/07 Criminal Proceedings Against A, Transcript of the Oral Hearing, file with the Court.

99 Walter van Gerven, The Genesis of EEA Law and the Principles of Primacy and Direct Effect, [1992–1993] 16 Fordham International Law Journal, 955.

100 Thomas Bruha, Is the EEA an Internal Market?, in: Müller-Graff and Selvig (eds.), EEA-EU Relations, [1999] Berlin, 97, 108, 116 ff.

North, said in 1994 while sitting on the EFTA Court that the principles of direct effect and supremacy were not as such among the obligations imposed on the EFTA States by the EEA Agreement[101]. In 1999, when sitting on the ECJ, he opined that they were part of EEA law[102]. *Fredrik Sejersted* wrote in 1997 that the ECJ case law concerning direct effect and primacy was not relevant within the meaning of Article 6 EEA. Whether there should be State liability could be argued both ways[103]. *Per Christiansen* who was the Registrar of the EFTA Court at the time said in the same year that whether the fundamental Community law principles such as that of direct effect formed part of EEA law, could be argued in both ways. If the answer was in the negative, State liability "could hardly be seen as relevant because of the close relationship to the principle of direct effect of Community law" [104]. But the former Swedish EFTA Court Judge *Sven Norberg* in 2000 took the view that direct effect and primacy were part of EEA law[105].

C. Cases on effect and primacy

Then came the cases on effect and primacy, before the EFTA Court in particular, but also before the Union courts. The EEA is a strange animal, a very complicated agreement, and it is not only the Court which is competent to give interpretation, it is also the ECJ and the European Court of First Instance. Whenever a case on EEA law originates from an EC country, but still is an EEA law case because EFTA operators are involved, e.g. a Norwegian exporter, or an Icelandic migrant worker, the ECJ is competent to give interpretation of the EEA Agreement because under Article 216(2) TFEU (ex Article 300[7] EC) the EEA Agreement has become part also of EU law. That is a very important point. Most government representatives in the EEA/EFTA States do not see that this is also of high relevance for the EFTA pillar. The only thing they are concerned with is to defend their traditional constitutional beliefs.

1. EFTA Court Restamark (1994)

In Case E-1/94 *Restamark*[106] the question of **direct effect** of EEA law came up for the first time. A Finnish court asked the EFTA Court, *inter alia*, whether a provision of the EEA Agreement had direct effect. That was the EFTA Court's very first case in the first

101 Leif Sevón, Primacy and Direct Effect in the EEA. Some Reflections, in: Liber Amicorum Ole Due [1994] 339, 352.

102 Leif Sevón and Martin Johansson, The protection of the rights of individuals under the EEA Agreement, [1999] 24 European Law Review, 380.

103 Fredrik Sejersted, Between sovereignty and supranationalism in the EEA context, in: Müller-Graff and Selvig (eds.), The European Economic Area: Norway's basic status in the legal construction of Europe, [1997] Berlin, 43, 53 et seq.

104 Per Christiansen, The EFTA Court, [1997] 22 European Law Review, 539, 547.

105 Sven Norberg, Perspectives on the Future Development of the EEA Agreement, in: Afmaelisrit Thór Vilhjálmsson, [2000] Reykjavik, 367, 374.

106 Case E-1/94 Restamark [1994-1995] EFTA Court Report 15.

year of its existence. Ten days after the entry into force of the EEA Agreement a Finnish company with the name of *Restamark* had imported from Italy 120 bottles of Italian red wine and from Germany 60 bottles of whisky and placed the beverages in a bonded warehouse. The Finnish authorities, invoking the State import monopoly, rejected *Restamark's* request the place to goods in free circulation. The Norwegian government argued that this was not a question to be answered by EEA law. This was a question to be answered by domestic law. It was the constitutional framework of each EFTA State that had to decide on whether there was direct effect or not. The Norwegian government said that the provision in question, the state monopoly provision of Article 16 EEA, had been implemented into Finnish law. Consequently, the question did not even pose itself. The EFTA Court need not answer this question[107]. The Court struck a balance. It did not say that EEA law was able to have direct effect, but held that **implemented provisions** of EEA law may have direct effect. The essential thing is that this effect follows from EEA law, not from the domestic law of the EFTA States. EEA law demands that such provisions are given direct effect in the legal orders of the EEA/EFTA States. The States cannot deviate from this without facing consequences, in particular State liability. I will discuss that in more detail later.

On the other hand, the Court also found that non-implemented provisions are not directly effective[108]. This could be called the EEA **compromise**. We did not go for full direct effect, but we went for this middle course. Since over 90 % of all EEA law provisions have been implemented in the Member States, we are almost where the EU is on this subject.

2. CFI Opel Austria (1997)

In 1997, the Court of First Instance of the European Communities had to deal with a case originating in Austria, whose facts had occurred when Austria was still an EEA/EFTA State. That was Case T-115/94 *Opel Austria*[109]. The CFI held that provisions of the EEA Agreement (*in casu* Article 10 EEA) were able to produce **direct effect** in the EC legal order. In this judgment, the CFI as the first Community Court also opened the dialogue with the EFTA Court when dealing with the EEA homogeneity rules[110]. I will extensively deal with that dialogue in my fifth lecture. The Court for its part made reference to the CFI's *Opel Austria* ruling in its 2003 judgment in E-2/03 *Ásgeirsson*[111].

107 Case E-1/94 Restamark [1994-1995] EFTA Court Report 15, Report for the Hearing, at paragraph 87.

108 See infra, 5.

109 Case T-115/94 Opel Austria [1997] ECR II-39, at paragraph 108.

110 See Bo Vesterdorf, EFTA Court 10th Anniversary, in: Carl Baudenbacher/Per Tresselt/Thorgeir Örlygsson (eds.), The EFTA Court Ten Years On, [2005] Oxford and Portland, Oregon, 187 et seq.

111 Case E-2/03 Ásgeirsson [2003] EFTA Court Report 185, at paragraph 28.

3. EFTA Court Einarsson (2002)

The same question as in *Restamark* with respect to direct effect came up some years later with regard to **primacy** in Case E-1/01 *Einarsson*[112]. Mr *Einarsson* was an Icelandic lawyer, a private attorney, who deeply disliked a certain piece of Icelandic legislation. Under Icelandic law, books were subject to different VAT rates, depending on whether they were written in Icelandic or in another language. Books written in Icelandic were subject to a VAT rate of 10 %, whereas books in a foreign language were subject to a VAT rate of 24.5 %. Mr *Einarsson* felt that this constituted discriminatory taxation and brought an action in the Reykjavík District Court, and that court made a reference to the EFTA Court. The Court held that the Icelandic rule constituted **discriminatory taxation** within the meaning of Article 14(2) EEA. That provision states:

> *"Furthermore, no Contracting Party shall impose on the products of other Contracting Parties any internal taxation of such a nature as to afford indirect protection to other products."*

Given this outcome, it is fair to state that Mr Einarsson acted as a private attorney general. He brought a lawsuit that was in the public interest, benefiting the general public and not just himself.

With regard to primacy, the Court used the same formulation as in *Restamark*, namely that **implemented provisions** of EEA law may take precedence over conflicting provisions of domestic law. That means that non-implemented provisions do not take precedence.

The Court's findings in cases *Restamark* and *Einarsson* have been greeted by academics. I just give you two examples. Professor *Hans Petter Graver*, probably the most influential Norwegian scholar in the field and now the Dean of the Law School of the University of Oslo, speaks of quasi-direct effect and quasi-primacy[113]. A Danish author, *Ole Spiermann* when referring to Opinion 1/91 and EFTA Court *Restamark*, wrote that the ECJ "suffered the indignity to be brushed aside by a much more open-minded EFTA Court"[114].

4. Liechtenstein State Court and Liechtenstein Supreme Administrative Court

The Liechtenstein State Court, in an expert opinion of 11 December 1995, found that provisions of EEA law are **effective in domestic law** as they enter into force as public international law insofar as they are self-executing; no national act of transformation is

112 Case E-1/01 Einarsson [2002] EFTA Court Report 1.

113 Hans Petter Graver, Supranationality and National Legal Autonomy in the EEA-agreement, ARENA Working Papers 00/23 <http://www.arena.uio.no/publications/working-papers2000/papers/00_23.htm> (last visited on 20 November 2009).

114 Ole Spiermann, The Other Side of the Story: An Unpopular Essay on the Making of the European Community Legal Order, [1999] European Journal of International Law Vol. 10 No. 4, 763 et seq.

needed[115]. In a judgment of 3 May 1999, the same Court held that EEA law takes **precedence** over conflicting domestic law including national constitutional law according to EEA Agreement Article 7 and Protocol 35 to the EEA Agreement. The primacy of EEA law is limited only by the fundamental principles and core content of fundamental rights laid down in the Constitution and in the European Human Rights Convention[116]. Accordingly, the Supreme Administrative Court of Liechtenstein sees no difficulty in setting aside provisions of national law that conflict with EEA law. In the alternative, the Court would try to give the national rule in question an EEA-friendly interpretation. In either case, the Supreme Administrative Court will not wait until the provision has been amended or abolished either by the legislature or the State Court[117].

The Liechtenstein Supreme Administrative Court held in a judgment of 9 February 2006, that Article 39a of the Liechtenstein Salaries Act which stated that part-time employees had a right to payment of a bridging pension provided they had worked at least 50 % under a service contract was incompatible with Articles 2(1) and 5 of the Equal Rights Directive 76/207/EEC and Clause 4 No 1 of the Framework Agreement on part-time work annexed to Council Directive 97/81/EC of 15 December 1997. The Supreme Administrative Court also ruled that those provisions had not been implemented into domestic law in due time and that they were sufficiently clear and unconditional to produce **direct effect**[118]. The court emphasised that during Austria's EEA/EFTA membership that country's supreme court had also assumed that EEA law was capable of having direct effect[119].

5. EFTA Court Karlsson (2002) and Criminal proceedings against A (2007)

In Cases E-4/01 *Karlsson* and E-1/07 *Criminal proceedings against* A the Court deduced from Article 7 EEA and from Protocol 35 that EEA law does not entail a transfer of legislative powers and therefore does **not** require that individuals and economic operators can **rely directly** on non-implemented EEA rules before national courts. Moreover, EEA law does not require that non-implemented EEA rules take precedence over conflicting national rules. The Court added in *Criminal proceedings against* A that in cases of violation of EEA law, the Contracting Party could be sued by ESA and will be obliged to **pay compensation** for loss and damage caused to individuals and economic operators if the conditions laid down in E-7/97 *Sveinbjörnsdóttir* and in E-4/01 *Karlsson* are fulfilled (see infra, D.)[120].

115 See Expert Opinion of the State Court 1995/14, [1996] LES 122.

116 Judgment of the State Court of the Principality of Liechtenstein in the capacity of a Constitutional Court, StGH 1998/60, [1999] ZBl. 585.

117 See the article of the President of the Administrative Court Andreas Batliner, Die Anwendung des EWR-Rechts durch liechtensteinische Gerichte – Erfahrungen eines Richters, Liechtensteinische Juristenzeitung, 4/04, 139.

118 Supreme Administrative Court, Judgment 2005/94 of 9 February 2006, at paragraphs 21 et seq.

119 Loc. cit., at paragraph 27.

120 Cases E-4/01 Karlsson [2002] EFTA Court Report 240, at paragraph 28; E-1/07 Criminal proceedings against A [2007] EFTA Court Report 245, at paragraphs 36–42.

D. Cases on State liability

1. EFTA Court Sveinbjörnsdóttir (1998)

The decisive step, however, was not so much *Restamark* and *Einarsson*, the decisive step was E-7/97 *Sveinbjörnsdóttir*[121]. An additional remark is due about how the vote was taken, since the judge who had been overruled went public.

Iceland had mis-implemented the Insolvency Directive 80/897/EEC. A worker, *Erla María Sveinbjörnsdóttir*, had been excluded from the wage guarantee after her employer had gone bankrupt. The point was that she was the sister of a major shareholder and under Icelandic law she was **excluded from the wage guarantee**. We will come back to the case when talking about methods of interpretation in lecture 4. After not having received any payment from the wage guarantee fund, *Erla María* sued the Icelandic government. The Court was asked by the Reykjavík District Court whether the State was liable in such a case. The Governments of **Iceland**, **Norway** and **Sweden** pleaded that to recognise EEA State liability was out of the question. State liability was said to be part of EC law, it could only be imagined together with EC style direct effect and primacy. Surprisingly for a lot of observers, the **European Commission** also pleaded against EEA State liability. The Commission's agent thought that direct effect, primacy and State liability were an EC invention, only available to EC players. Others could not play with these sacred toys. One could call this the "Toys R Us" approach. Two things may be added in that respect: In E-1/94 *Restamark*, the Commission had urged the Court to acknowledge direct effect of Article 16 EEA, the monopoly provision which mirrors Article 31 EC[122]. The agent of the Commission in *Sveinbjörnsdóttir*, *Pieter-Jan Kuijper*, was a well-known member of the Legal Service who later became Director for External Relations and is now a professor of the Law of International Organisations at the University of Amsterdam. Most recently, he was on the shortlist of the European Union for the nomination of a new member of the WTO Appellate Body. Given his standing in the Commission's Legal Service at the time, it could be that Mr *Kuijper* acted on his own initiative. One must not overlook in this context that in 2005, Professor *Kuijper* basically called on the ECJ to overrule its *Kupferberg* judgment and to generally make the recognition of direct effect of international treaties in Community law dependent on reciprocity [123]. But it is also possible that the Head of the Legal Service at the time wanted to keep the EEA at arm's length from the EC and instructed him accordingly.

---

121 Case E-9/97 Sveinbjörnsdóttir [1998] EFTA Court Report 95; see with regard to that judgment Carl Baudenbacher, If Not State Liability, Then What? Reflections Ten Years After the EFTA Court's Sveinbjörnsdóttir Ruling, 10 Chi. J. Int'l L. 333 et seq. [2009].

122 E-1/94 Restamark [1994-1995] EFTA Court Report 35, Report for the Hearing, at paragraph 96.

123 See his contribution in Pieter Jan Kuijper/Marco Bronckers, WTO Law in the European Court of Justice, [2005] CML Rev., 1313, 1317 et seq.

The Government of Iceland further elaborated on the point mentioned and argued that whether State liability should be part of EEA law was not for the Court to decide, but for the governments. If there should be inhomogeneity because of lack of State liability, you judges should stay out of the game, we, the politicians and civil servants, will take care of that on a **political level** and through **diplomatic channels**[124]. The argument is classic. The claim is that judges are trying to do the job of the legislature, that they should mind their own business, which – allegedly – is merely to apply the law and not to rewrite it. Otherwise, the reasoning goes, judges who have not been democratically elected but only appointed interfere with the sovereignty of the Contracting Parties.

ESA was the only participant in the case pleading in favour of State liability. It argued that State liability was part of EEA law due to the similarities between the EEA Agreement and the EC Treaty, the homogeneity objective of the EEA Agreement, the recognition of the important role that individuals play through the exercise of their rights in judicial proceedings and the intention of ensuring equal treatment of individuals and economic operators[125].

The Court found State liability to be **part of** EEA **law**, mainly for three reasons. First: homogeneity, second: protection of individuals and economic operators, and third: the duty of loyalty laid down in Article 3 EEA, the provision mirroring Article 10 EC (now: Article 4[3] TEU)[126]. Then came the second part, like in every State liability case. If you read State liability judgments, you always have the theoretical part and then the practical part. The latter deals with the application of the famous **three conditions** which the ECJ has set up on the question whether the State in fact has to pay. First condition: Does the breached provision confer rights upon individuals? Second condition: Is the breach sufficiently serious? Third condition: Is there a causal link between the breach and the damage sustained? We dealt with the first question ourselves and answered it in the affirmative, while leaving the answer to the second and the third condition to the national court.

I mentioned that one judge **went public** over the way the judgment was reached. In 1999, the Nordic Law Conference was held in Oslo. The judge indirectly, but clearly distanced himself from the Court's *Sveinbjörnsdóttir* judgment. He quoted the case and criticised the lack of a dissenting opinion system by saying that he found "it very difficult to function if we [sc. the judges], if the occasion arises, are not given the opportunity to give 'a dissenting, or even concurring opinion'. One is bound by the majority, not only with regard to the conclusion, but also with regard to the reasoning leading

124 [1998] EFTA Court Report 115, Report for the Hearing, at paragraph 62.

125 [1998] EFTA Court Report 115, Report for the Hearing, at paragraphs 84, 94, 95.

126 For the significance of Article 10 EC (see now Article 4[3] of the EU Treaty) in Community law, compare John Temple Lang, The Duties of National Courts Under Community Constitutional Law, [1997] 22 Eur. L. Rev., 3; see also Eleanor Cashin Ritaine/Eva Lein, La notion de proportionnalité appliquée au droit des jeux de hasard – Les cas Placanica et Autorité de surveillance de l'AELE/Royaume de Norvège, Schweizerisches Jahrbuch für Europarecht = Annuaire suisse de droit européen 2006/2007 355.

to the conclusion." He then added that he did "not intend to break this rule by saying something which could be interpreted as a further reasoning". This is documented in the book from the Nordic Law Conference from 1999[127]. That was the gentleman from Norway, at the time he was the President of the Court and in that capacity he had assigned the case to himself and acted as the judge rapporteur.

Allow me a parenthesis here: A lot of people talk about the need to protect the sovereignty of the EEA/EFTA States. If you ask them, what they exactly mean, they have difficulties to explain their position. I sometimes have the feeling that much of this sovereignty talk is nothing else than an attempt to protect the power of high civil servants in ministries or of the ministers themselves as well as lobbyists having access to them whose special interests are affected [128]. This is in fact understandable because if a court decides dynamically, these players will lose influence. The focus of the EEA Agreement is not primarily on safeguarding this kind of Member State sovereignty. It is rather on protecting the **sovereignty of the people**. This message is important: the EEA Agreement is about the protection of individuals and economic operators. It is not about the protection of ministers. It is not about the protection of judges, of high civil servants, or of diplomats. What is the purpose of the EEA Agreement? The purpose of the EEA Agreement is to extend the EC single market to the EFTA States and at the same time to give free access to the players from the EC States to the markets of the EEA/EFTA States. Seen from this perspective, things become crystal clear: Who are the players in a market? It is **manufacturers**, **employees**, **consumers**, **dealers** and **investors**. They need to be safeguarded, otherwise a market does not function. Many people in the EEA/EFTA States have still not understood this. They still think that stone walling is the most important thing. The EFTA Court has been around for more than fifteen years and I think the time has come to change this attitude. In fact, it is high noon to change it.

2. ECJ Rechberger (1999)

Half a year after the EFTA Court had rendered its *Sveinbjörnsdóttir* ruling, the ECJ had to deal with EEA State liability in two interesting cases. **Austria** and **Sweden** had been EEA/EFTA States in 1994 and the facts of the cases occurred during this year. In Cases C-140/97 *Rechberger*[129] and C-321/97 *Andersson*[130] the ECJ was asked by way of reference from an Austrian and a Swedish first instance court whether State liability was part of EEA law. Austria had not implemented the Package Tour Directive 90/314/EEC in due time and travelers had suffered damage. Sweden had misimple-

127 Forhandlingene ved Det 35. nordiske juristmøtet i Oslo, 18.–20. august 1999, Del 2, Utgitt av Det norske lokalstyret, 1005 et seq.

128 See Henry G. Schermers, The International Court of Justice in Relation to Other Courts, in: Sam Muller/David Raič/Hanna Thuránszky (eds.), The International Court of Justice: its Future Role After Fifty Years, Editorial Introduction, The Hague Boston London 1997, 261 et seq.

129 Case C-140/97 Rechberger [1999] ECR I-3499.

130 Case C-321/97 Andersson [1999] ECR I-3551.

mented the Insolvency Directive 80/897/EEC, the same directive that had been at stake in *Francovich* and in *Sveinbjörnsdóttir*. Two workers had suffered damage and sued the Swedish State (*Svenska Staten*). In view of the planned accession of four of them to the EU, the five EEA/EFTA States had entered into an Agreement on transitional arrangements for a period after the accession of certain EFTA States to the EU on 28 September 1994[131]. According to Article 5 of this Agreement, after accession, new preliminary reference proceedings could only be brought before the EFTA Court in cases in which the facts occurred before accession and the application was lodged with the Court within three months after accession. Under Article 7 of that Agreement, the EFTA Court of five judges was to conclude all pending cases within six months of accession. On 1 January 1995, Austria, Finland, and Sweden joined the EU. The ECJ held that it had no jurisdiction to answer these questions because the facts occurred before the two countries became Member States of the European Union. But, the ECJ added in *Rechberger*, in *dicta*, that the EFTA **Court** found State liability to be part of EEA law in its *Sveinbjörnsdóttir* judgment[132]. However, in *Andersson*, this statement was not made. Both judgments were rendered on the same day, 15 June 1999. Nobody knows about the reason for this difference in dealing with the two cases. If you believe in the teachings of Legal Realism, the first thing to do when confronted with such a phenomenon is to look at the **names of the judges** who have been sitting. In fact, the ECJ sat in slightly different composition in the two cases. In *Rechberger*, the Italian judge was sitting, but not in *Andersson* and in *Andersson* the Swedish judge participated, but not in *Rechberger*. *Svenska Dagbladet* wrote an article and guessed that the Swedish judge had seen to it that his government did not have to pay[133]. I do wish to not comment. In any case, the ECJ's reference to EFTA Court *Sveinbjörnsdóttir* in *Rechberger* turned out to be very important when the second State liability case, the *Karlsson* case, came before the Court.

3. EFTA Court Karlsson (2002)

Case E-4/01 *Karlsson*[134] was again based on a reference from the Reykjavík District Court. The *Karlsson* firm was the sole importer for *Cointreau*, the French brandy. Since Iceland did not abolish its **alcohol import monopoly** upon the entry into force of the EEA Agreement, *Karlsson* could not sell for almost two years. When the monopoly finally was abrogated, *Karlsson* sued the government for compensation of its lost profit. That Article 16 EEA had been breached was clear. The Icelandic government observed that it was prepared to live with *Sveinbjörnsdóttir*, but the Norwegian government urged the Court to overrule that judgment. Had we followed this advice, we could have

131 Agreement on transitional arrangements for a period after the accession of certain EFTA States to the European Union of 28 September 1994, printed in [1994–1995] EFTA Court Report, 161 ff.

132 Loc. cit., at paragraph 39; see with regard to the importance of that reference John Forman, The EEA Agreement Five Years On: Dynamic Homogeneity in Practice and Its Implementation by the Two EEA Courts, 1999 C.M.L.Rev. 751, 753.

133 See Svenska Dagbladet Mndagen 8 (21 June 1999).

134 Case E-4/01 Karlsson [2002] EFTA Court Report 240.

closed down and gone home. But we confirmed *Sveinbjörnsdóttir*. And we mentioned the reference to our ruling in the ECJ's *Rechberger* judgment. You see how important judicial dialogue can be in such a power game. We even went one step further than in *Sveinbjörnsdóttir* in that we not only answered the first question but also the second question, namely whether there was a sufficiently serious breach. We found that the breach was indeed a **sufficiently serious** one and thereby excluded the possibility that a national court would find that there is no liability at the end of the day. That is what the German Supreme Court did in its judgment in the *Brasserie du Pêcheur* case. As far as the provision prohibiting the use of the name "beer" was concerned if the ingredients did not correspond to German law, the Supreme Court found the breach to be sufficiently serious. In further examining the issue of the designation "beer", the Supreme Court could, however, not see a direct causal link between the breach of EC law and the damage suffered. With regard to the prohibition to use certain additives, the *Bundesgerichtshof* held that the breach was not sufficiently serious[135]. The French brewery which like the *Karlsson* firm had been unlawfully prevented from selling its products left the courthouse empty-handed.

4. Further EFTA Court case law

There have been further cases on State liability before my court. In the meantime, it is settled case law[136].

5. Acceptance by the national courts

The **Icelandic courts** accepted State liability but the Supreme Court did not do it with enthusiasm. Following dualist theory, the Justices did not approve State liability because it is part of EEA law, but because they found a legal basis for it in Icelandic tort law[137]. What a coincidence and what a piece of luck that the Justices found that basis!

The **Norwegian Supreme Court** accepted EEA State liability in the second *Finanger* case by nine votes against four[138]. I will come back to the *Finanger* saga later.

---

135 See Judgment of the German Supreme Court of 24 November 1996, III ZR 127/91, Europäische Zeitschrift für Wirtschaftsrecht 1996, 761.

136 Case E-8/07 Celina Nguyen [2008] EFTA Court Report 223; see also Case E-1/07 Criminal proceedings against A [2007] EFTA Court Report 248, at paragraph 42.

137 Judgment of the Supreme Court of 16 December 1999 Sveinbjörnsdóttir, Case No. 236/1999, Hæstiréttur Íslands Report as H 1999 4916; see Thorgeir Örlygsson, Iceland and the EFTA Court, Twelve Years of Experience, in: Mario Monti, Prinz Nikolaus von und zu Liechtenstein, Bo Vesterdorf, Jay Westbrook (eds.), Economic Law and Justice in Times of Globalisation, Festschrift for Carl Baudenbacher, Baden-Baden/Berne/Vienna 2007, 225 et seq.

138 Norges Høyesterett (Supreme Court of Norway), Rt. 2005, 1365 (Finanger II).

The **Swedish Supreme Court** opted for EEA State liability in the *Andersson* case by three against two votes[139]. Andersson was the case in which the ECJ had not made reference to EFTA Court *Sveinbjörnsdóttir*[140]. The referring Stockholm tingsrätt found nevertheless in favour of the plaintiffs, but the judgment was reversed by the Appeals Court[141].The Swedish Supreme Court by three votes against two accepted EEA State liability and ruled in favour of the plaintiffs. In doing so, it based itself on the Court's and the Icelandic Supreme Court's judgments in the *Sveinbjörnsdóttir* case. Professor *Ulf Bernitz* has argued that the *Andersson* ruling of the Supreme Court had important legal consequences. First, the judgment made it clear that "**a monistic view** in line with what is Community law has been adopted in Sweden also in relation to the application of EEA law", and second, "the Swedish Supreme Court's stance in the *Andersson* case concerning liability for damages according to the EEA Agreement has become an important precedent also in relation to the long disputed issue of the Swedish courts' possibilities to award damages to be paid by the Swedish State for violations of the European Convention (sc. on Human Rights and Fundamental Freedoms) connected to flaws in Swedish legislation or practices by Swedish courts or other authorities" [142].

We are having a peculiar situation in **Liechtenstein**, the only monist country in the EFTA pillar of the EEA. I mentioned the case in which three Austrian doctors had applied for a licence to practice in Liechtenstein. Liechtenstein had enacted legislation based on the so-called "Single Practice Rule". The single practice rule stated that every doctor could only run one medical practice, either in Austria or in Liechtenstein, but not in both countries. The Austrian doctors did not want to close down their offices, they only wanted to practice part time in Liechtenstein. The Court found this to constitute a violation of the freedom of establishment[143] and as a consequence Liechtenstein abolished the single practice rule. Subsequently, one of the doctors sued the Liechtenstein State for compensation because he had been unable to practice in Liechtenstein in all these years. The Court of Appeal found in favour of the plaintiff, but the **Supreme Court** ruled against him. Strictly speaking, the Supreme Court did not base its ruling on EEA law, but rather on domestic State liability law[144]. In Liech-

---

139 Cases Nos. T-2593/01 and T-2595/01 Susanne Wåkerås Andersson and Ulla-Brith Andersson v The State of Sweden, reported in NJA 2004, 662.

140 See supra, D.2.

141 T G-16/97 and T 6-17/07 Stockholm tingsrätt; Appeals Court (Hovrätten) judgment of 7 June 2001, see Martin Johansson, State liability within the EEA from a Swedish perspective – Sveinbjörnsdóttir confirmed, [2005] European Law Reporter, 50 et seq.

142 Ulf Bernitz, The Application of EEA Law in Sweden, in: Mario Monti, Prinz Nikolaus von und zu Liechtenstein, Bo Vesterdorf, Jay Westbrook (eds.), Economic Law and Justice in Times of Globalisation, Festschrift for Carl Baudenbacher, Baden-Baden/Berne/Vienna 2007, 29, 35 et seq, emphasis added.

143 Cases E-4/00 Dr Johann Brändle [2000–2001] EFTA Court Report 123; E-5/00 Dr Josef Mangold [2000–2001] EFTA Court Report 163; E-6/00 Dr Jürgen Tschannet [2000–2001] EFTA Court Report 203.

144 Beschluss, Oberster Gerichtshof, CO.2004.2-25 (7 December 2006), Jus & News 137 (January 2007); critical remarks were made by Bernhard Hofstötter, Rechtsfehlerhafte Abweisung einer EWR-Staatshaftungsklage als judikatives Unrecht?: (Urteil des Obersten Gerichtshofs vom 7. Dezember 2006 [CO.2004.2-25]), Jus & News Jan 2007, 33 et seq., and Constanze Semmelmann, Staatshaftung in Liechtenstein – ein Sonderweg im EWR?: (Fürstlicher Oberster Gerichtshof Liechtenstein, Urteil vom 7. Dezember 2006, CO.2004.2-25.), [1997] 4 European Law Reporter, 131 et seq.

tenstein State liability law there is a fault requirement. The Supreme Court held that the government was not at fault because it had not been known in advance that the single practice rule was incompatible with EEA law. The State Court (= Constitutional Court) quashed this judgment in 2007 [145] and sent it back to the Supreme Court. The Austrian plaintiff asked the Supreme Court to make a reference to the EFTA Court. However, the Supreme Court refused to do that and made basically the same ruling again against the doctor. This time the Supreme Court found that the breach was not sufficiently serious[146]. On 24 June 2009, the State Court overruled also the Supreme Court's second judgment[147]. For the sake of order, it may be added that the **Supreme Administrative Court** made it clear in the aforementioned Case VGH 2005/94 *in dicta* that it fully accepted the Court's State liability jurisprudence[148].

E. EEA law friendly interpretation

The Court adopted the principle of EEA law friendly interpretation in two cases: *Karlsson*[149] and *Criminal Proceedings against A*[150]. This is the same principle as has been recognised by the ECJ in cases such as *Marleasing*[151].

F. Lack of horizontal direct effect – State liability: The *Finanger* saga

Veronika Finanger was a young woman who participated in a moonshine party in Norway, and at the end of the party she went on the car of her boyfriend. This man was heavily drunk, drove off the road, and as a result, she was severely injured and has been unable to work since. *Veronika Finanger* brought an action against the driver's insurance company, *Storebrand. Storebrand* invoked a provision in Norwegian law which by tradition also has a counterpart in the laws of other Nordic countries. According to that rule, **a passenger of an intoxicated motor vehicle driver** was basically excluded from insurance coverage if he or she knew or must have known that the driver was under the influence of alcohol. The Norwegian Supreme Court referred the question to the Court whether that provision was compatible with EEA law, namely with the so-called

145 Dr med T v Liechtenstein, StGH 2007/15 (Staatsgerichtshof [State Law Court] acting as Verfassungsgerichtshof [Constitutional Court] 2007) (Liechtenstein), available online at <http://www.stgh.li/Inhalte/themen/StgHPDF/StGH2007-15.pdf> (visited 9 March 2009).

146 Judgment CO.2004.2-38 (5 June 2008).

147 Judgment StGH 2008/87.

148 Judgment of 9 February 2006, at paragraph 31.

149 Case E-4/01 Karlsson [2002] EFTA Court Report 240.

150 Case E-1/07 Criminal proceedings against A [2007] EFTA Court Report 245.

151 Case C-106/89 Marleasing [1990] ECR I-4135; see with regard to the EEA relevance of that judgment Knut Almestad, The duties of co-operation of national authorities and the Community institutions under Article 10 (ex Article 5) of the Treaty of Rome : the EEA variant, FIDE: XIX congress. Vol. I [2000], 427.

"Motor Vehicle Insurance Directives". We found that it was not compatible[152]. The Supreme Court followed our ruling by holding that in fact the State had breached its obligations under the EEA Agreement. However, by a majority of 10:5, the Chief Justice being in the minority, it found that it **could not set aside** a clear provision of Norwegian law, also because predictability for private parties, in the case at hand the insurer, was important[153]. That means that the court denied direct effect in this case. The case was about the application of provisions of a directive and obviously it concerned the **horizontal relationship** between the insurer and the victim. A well-known Norwegian professor said that had the case been about a vertical relationship, the Supreme Court would most probably have found some kind of a construction to come to another result[154]. *Veronika Finanger* then brought an action against the Norwegian State based on the EFTA Court's State liability jurisprudence. She claimed the same amount of money from the State which she had not obtained from the insurance company. This time the Supreme Court ruled in her favour[155]. As I said, the Supreme Court acknowledged **State liability** as being part of EEA law. It also found that the conditions for liability were fulfilled in this case and, most importantly, it rejected the argument of the Norwegian government that the second condition according to which the breach must be sufficiently serious is to be interpreted in a more government-friendly way in EEA law than in EC law. In the oral hearing in Case E-8/07 *Nguyen*, nobody contested EEA State liability anymore[156]. All the governments based their pleadings on the assumption that State liability is part of EEA law. Also the question of whether the condition of there being a sufficiently serious breach should be construed in a more government-friendly way than in EC law was no more an issue. To the contrary, the question was discussed whether the threshold for a sufficiently serious breach should be lower in EEA law than in EC law given the lack of EC style direct effect in EEA law[157]. But the Court stuck to its case law according to which the condition of there being a sufficiently serious breach must be dealt with in the same way in EEA law as in EC law[158].

---

152 Case E-1/99 Storebrand Skadeforsikring AS v Veronika Finanger [1999] EFTA Court Report 119.

153 Norges Høyesterett, Case 55/1999, 16 November 2000, Rt. 2000, 1811 (Finanger); with respect to the predictability issue Henrik Bull, European Law and Norwegian Courts, in: Mueller-Graff/Selvig (eds.), The Approach to European Law in Germany and Norway, Berlin 2004, 95, 102 f.

154 Hans Petter Graver, EEA, Supremacy and the Liquidity of Law – does EU Law Trump the Norwegian Constitution?, ARENA Working Papers, 2005, 7 <http://www.arena.uio.no/news/news2005/Arena%20Conference%20Nov05/Graver.pdf> (last visited on 20 November 2009).

155 Norges Høyesterett, Case 412/2005, 28 October 2005, Rt. 2005, 1365 (Finanger II).

156 Case E-8/07 Nguyen [2008] EFTA Court Report 223.

157 Case E-8/07 Celina Nguyen, Transcript of the Oral Hearing, file with the Court.

158 Loc. cit.

Lecture 4
Methods of interpretation

A. General

1. ECJ Opinion 1/91: The EEA Agreement – A simple treaty under public international law

In Opinion 1/91 the ECJ characterized the EEA Agreement as a **classic public international law treaty**[159]. If taken seriously, this statement would have consequences with regard to the **choice of methods**. The method of interpretation in public international law has been codified in Articles 31 and 32 of the Vienna Convention on the Law of Treaties. Those provisions are conservative rules under which you have to stick to the purpose, but in a historical, not in an actual sense, not in a sense which the European Court of Human Rights calls interpretation in the light of present day conditions. Under the rules of the Vienna Convention, you also may take into account the history of the treaty-making. It is to be noted that the ECJ does not adhere to Articles 31 and 32 of the Vienna Convention when interpreting Community law. It has developed its own methods of interpretation, methods which resemble those used by national supreme and constitutional courts. Special consideration is given to *effet utile*, and dynamic interpretation, i.e. judicial lawmaking, is not ruled out.

2. Falsification of the ECJ's assumption in Opinion 1/91

But Opinion 1/91, with respect, is not an expression of particularly sophisticated thinking. In the ECJ, a fraction prevailed when this Opinion was written which obviously feared that the then planned EEA Court could become a competitor. In fact there are other elements, pointing to another direction. There is the homogeneity goal which is underlying the EEA Agreement. How should we have reached homogeneity if we had used the interpretation methods of the Vienna Convention while the ECJ uses *effet utile* and dynamic interpretation? There is the **role of individuals and economic operators**, I have spoken about that before. This role is also emphasised to be played on the judicial level, in the judicial defense of the rights given to citizens and undertakings[160]. The

159 Opinion 1/91 [1991] ECR I-6079.
160 E.g. Recital 4 of the preamble to the EEA Agreement.

statements in ECJ Opinion 1/91 on the legal nature of the EEA Agreement have been an exaggeration already when they were formulated. In the meantime, not only the part on the legal nature of the EEA Agreement, but also the part on direct effect and supremacy has been largely **falsified** by the development of the case law in both EEA pillars.

Milestones on this path were the Court's *Restamark* judgment[161], where direct effect of implemented rules was recognised, the *Einarsson* judgment[162], where primacy of implemented rules was accepted, the CFI's *Opel Austria* judgment on direct effect of EEA law[163], then *Sveinbjörnsdóttir* and *Karlsson* and ECJ *Rechberger* on State liability[164]. Treaty friendly interpretation was recognised by the Court in *Karlsson* and in *Criminal proceedings against* A[165]. In editorial comments published after the ECJ had handed down its judgment in *Rechberger*, the Common Market Law Review said that with its reference to *Sveinbjörnsdóttir* the EC Court admitted that the thesis according to which the EEA Agreement only creates rights and obligations between governments "has been too one-sided ... This is more than a 'coup de chapeau', a salute to the EFTA Court. With this statement, it is important to note, the EC Court appears to endorse the EFTA Court's judgment."[166]

3. The EEA Agreement as a public international law treaty sui generis

The EEA Agreement cannot be characterized as an agreement under classical public international law. In E-9/97 *Sveinbjörnsdóttir* and in E-2/03 *Ásgeirsson*, both cases originating from Iceland, the Court held that the EEA Agreement is a public **international law treaty *sui generis***, which has created a distinct legal order of its own that is characterized by the making of an internal market, the protection of the rights of individuals and economic operators, and an institutional framework providing for effective surveillance and judicial review[167]. The EEA is a strange animal, an agreement *sui generis* if we look at it from the perspective of classic international law as well as from the perspective of supranational Community law. It is, as I said before, a ***tertium***, a mixed breed. The agreement was created by making use of the tools that were available. International law was taken in order to link the EFTA States as closely as possible to the supranational European Community. A lot of people said at the time, it is an attempt to **square the circle**. This may be so, but it is more a problem on the brains

161 Case E-1/94 Restamark [1994–1995] EFTA Court Report 15.
162 Case E-1/01 Einarsson [2002] EFTA Court Report 1.
163 Case T-115/94 Opel Austria [1997] ECR II-39.
164 Cases E-9/97 Sveinbjörnsdóttir [1998] EFTA Court Report 95 and E-4/01 Karlsson [2002] EFTA Court Report 240; C-140/97 Rechberger [1999] ECR I-3499.
165 Cases E-4/01 Karlsson [2002] EFTA Court Report 240 and E-1/07 Criminal proceedings against A [2007] EFTA Court Report 245.
166 Editorial comments: European Economic Area and European Community: Homogeneity of legal orders?, CMLRev 1999, 697, 700.
167 Sveinbjörnsdottir, loc. cit., at paragraph 59, and E-2/03 Ásgeirsson [2003] EFTA Court Report 185, at paragraph 28.

of certain constitutional law scholars. What counts in practice is the outcome, not so much the constructions. Constructions are important and lawyers must base themselves on them, otherwise we risk losing the rule of law. At the same time constructions are not a goal in themselves. They serve a certain purpose.

Most importantly, the Court also recognised **fundamental rights** under the EEA Agreement in three cases, *TV 1000*, *Bellona*, and *Ásgeirsson*[168]. *Ásgeirsson* was a reference case from a district court south of Reykjavík, Reykjanes. Vessels not showing the Icelandic flag had been fishing cod in the waters off the coasts of Alaska and of Russia. The cod was then processed, and since I have been sitting in this case I know how that is done. You have to take off the head, the skin, you fillet the fish and you take out the bones, you salt it and dry it. And then you sell it, not so much here, but in Portugal, in Spain, or in Italy. The cod was sold in these countries as *Bacalhau de Islandia* although it had not been caught by a vessel showing the Icelandic flag and not in the waters of Iceland. Criminal proceedings were opened against three managers. One of the questions referred by the Reykjanes Court was whether the fish had become a new product under the rules of origin by way of the processing. I remember that I had an interesting discussion with one of the attorneys in this case. If you go to one of the temples of molecular cuisine in Catalonia or in the Basque country and order a portion of *Bacalhau* you pay a fortune. The lawyer argued that by processing the cod a new product was generated. But as the rules of origin are dull rules, he was unsuccessful with that. He could have pleaded a new product if they had taken the skin, e.g., and made a pair of shoes or a handbag out of it. Be that as it may, the most interesting point was another one. One of the three defendants argued that the reference to the Court in itself would lead to a delay of the proceedings and would violate Article 6(1) of the European Human Rights Convention where the right to a **fair trial within a reasonable time** is guaranteed. We held that the preliminary reference procedure is part of granting citizens' fundamental rights and that the delay was minimal. In fact, it only took five months in this case. In the ECJ such proceedings lasted more than 2 years at the time. We used the good opportunity to clearly state that EEA law must be interpreted in the light of fundamental rights and that the provisions of the European Human Rights Convention and the judgments of the European Court of Human Rights are important sources for determining the scope of these rights. We did this in the three cases mentioned, and this is a very important development.

4. Consequences for the choice of the interpretation method

The characterisation of the EEA Agreement as an international law treaty *sui generis* as such leaves open the question of whether the interpretation methods laid down in the Vienna Convention on the Law of Treaties or the ones developed by the ECJ

168 Cases E-8/97 TV 1000 [1998] EFTA Court Report 68, E-2/02 Bellona [2003] EFTA Court Report 52, and E-2/03 Ásgeirsson, loc. cit.

should apply. But the Court has made it clear from the beginning that it uses the same rules when interpreting EEA law as the ECJ when dealing with Community law. This may include judicial law-making. The reason for this choice is the fact that EEA law is much **closer to supranational Community law** than to public international law. The Vienna Convention rules have been invoked once or twice by governments in the early days and I remember that we also had a discussion among the judges. The Vienna Convention would have given the governments more leeway and would have left more sovereignty untouched.

I wrote an article in *Tímarit lögfræðinga* some time ago in which I took the view that being law in action the EEA Agreement had become a supranational treaty[169]. The then Icelandic Minister of Justice felt prompted to protest on his website. He stated that four wise men in his country had told the government in 1991 that the EEA Agreement would not be a supranational treaty. I was rather amused by this, and I happen to know that those wise men said that in 1991, it appeared that the EEA Agreement was not supranational in nature, but that it could develop into that direction. Obviously, this is to a large extent a matter of definition. What counts are the outcomes, not the labels.

B. Interpretation of the EEA Main Agreement

1. Introduction

Although EEA law does not explicitly recognise the distinction between primary and secondary law, in substance this differentiation is also there. We have the main agreement on the one hand, and the directives and regulations and decisions etc. on the other. The main agreement is more important than secondary law. Here, the Court would proceed like the ECJ when dealing with the EC Treaty. Like the supreme courts of our Member States when interpreting their constitution we would look at the **text** first. That is the starting point of every interpretation. Then we would look at the position of the norm in the **scheme** of the Agreement, i.e. systematic interpretation and the **purpose**. With regard to the purpose you have to make a fundamental decision whether you take the purpose in the historic meaning or in the present day meaning. It is quite clear that since we are bound by homogeneity rules and the ECJ looks at the **present day meaning**, we would do the same.

Further factors to be taken into account and actually being taken into account are the Court's **own precedents**, the case law of the ECJ and, as the case may be, of the CFI. The homogeneity rules are a special feature and if there is clear case law of the ECJ, the homogeneity rules would basically replace our own interpretation process, at least in theory. In practice there are, however, always new legal questions. There are always

169 Carl Baudenbacher, Erla María: Viðurkennd réttarsköpun dómstóla, [2007] Tímariti lögfræðinga, 147 (175).

points on which we have to go our own way and most importantly, homogeneity relates to the **outcome** of a case and not so much to the reasoning.

Let me make a point with regard to the significance of **citing your own precedents**. That practice actually stems from the common law. In civil law countries this was never seen as being so important, and in fact I think the ECJ only started to do that after the accession of the common law countries United Kingdom and of Ireland to the community in 1973. Even today they do it in a rather unsystematic way, but they do it. I spoke with the then Chairman of the WTO Appellate Body in Geneva, *Jim Bacchus*, about this in the early years of that institution and he said it will be important for us, too, in order to build up a system of precedents. Governments do not necessarily like this because it gives an international court **more standing**. In the early days of the Court, we sometimes had discussions about whether making reference to our earlier case law or not. We decided to do it. We considered this to be a fundamental element of our activity in the interest of foreseeability of future developments and of legal certainty. In the end citizens and economic operators benefit.

I want to make a general remark here. When it comes to the **reasoning** of the judgment, we try to be as comprehensive as possible. Commentators have found laudable words for the Court's judicial style. Members of the European Commission's Legal Service who represent the Commission in the proceedings before the Court have repeatedly made such remarks. Professor *John Temple Lang*, a former Director in the Commission's DG Competition, who now practices law in a major American law firm, stated in that respect:

> *"The judgments of the EFTA Court are in general shorter, clearer, and more concise than the judgments of the Court of Justice. They are more practical, and for many lawyers easier to read, than the judgments of the Court of Justice used to be, when they were shorter but more abstract. The EFTA Court judgments are straightforward, clear and authoritative."*[170]

I will not comment on this. But let me be clear about one thing. There is no reason to put blame on the ECJ. If you have hundreds and hundreds of cases to deal with, you are in a difficult situation. On the other hand, we do have time and it would be unforgivable if we did not work hard. By the way, it also has its downsides when you do not have many cases. You may tend to repeatedly come back to questions, and you literally discuss every comma. We go over the final version, we, the judges, go over the translation – all this is no more possible at the ECJ.

Now, I have said the text, precedent, the position of the norm in the law, the purpose, and the homogeneity rules are relevant. The homogeneity rules basically state that the

---

170 John Temple Lang, The Importance of the EFTA Court, [2006] in: Porritt, J. (ed.), European Current Law, March 2006, xii.

Court ought to follow relevant ECJ case law. Important elements are also the opinions of **Advocates General** of the ECJ. Advocates General may be the Court's best friends on the EC side. It was always one of my personal goals to establish a good contact with the Advocates General because their opinions may constitute the entrance door for our case law into the case law of the ECJ. How do you establish good contacts with the Advocates General? In many ways. You talk to them, you publish articles, you give speeches, you make them aware of your cases, not to mention participation in social events. As a small dog you must bark louder than a big dog. Most importantly, we started quoting them. Vanity is a human sentiment, and once they see that we are making reference to them, they will be more inclined to take us into account. In one case we have even made reference to judgments of national courts of EC Member States[171]. I said at the Nordic Law Conference here in Reykjavík a couple of years ago that we should start to systematically quote the **supreme courts** of our Member States[172]. That would make them much more inclined to refer cases to us.

The Court has early on been faced with a couple of very fundamental questions concerning interpretation. In the first years all the EEA/EFTA governments argued that given the **alleged difference of goal and context** emphasised by the ECJ in Opinion 1/91, the EEA Agreement must be interpreted in a different way from the EC Treaty. Again, the assertion was that we should be more government-friendly. We also heard the argument that the fundamental freedoms include a *de minimis* rule. Furthermore, we were told that under the EEA Agreement, there are additional justification grounds, more justification grounds than under the EC Treaty. I have written an article on this in the Festschrift for *Claus Gulmann*, the former Danish Advocate General and Judge of the ECJ[173]. We rejected all these arguments, as they were totally unfounded. However, an interesting question is whether **climate** and **geography** can be invoked as a justification ground. We are half way to the United States here, in the middle of the Atlantic Ocean and far in the North. Basically there could be cases in which the climate and geography argument is relevant, but there are other cases where it cannot be deemed to be decisive. We had to decide the *Fagtún* case (E-5/98)[174], a case referred to us by the Supreme Court of Iceland. It was a public procurement case where the procurement conditions stated that due to the specific weather conditions in Iceland the roof for a school here in Reykjavík had to be made of self ventilating elements and these elements could only be manufactured in Iceland, because only Icelanders had the necessary experience. This we threw out as an argument. But you can imagine cases in which you could take climate and geography into account. In fact, in the *Finnmark* case (E-3/05), the Court found that a regional residence requirement for family benefits could be justified as a means to promote sustainable settlement in an area "where there has been a decline in population, and where living condi-

---

171 Case E-3/02 Paranova v Merck [2003] EFTA Court Report 101.

172 Det 37. nordiske Juristmøde I Reykjavík, 18.-20. august 2005, Bind II, p. 79.

173 Carl Baudenbacher: Governments before the EFTA Court, in: Festskrift til Claus Gulmann, Kopenhagen: Thomsen, 2006, 23 et seq.

174 Case E-5/98 Fagtún [1999] EFTA Court Report 51.

tions are particularly difficult due to, *inter alia*, harsh climate, vast distances and sparse population"[175].

I come to another important point. We have heard many times by parties and in particular by governments that under Articles 6 EEA and 3(2) SCA, we are bound by old ECJ case law, but not by new case law. We never spelled it out the way I am doing it now, but we tend to follow ECJ case law **no matter whether it is old or new**. In fact, you cannot uphold homogeneity otherwise. I would not rule out that in an extreme case one day we will rely on this distinction but we have not done it so far. If I may open a parenthesis here: This is exactly the point where the EEA Agreement differs from the bilateral treaties Switzerland concluded with the European Union. The Swiss Supreme Court has always followed old ECJ case law, but occasionally it has refused to adopt new ECJ case law[176]. This has caused irritation on the side of the EC Council. Although the Swiss Supreme Court is entitled to proceed the way it did under the homogeneity rules of the bilateral agreements, the Council published a paper in December 2008 containing critical remarks. It commended the EEA judicial mechanism and called upon the responsible Swiss institutions to look for solutions that would secure **present day homogeneity**[177]. Thus, even under the bilateral agreements Switzerland has concluded with the European Union there may be this dynamic element in the future.

2. Existence of "relevant" case law of the ECJ

General

The EFTA Court had to answer the question of whether judgments of the ECJ which have recognised **general principles** in EC law were "relevant" within the meaning of the EEA homogeneity rules.

The expression "relevant" is mentioned in Article 6 EEA and in the second paragraph of Article 3 of the ESA Court Agreement. The case law must be relevant in order to be followed or taken into account. We heard pleadings by **government agents** that the ECJ's case law concerning direct effect, primacy and State liability was not relevant for the interpretation of the EEA Agreement. As I said in my second lecture, we found judgments of the ECJ concerning State liability, the principle of EEA friendly inter-

175 Case E-3/05 ESA v Norway (Finnmark) [2006] EFTA Court Report 101, at paragraph 57; see generally Peter Christian Müller-Graff, The Impact of Climate, Geography and Other Non-Legal Factors on EC law and EEA law, in: Carl Baudenbacher/Per Tresselt/Thorgeir Örlygsson (eds.), The EFTA Court Ten Years On, 55 et seq.

176 ATF 132 V 423.; see supra, lecture 2

177 Draft Council conclusions on EU relations with EFTA countries, Doc. No. 16651/1/08, <http://register.consilium.europa.eu/pdf/en/08/st16/st16651-re01.en08.pdf> (last visited on 27 July 2009); see Carl Baudenbacher, Wachsende Dynamik im Bilateralismus, Neue Zürcher Zeitung of 14 January 2009.

pretation and fundamental rights to be relevant. With regard to effect and primacy we went the middle course as I mentioned.

Creative homogeneity

I said previously that the Court is bound by homogeneity rules to follow or to take into account relevant case law of the ECJ and that the dichotomy between old and new case law is hardly of any significance in practice. I also explained that the homogeneity rules relate primarily to the outcome of a case and not so much to the reasoning. In fact, in a number of cases we have given **different reasons** than the ECJ and I think in some of these cases we were more convincing. This has been confirmed with regard to one important area by a longstanding judge of the ECJ, Professor *Christiaan Timmermans*. As president of the second chamber, he is also a born member of the Grand Chamber of the ECJ. As a parenthesis I may mention that some people think that at the ECJ there is now some sort of a two class society. The judges belonging to the Grand Chamber have more influence on the case law as a whole than those not belonging to it.

Mr *Timmermans* created a notion which he calls "creative homogeneity"[178]. By this, he describes a constellation in which the EFTA Court basically follows the ECJ with regard to the outcome of a case, but uses different reasons, and maybe the outcome might be **slightly different**. This is obviously a fine line to walk. We are not supposed to become inhomogeneous, but at the same time we want to use our good judgment and in certain circumstances we may be unwilling to follow the ECJ on a track which we think is not optimal. The example for this given by Mr *Timmermans* is the Court's case law concerning the written **justification grounds** in Article 13 EEA which is the equivalent of Article 36 TFEU (ex Article 30 EC, and the so-called **mandatory requirements** which have been acknowledged by the ECJ in the *Cassis de Dijon* case[179] under what is now Article 34 TFEU (ex Article 28 EC). In our Agreement the corresponding provision is Article 11. The ECJ has developed a very sophisticated, but also confusing system: In case of indistinctly applicable measures you may invoke the mandatory requirements but in the case of distinctly applicable measures you may not do that. We just disregarded this distinction. We treat the written justification grounds in Article 13 of the EEA Agreement in exactly the same way as the unwritten mandatory requirements. That Mr *Timmermans* has called "creative homogeneity".

Other examples of creative homogeneity can be found in Cases E-5/96 *Nille*, E-6/96 *Wilhelmsen*, E-8/00 *LO*, E-1/06 *Gaming Machines*, and E-3/06 *Ladbrokes*[180]. As regards

---

178 Christiaan Timmermans, Creative Homogeneity, in: Martin Johansson, Nils Wahl, Ulf Bernitz (eds.), A European for all seasons: Liber Amicorum in Honour of Sven Norberg, Brussels 2006, 471–484.

179 Case 120/78 Cassis de Dijon [1979] ECR 649.

180 Cases E-5/96 Nille [1997] EFTA Court Report 30, E-6/96 Wilhelmsen [1997] EFTA Court Report 53, E-8/00 LO [2002] EFTA Court Report 114, E-1/06 Gaming Machines [2007] EFTA Court Report 7, E-3/06 Ladbrokes [2007] EFTA Court Report 85.

LO, it is the only case so far referred from a Labour Court. It concerned the question of whether **collective bargaining agreements** which have been concluded between the unions and the employers' associations are fully sheltered from EEA competition law or whether there are limits to this immunity. The ECJ had previously adopted a rather union-friendly approach. In C-67/96 *Albany* and in related cases, it found that collective agreements aim at improving the working conditions and therefore are out of the reach of European competition law[181]. In contrast to Advocate General *Jacobs*, the EC Court did not examine the limits of such immunity. *Francis Jacobs* had carried out a comparative study which included the law of the United States and had come to the conclusion that in all the systems examined collective agreements are to some extent sheltered from the cartel prohibition, but that immunity is not unlimited[182]. The Court reproduced this statement almost verbatim and cited the respective point in the Advocate General's opinion[183]. The ECJ did not mention the opinion in *Albany*. The Court also held that the good faith of the parties in concluding and implementing a collective agreement had to be taken into account[184]. Advocate General *Jacobs* pointed to that requirement in his opinion[185], but the ECJ did not. What we did was an act of **dialectic judicial dialogue**. In the meantime, another Advocate General, Professor *Poiares Maduro*, made reference to us on that very point in his opinion in C-438/05 *Viking Line* where he, too, argued for a concept of limited antitrust immunity of collective agreements[186].

LO was also interesting from a **political point of view**. In its written submissions, the Norwegian government urged the Court to stick to the line of argument followed by the ECJ in *Albany*. In the oral hearing, however, the Norwegian agent withdrew her government's written submissions and asked the Court to decide in accordance with the opinion of Advocate General *Jacobs* in Albany [187]. The reason for this shift was that between the written and the oral procedure, a new conservative government had been established in Norway. The Commission for its part unsuccessfully recommended the Court to limit itself to marginal control of the clauses of the collective agreement[188].

181 Cf. case C-67/96 Albany [1999] ECR I-5751.

182 Loc. cit., at paragraph 109.

183 Loc. cit., at paragraph 35.

184 Loc. cit., at paragraph 56.

185 Loc. cit., at paragraphs 192, 194, 296.

186 Opinion of AG Maduro delivered on 12 September 2007, C-438/05 Viking Line [2007] ECR I-10779, at paragraph 27. AG Poiares Maduro also referred to AG Jacobs in Albany.

187 Transcript of the Oral Hearing, 47 et seq., file with the Court.

188 Transcript of the Oral Hearing, 64 et seq. (76 et seq.), file with the Court.

3. Lack of "relevant" case law of the ECJ

General

A more challenging situation exists if there is no relevant case law of the ECJ. It is quite clear that in such a case the Court has to find its own solution. That is the **"going first"-constellation**. I called it so more than ten years ago in a speech and it has meanwhile become a technical term. The "going first"-constellation has not been foreseen by the drafters of the EEA Agreement. They have not inserted any provision on this. The ECJ is under no written obligation to take us into account, but experience shows that it does so in certain circumstances.

Teleological interpretation

When we have to answer a fresh legal question, teleological considerations which focus on the purpose of a provision are of paramount importance. An example I want to mention concerns Case E-5/98 *Fagtún*[189]. It is one of two references from the Supreme Court of Iceland to the EFTA Court. *Fagtún* was about the roof elements which were said to be only acceptable if they stemmed from an Icelandic source, I mentioned this. But the first question was a different one. The Icelandic authorities had inserted this new condition into the specifications after the closure of the tender procedure. We said that from a teleological perspective, it cannot be decisive whether you insert such a clause into the specifications before the tender takes place or after the tender procedure has been closed.

Functional interpretation

In German and in Swiss methodology there is a further distinction when we speak about teleological interpretation between what some authors call micro-teleology on the one hand and macro-teleology on the other[190]. Micro-teleology asks about the purpose of the norm for the parties concerned whereas **macro-teleology** would ask the question what are the consequences for the system as a whole. Functional interpretation is similar to interpretation according to the *effet utile*. It means that we ask what the consequences of a certain interpretation for the well-functioning of the EEA single market are or, as the case may be, for the well-functioning of the competition system in

---

189 Case E-5/98 Fagtún [1999] EFTA Court Report 51.

190 See Walter R. Schluep, Was ist Wirtschaftsrecht?, Festschrift for Walter Hug, Berne 1968, 25 et seq., 66 et seq.; Ernst Steindorff, Politik des Gesetzes als Auslegungsmassstab im Wirtschaftsrecht, Festschrift for Karl Larenz, Munich 1973, 217 et seq.; Carl Baudenbacher, Wirtschafts-, schuld- und verfahrensrechtliche Grundprobleme der Allgemeinen Geschäftsbedingungen, Zurich 1983, 82 et seq.

the EEA. This has been used in the *LO* case[191] which I have spoken about briefly, when the Norwegian labour associations were of the opinion that their collective agreements were sheltered from EEA competition law. The Court found that it had to give an interpretation that takes into account the significance of the **competition law rules** for the good functioning of the EEA. That was clearly functional. The same happened in *Husbanken*[192] when we as the first court in Europe said that state guarantees for publicly owned banks constituted state aid within the meaning of Article 61(1) EEA, the provision mirroring Article 107(1) TFEU (ex Article 87[1] EC) since it was capable of **distorting competition**. This was confirmed in E-1/00 *Íslandsbanki*[193] and in E-9/04 *HFF*[194].

An interesting case of functional interpretation is E-1/98 *Astra Norge*[195]. Most commentators of our case law focus on the sovereignty issue. They speak about *Sveinbjörnsdóttir*, they speak about *Restamark* giving the impression as if all this was only a matter between a supranational level and a national level. This may be a consequence of the fact that EEA law specialists often have a public international law background. However, there are also private law cases or cases in which **private interests** are at stake on both sides. The Court did not have many cases of this type so far, but it had a couple of them and *Astra Norge* is such a case. In EEA law as in EC law there is a fundamental principle with regard to intellectual property rights. If you own a patent, a trade mark or a copyright, you cannot control the distribution of your protected goods in an unlimited way. Once you have put your goods on the market in another Member State, your distribution right is exhausted. The **principle of exhaustion** is of particular relevance for the pharmaceutical industry and as you can imagine this industry is rather critical about it. They therefore look for measures that would make parallel importers' lives difficult. *Astra Norge* knew it could not stop parallel imports as such, but it claimed that it owned a **copyright** in the respective Summary of Product Characteristics (SPC). The SPC is the sheet of paper which comes with the pills in the box and lists the components, informs about the forms of intake, the side effects and the like. Surprisingly enough, the Oslo City Court recognised a copyright in *Astra's* SPC. That was obviously a mistake, but we could not look into this because it was a matter of national law. However, when *Astra* tried to invoke its copyright in order to prevent a parallel importer from using its SPC, we found that this amounted to a restriction of the free movement of goods. To be exact, it was deemed to constitute a disguised restriction on trade within the meaning of Article 13(2), second sentence, of the EEA Agreement. With this, the Court set aside the **core matter of the copyright** which was quite a revolutionary step. The setting aside of the copyright was the result of a functional interpretation. To allow such a bogus copyright to be invoked would have constituted a serious threat to a free market system.

191 Case E-8/00 LO [2002] EFTA Court Report 114.
192 Case E-4/97 Husbanken II [1999] EFTA Court Report 1.
193 Case E-1/00 Íslandsbanki [2000–2001] EFTA Court Report 8.
194 Case E-9/04 HFF [2006] EFTA Court Report 41.
195 Case E-1/98 Astra Norge [1998] EFTA Court Report 140.

I give you another example, on a similar track: The pharmaceutical companies not only tried to make the parallel importers' lives miserable by attempting to enforce a copyright in the SPC, they also pursued another strategy. They used different box sizes, different marketing, different colors, all sorts of differences in the appearance of the products in various Member States. That's why the ECJ held early on that a parallel importer may **repackage** the pharmaceuticals if this is **necessary** for him to gain market access in the second country. In Joined Cases C-427/93, C-429/93 and C-436/93 *Bristol-Myers Squibb*[196] the ECJ listed a number of requirements which a parallel importer must fulfill in order to be considered to have lawfully repackaged. E.g. the repackaging must not affect the inner layer, the blister stripes, only the outer box, the trade mark owner must be informed in advance, the trade mark owner must be sent a sample, the parallel importer must make it clear on the box who has repackaged, and finally, he must put on the trade mark.

The Supreme Court of Norway which does not have the reputation of being keen to ask for preliminary rulings referred questions to the Court in Case E-3/02 *Paranova v Merck*[197] that had not been answered by the ECJ. *Paranova*, a well-known parallel importer in the North based in Denmark, had started a new scheme. Not only would they repackage the pharmaceuticals but they would do the following: On the original *Merck* box, there are two color stripes in the middle of the box. *Paranova* used its own boxes, affixed the trade mark *Merck* on them and said "repackaged by *Paranova*", but instead of putting the color stripes in the middle it moved them to the edges. In other words, *Paranova* added its **own design elements**.

Since *Paranova* did that with all the pharmaceuticals it repackaged, it created its own product line. In the case of *Merck* it was black and green, in the case of *Novartis* it was black and yellow, in the case of *Bayer* it was black and red, etc. *Merck* argued before the Norwegian Supreme Court that this amounted to a violation of its trade mark. It stated that the **necessity test**, as developed by the ECJ, also applied to the change of design, that there was not the slightest necessity for the parallel importer to add new design elements in order to gain market access, that the parallel importer should use the original design. The Court rejected this contention. Once the right to repackage and to depict the original trade mark is established, and market access is thereby assured, the necessity test no longer applies. Instead, one has to make an **open balancing test**, balance the interests involved and then one must take into account also the function of the parallel importer for the regulation of prices in the field. The Court even held that the parallel importer is to be considered as an operator on basically **equal footing** with the manufacturer and trade mark proprietor within the framework of the Trade Mark Directive. This was obviously functional interpretation, focusing on the good functioning of a free market system. The pharmaceutical industry was unhappy about this. They said that this was bad case law which the ECJ should not follow. The line

196 Joined Cases C-427/93, C-429/93 and C-436/93 Bristol-Myers Squibb [1996] ECR I-3457.
197 Case E-3/02 Paranova v Merck [2003] EFTA Court Report 101.

of argument was in particular that judgments like this one constitute a disincentive for research and development.[198]

I will come back to this case in my fifth lecture because it is a case in which we have influenced the ECJ's case law. There was also a special constellation because our judgment prompted the Court of Appeals of England and Wales to make a reference to the ECJ[199].

Dynamic interpretation

Dynamic interpretation may be an option for the Court also in going first cases, i.e. not only when we have to close a gap between EEA and EU law, but also when we decide a fresh legal question. The most important example is the judgment in the *Kellogg's* case[200]. *Kellogg's* concerned the following factual situation: All over Europe *Kellogg's* cornflakes which are **fortified** with certain vitamins and with a certain amount of iron could be freely sold. However, the Norwegian health authorities banned the marketing in Norway and ESA brought an infringement action against Norway. ESA took the view that this was an unlawful restriction on the free movement of goods. The Norwegians argued firstly that there was **no nutritional need** in their country for this, because the population had enough vitamin and enough iron. We, the State, they said, see to it that our people get enough iron by giving them a piece of goat cheese fortified with iron in school every morning until they are fifteen years, and after these fifteen years they have enough iron for the rest of their lives. The nutritional need argument was based on a certain reading of an ECJ judgment from the early 1980's[201]. We rejected it. Secondly, the Norwegian government invoked the **precautionary principle**, and the Court accepted that in principle. According to this maxim, a national government is entitled to take action even if there is no final proof that a product is dangerous as long as qualified scientists in the field have taken this view. The government must have carried out a comprehensive risk assessment. It cannot base itself on hypothetic considerations and it may only aim at zero risk in the most exceptional circumstances. Measures must be transparent, proportionate, non-discriminatory, and the fortification policy as a whole must be consistent. The Norwegian policy obviously was inconsistent. If you give away cheese fortified with iron to all school children and if you allow pharmacists to sell vitamin products without a prescription requirement, then you are not consistent. So Norway lost the case, but in a future case it could possibly invoke the precautionary principle.

---

198 Arguments against this position have been put forward by Jonas Myhre, Parallel imports and "co-branding" of pharmaceuticals – analysis and comments, [2008] Nordiskt Immateriellt Rättsskydd, 388 (394 et seq.).

199 Case C-348/04 Boehringer Ingelheim II [2007] ECR I-3391.

200 Case E-3/00 EFTA Surveillance Authority v Norway ('Kellogg's') [2000–2001] EFTA Court Report 73.

201 Case C-174/82, Sandoz B.V. [1983] 2445.

That the EFTA Court's *Kellogg's* judgment was based on dynamic interpretation became clear when AG *Mischo* presented his opinion in the subsequent ECJ case C-192/01 *Commission v Denmark*. The case was about very similar facts as *Kellogg's*. Mr *Mischo* invited the ECJ to accept the nutritional need argument put forward by the Danish government, to disregard the EFTA Court's *Kellogg's* ruling and to dismiss the Commission's action. The ECJ found in favour of the Commission[202]. The Commission had characterized the Court's *Kellogg's* judgment "as an element in the development of the law"[203], which reflected the considerable changes in the methods used to determine health risks in the past 20 years.

In E-1/04 *Fokus Bank* the Court held that a Contracting Party (Norway) which granted a tax credit to shareholders residing in that State on dividends paid by domestic companies (so-called **outbound dividends**), but denied such a favour to shareholders residing in other EEA countries violated the free movement of capital[204]. In making the differentiation in question, national legislation was based on the assumption that non-resident shareholders were reimbursed in their respective home state. The Court admitted that Contracting Parties are, within the framework of bilateral double taxation agreements, at liberty to determine the connecting factors for the purposes of allocating powers of taxation as between themselves. However, that does not mean that in the exercise of the power of taxation so allocated, a Contracting Party may disregard EEA law. Possible tax advantages in the home state could not offset the restriction and discrimination. A Contracting Party cannot shift its obligation to comply with the EEA Agreement to another Contracting Party by relying on the latter to make good for discrimination and disadvantages caused by the former's legislation. Likewise, the principle of **legal certainty** would require that the granting of an imputation tax credit to a non-resident shareholder may not depend on whether a tax credit is granted in his or her state of residence in respect of dividend payments.

Attempts of the Norwegian government to justify the violation of Article 40 EEA were rejected. The Court held that derogations from the fundamental principle of the free movement of capital were to be interpreted strictly. It considered resident and non-resident shareholders in Norway to be in an objectively **comparable situation**, referring to the judgment of the Court of Justice of the European Communities in Case C-319/02 *Manninen*[205]. The Court did not accept cohesion of the international tax system as a justification, since permitting derogations from the fundamental principle of free movement of capital laid down in Article 40 EEA on the grounds of safeguarding the cohesion of the international tax system would amount to giving **bilateral tax agreements** preference over EEA law. A Contracting Party therefore cannot make the rights conferred by Article 40 EEA subject to the contents of a bilateral agreement

202 Case C-192/01 Commission v Denmark [2003] ECR I-9693.

203 Cf. Opinion of AG Mischo in Case C-192/01 Commission v Denmark [2003] ECR I-9693, at paragraph 79.

204 Case E-1/04 Fokus Bank ASA, [2004] EFTA Court Report, 11.

205 Case C-319/02 Manninen [2004] ECR, I-7477, at paragraphs 35–37.

concluded with another Contracting Party. Also, the legislative history of the Corporate Tax Act gave rise to the assumption that the real purpose of the Act was not to preserve the cohesion of the international tax system but to protect the Norwegian tax base, a requirement of purely econo mic nature.

At the time, our *Fokus Bank* judgment did not seem to be a particularly revolutionary step. What we did was to extend the *Manninen* jurisprudence of the ECJ which had acknowlegded the same principles in the context of inbound dividends into the sphere of outbound dividends[206]. Both ESA and the European Commission had asked the Court to rule accordingly. After some controversy, the judgment was implemented in Norway. However, in those EC countries which had a **huge budget deficit**, the Court's ruling caused irritation. The German Law Journal *Finanz-Rundschau* published an article bearing the title „Wie drei Richter aus Island, Liechtenstein und Norwegen auszogen, die EU-Staaten das Fürchten zu lehren!" ("How three Judges from Iceland, Liechtenstein and Norway went out to teach the EU States a lesson!")[207] The *Süddeutsche Zeitung*, one of the most prominent German newspapers, wrote: „Geradezu bizarr erscheint, dass nun auch Richter von ausserhalb der Europäischen Union die Gesetzgebung der nationalen Parlamente eingrenzen wollen." [208] ("It is downright bizarre that meanwhile also judges from outside of the European Union are trying to restrict the law making powers of the national parliaments.") When the ECJ was asked similar questions as the EFTA Court in *Fokus Bank*, it basically acknowledged the right of the Members States to invoke the provisions of bilateral Double Taxation Agreements[209]. I will come back to that in my fifth lecture.

Teleological and dynamic interpretation

In E-4/04 *Pedicel* the Court ruled that the exclusion of wine from the product coverage of the EEA Agreement meant also that the provisions concerning the free movement of services did not apply to the **advertising of wine** since in the conditions of the case at hand, the service was inseparably linked to the sale of wine[210]. ESA and the Commission had unsuccessfully argued that the advertisement of wine should be deemed to be covered by Article 36 EEA, the provision mirroring Article 56 TFEU (ex Article 49 EC).

206 Case C-319/02 Manninen [2004] ECR, I-7477.
207 2005, 345.
208 Süddeutsche Zeitung of 25 April 2005.
209 Cases C-374/04 Test Claimants in Class IV [2006] ECR I-11673 and of 27 April 2006, Case C-170/05 Denkavit [2006 ECR I-11919; see also Opinion of Advocate General Geelhoed of 23 February 2006 in Case C-374/04 Test Claimants in Class IV [2006] ECR I-11673 and of 27 April 2006, Case C-170/05 Denkavit [2006] ECR I-11919.
210 Case E-4/04 Pedicel [2005] EFTA Court Report 1.

4. "Widening gap"

The EC Treaty, the model of reference of the EEA Agreement, has been amended no less than four times since the conclusion of the EEA Agreement in 1992, namely in Maastricht, Amsterdam, Nice and Lisbon. At Lisbon the EC Treaty has been renamed "Treaty on the Functioning of the European Union" (TFEU). The question has arisen whether the competent courts – and in particular the EFTA Court – should understand the homogeneity principle in the light of **present day conditions** and thereby implement elements of EU law into EEA law by way of creating case law. The EEA Joint Committee does not have the competence to amend the EEA Main Agreement, and the Contracting Parties will hardly reopen negotiations. The Court may therefore face the task of closing the gap once there has been a further development on the EC side. In a way, the Court laid the methodological ground for this in E-4/04 *Pedicel* where it explicitly held that the objective of creating a dynamic and homogeneous European Economic Area "may make dynamic interpretation of EEA law necessary"[211]. To my knowledge, the ECJ never made such a statement. The EFTA Court made it clear that it is in a special situation if homogeneity of the case law is to be preserved. The other side moves faster than we do. I sometimes describe that as the EFTA pillar dancing slow fox and the EC pillar dancing rock 'n' roll and then somebody must increase the tempo in the EFTA pillar if **homogeneity** is to be maintained. The Court deals with this challenge on a case by case basis[212]. I will give you two examples.

One is the *Einarsson* case E-1/01[213]. I spoke about it in my second lecture. Icelandic tax legislation stated that there was a 24.5 % VAT on books in foreign languages but only a 10 % VAT on books in Icelandic. The Icelandic government attempted to justify this taxation by invoking the justification ground of the need to protect cultural heritage. The argument was that Icelandic is spoken by only a little more than 300'000 people, that the sagas, which constitute **world heritage**, are written in Icelandic, and that therefore the Icelandic VAT regime was justified. The EEA Agreement does not mention such a justification ground nor was there any ECJ case law to that effect. But the Icelandic government invoked Article 151(4) EC (now: Article 167[4] TFEU), which had been inserted into the EC Treaty by the Treaty of Amsterdam and asked the Court to apply this provision by analogy. According to this provision the Community had to take cultural aspects into account in its action under other provisions of the Treaties, in particular in order to respect and to promote the diversity of its cultures. In other words, the government urged the Court to become a **judicial activist**. As you can see, whether being a judicial activist is seen in a negative or in a positive way always depends on where an observer stands. Our position was that you do not need this sort of discriminatory tax legislation in order to protect your language.

---

211 Case E-4/04 Pedicel [2005] EFTA Court Report 101, at paragraph 28.

212 See Carl Baudenbacher, Der EFTA-Gerichtshof, das EWR-Abkommen und die Fortentwicklung des EG-Vertrags, Festschrift für Herbert Batliner, Vaduz 2004, 59 et seq.

213 Case E-1/01 Einarsson [2002] EFTA Court Report 1.

Another example is E-1/02, the *Oslo University* case[214]. Norwegian legislation had gone one step beyond what had been common in the EC Member States with regard to positive discrimination or, as it is called in the U.S., affirmative action. A law had been enacted that stated that a certain number of university posts were **earmarked for members of the underrepresented sex**. The Court did not use the term sex, but spoke of gender. The members of the underrepresented gender in the universities in Norway were women. ESA sued the Norwegian government claiming that the legislation in question was incompatible with the Equal Rights Directive 76/207/EEC[215]. The ECJ had interpreted the Equal Rights Directive as not recognising the concept of group rights. Women could in theory have group rights like, e.g., Indians in Canadian law. The ECJ, however, held repeatedly that every individual case must be assessed on its own merits[216]. Under the EEA homogeneity rules, we were bound to take into account this case law, and we did. The case has some interesting aspects. First of all, after the ECJ's judgment in Case C-450/93 *Kalanke* where the principle that every individual case must be assessed on its own merits had been spelled out for the first time, the Norwegian government declared its intention to ignore this decision[217]. In *University of Oslo* the Norwegian government's agent used two lines of argument. The first line was that the Court should follow the ECJ's case law because that case law, if rightly understood, allowed the earmarking of the posts. The second line of argument was that we should distance ourselves from the ECJ. Again, the Court was called upon **to be a judicial activist**. Then, and that is why I speak about the case under the heading of the "widening gap", the government argued that we should base ourselves on the Amsterdam Treaty and no more on the old EC Treaty as it was relevant when the EEA Agreement was signed. We did not do that. But in a later case, in a half sentence, a little bit hidden, we did make reference to this new Article 141(4) of the EC Treaty (now: Article 157[4] TFEU)[218].

University of Oslo was, by the way, the first time that the Court was composed of two men and **a woman**. No woman has served on the EFTA bench as a regular judge so far. In this case the Icelandic judge at the time, *Thor Vilhjálmsson*, fell ill and we called on his replacement, *Dora Gudmundsdóttir* to sit. It did not look bad for us to have a woman on the bench in this case. This is not to say that women are, as a rule, in favour of affirmative action. My experience is that those who made it to the top are quite critical of positive discrimination.

We inserted what some called a golden paragraph into this judgment. What counts when you have an application by a man and an application by a woman for a chair

---

214 Case E-1/02 EFTA Surveillance Authority v Norway ("University of Oslo") [2003] EFTA Court Report 1.

215 Directive 76/207/EEC of 9 February 1976 on the implementation of the principle of equal treatment for men and women as regards access to employment, vocational training and promotion, and working conditions, [1976] OJ L 39, 40–42, referred to in point 18 of Annex XVIII to the EEA Agreement.

216 See e.g. Cases C-450/93 Kalanke [1995] ECR I-6363 and C-407/98 Abrahamsson [2000] ECR I-5539.

217 See Laura Molinari, The Effect of the Kalanke Decision on the European Union: A Decision With Teeth, But Little Bite, 71 St. John's L. Rev. 591, 629 f. (1997).

218 Case E-2/07 EFTA Surveillance Authority v Norway ("Golden widows") [2007] EFTA Court Report 279, at paragraph 25.

at a university? You compare the length of the publication list, the number of courses taught and all other academic activities. The result is that the man's list has one hundred titles whereas the woman's list has only sixty. What does not show up on the list is what the woman did in addition to that, gave birth to children, raised children – you name it. Our judgment acknowledges that **female life experience** may be taken into account in certain fields. This is a paragraph which is often overlooked, but I am a little bit proud that the Court included it[219].

C. Interpretation of EEA secondary law

1. General

So much for the interpretation of the main agreement. What about the interpretation of secondary law, in particular directives? These measures have exactly the same function as in the EC. If there were no harmonised law, there would just be national statutory law and then courts would use the **usual interpretation canon**: the text, the purpose, the scheme, sometimes even the history. Again, in an unusual move, the EFTA Court has openly stated what kinds of methods of interpretation it adheres to. In two labour law cases originating from Norway, we said that if there is no ECJ jurisprudence which is relevant under the homogeneity rules, then we proceed based on "recognised methods of interpretation"[220]. If there is ECJ case law, we will, as a matter of principle, follow it, but there is the possibility to aim at creative homogeneity.

2. Existence of "relevant" ECJ case law

The Court has oriented itself towards ECJ case law with regard to the structures and basic concepts of secondary law. In a clear majority of cases, the Court has, however, been confronted with new legal questions.

3. Lack of "relevant" ECJ case law (EFTA Court going first)

Textual and teleological interpretation

A case of interpretation of secondary law has been the interpretation of the term **"direct relative"** in the Insolvency Directive. That was at stake in the "*Erla María*" case as the Icelanders call it (E-9/97). For foreigners it is *Sveinbjörnsdóttir*[221]. The question arose

219 Loc. cit., at paragraph 57.

220 Case E-2/95 Eidesund [1995-1996] EFTA Court Report 1, at paragraph 56; and Case E-3/95 Langeland [1995-1996] EFTA Court Report 36, at paragraph 28.

221 Case E-9/97 Sveinbjörnsdóttir [1998] EFTA Court Report 95.

who would be excluded from the wage guarantee. Mrs *Sveinbjörnsdóttir* was the sister of the main shareholder of the bankrupt company. The Court had to answer the question of whether the expression "direct relative" was to be interpreted so as to include the sister of the main shareholder. If that question was answered in the affirmative, she was excluded from the wage guarantee. In other words, the Court had to decide whether direct relatives were only father and mother and daughter and son **or** also siblings. We used **textual interpretation**, looked into a number of language versions. The English wording "direct relative" was not clear. The Icelandic version ("ættingi í beinan legg") had the clear and limited scope of ascendants and descendants, excluding siblings. But from a **teleological** point of view we came to the result that the directive aims at protecting workers and from this perspective it was correct to construe that exclusion as narrow as possible and to have siblings covered by the wage guarantee.

A clear example of teleological reasoning can be found in a case originating from Iceland decided ten years ago, E-2/98 *Federation of Icelandic Trade*[222]. It shows that the EFTA Court often gets good cases first: Ten years later, the ECJ faced exactly the same question. Advocate General Professor *Verica Trstenjak* proposed the ECJ to follow us[223]. In *Federation of Icelandic Trade* the Court had to give interpretation to the so-called Transparency Directive in the field of pharmaceuticals. Article 4 of the Directive states that the competent authorities in a Member State may decide to **freeze the prices**, but they then must conduct a review at least once a year. A price freeze is clearly a restrictive measure. The review must ascertain whether the macroeconomic conditions justify that the freeze continues. Within 90 days from the start of this review, the authorities shall announce what increases or decreases in prices are being made, if any. The Icelandic authorities had not ordered a price freeze, but a **price cut**. They declared that everyone in the pharmaceutical business had to reduce the prices by 2 % or the like. The Directive did not address the issue of price cuts. The Court found that the words price freeze cannot be interpreted so narrowly that they only cover a status quo to the prevailing or pre-existing price level. It pointed to the aim of the Directive to ensure transparency regarding national measures for controlling prices of medicinal products as well as to contextual issues. Furthermore, the Court held that this interpretation was supported by the fact that otherwise the Contracting Parties might easily circumvent their obligations to provide minimum procedural guarantees under Article 4 by adopting general pricing decisions containing modest or minor price cuts instead of freezing prices at the prevailing level. Therefore a price cut was held to be covered by this provision. The consequence is that the authorities have to come up with an assessment within 90 days, and that they have to look into the matter so that the price cut may only be of limited duration.

222 Case E-2/98 Federation of Icelandic Trade [1998] EFTA Court Report 172.

223 See infra, lecture 5.

Principle of effectiveness

In E-8/07 *Celina Nguyen* the Court recognised almost between the lines the principle of effectiveness by stating that national provisions governing compensation for road accidents cannot deprive the Motor Vehicle Insurance Directives of their effectiveness[224]. In this case, the EFTA Court as the first European court also held that under the Motor Vehicle Insurance Directives, insurers are obliged to pay not only for material damages but also for **immaterial damages**, that means pain and suffering. Since Norway had wrongly implemented the measure, the country was found to be liable under the Court's State liability jurisprudence. We also found that this was in fact a sufficiently serious breach of EEA law to be able to entail State liability.

D. Accusation of judicial activism

The ECJ has occasionally been criticised of overstepping the boundaries which are set by the separation of competences between the EC and its Member States[225]. My Court too has been accused of being a **judicial activist**. Norwegian Prime Minister *Jens Stoltenberg* criticised alleged judicial activism in the context of the EFTA Court's case law concerning taxation in 2003 (at that time he was opposition leader)[226]. According to that jurisprudence, the tax systems of the EEA/EFTA States are not, as a rule, covered by the EEA Agreement. However, they may have consequences that would bring them within the scope of application of provisions of the EEA Main Agreement such as those concerning the fundamental freedoms and State aid[227].

In view of the then upcoming *Gaming Machines* case, in which the compatibility of the newly created State monopoly with the fundamental freedoms was at stake, I personally have been described in the Norwegian press as "a supporter of the free market and a liberalist" who would be prepared to expand EEA authority "by handing down judgments which widen the European markets" and thereby take an "activist" position[228]. Obviously this was based on hints given by somebody from the Norwegian government. By the way: I can very well live with the characterisation in question because in fact the EEA Agreement is first and foremost about creating and securing a free market and to a much lesser extent about securing State monopolies. In any case, the

224 Case E-8/07 Nguyen [2008] EFTA Court Report 223, at paragraph 24.

225 See, e.g., Hjalte Rasmussen, On Law and Policy in the European Court of Justice, Dordrecht 1986, 51 et. seq.; Roman Herzog and Lüder Gerken, Stoppt den Europäischen Gerichtshof, Frankfurter Allgemeine Zeitung of 8 September 2008, 8.

226 Oslo Newspaper 'VG' of 20 March 2003, http://www.vg.no/pub/vgart/hbs?artid=51776, cited by Peter Orebrech, The EU Competency Confusion: Limits, 'Extension Mechanisms', Split Power, Subsidiarity, and 'Institutional Clashes', 13 J. Transnat'l L. & Pol. 99, 144, footnote 191 (2003).

227 See Carl Baudenbacher, EFTA Court – Legal framework and case law, 3rd ed., Luxembourg 2008, <http://www.eftacourt.int/images/uploads/Legal_Framework_Finalweb.pdf> (last visited on 19 November 2009).

228 Dagens Naeringsliv, 16 January 2006, 33.

qualification of a court or of a judge as a judicial activist is of political nature, it is as such an **empty formula**[229]. Whether dynamic interpretation by a court is successful or not and whether it is legitimate, depends essentially on whether it is being accepted by the court's audiences.

As I said, in the case of the EEA Agreement we also have to bear in our mind that it can probably not be re-negotiated, it cannot be amended anymore. There has been an attempt by the EEA/EFTA States a couple of years ago to have the Agreement renegotiated. I was always critical towards such a step because the EEA Agreement was negotiated from 1989 to 1991 by seven EFTA States versus 12 EC States. It is a very **good agreement** for the EFTA States, no doubt about that. If negotiations were to be re-opened between now three small countries on the EFTA side – the Swedes, the Swiss, the Finns and the Austrians no more there – and 27 on the other side, this could amount to opening Pandora's box. The outcome could be devastating. To ask for this out of stubbornness would be unwise. Then you may rather accept that the EFTA Court acts as a judicial activist from time to time in order to **close the gap** to the ECJ if the Community has amended a new Treaty or the ECJ has decided dynamically. It is virtually impossible to re-negotiate and we, the judges, are aware of this. But as I will show, we have not in every case used dynamic interpretation when faced with the question of whether we should close a gap between EC and EEA law.

E. Conclusions

1. General

In Opinion 1/91, the ECJ called the EEA Agreement an international treaty which creates obligations only among the Contracting Parties. This characterisation has turned out to be inadequate. The prognosis that the so-called "constitutional principles" of Community law would be incompatible with the peculiarities of the EEA Agreement has been largely falsified with the recognition of quasi-direct effect, quasi-primacy, the obligation of treaty-friendly interpretation, and State liability by the EFTA Court. When I speak of falsification, the term is used within the meaning of science theory (*Thomas S. Kuhn*). EEA law is **no classical public international law** in spite of what we heard for years from government representatives from the Nordic countries. It is a *sui generis* animal. However, it is closer to supranational EC law than to traditional public international law. The Norwegian government as well as one of

229 See Keenan D. Kmiec, The Origin and Current Meanings of 'Judicial Activism', 92 Cal. L. Rev., 1441, 1477 [2004].

the leading Norwegian scholars in the field even speak of a supranational agreement[230]. So does the government of the Principality of Liechtenstein[231].

In Opinion 1/91, the ECJ has also erred with its statement that EEA law ought to be construed in accordance with the interpretation rules of the Vienna Convention on the Law of Treaties. The EFTA Court has never relied on these rules. The ECJ too has never made such a statement when dealing with EEA law. It has in particular not based itself on alleged differences with regard to goals and context, but applied the same methods as when interpreting Community law.

Dynamic interpretation may be an option not only where we have to keep up with the ECJ, but also where we have to "go first". We tend to be cautious on such occasions since we cannot know what the ECJ will do in a later case. And we do stick to the law. If the ECJ does not follow us in a later case, that does not mean that we had it wrong. It may well be that the ECJ has got it wrong. There is the famous saying of a former Justice of the US Supreme Court, Justice *Robert Jackson*, who concurring in *Brown v Allen*, stated in 1953: "We are not final because we are infallible, but we are infallible only because we are final."[232] In the EEA, the ECJ is not final, but in case of a judicial conflict, the Community could open dispute settlement proceedings, and in view of the size of the two EEA pillars it is questionable whether the EFTA side would be in a rather favourable position.

2. Dynamic interpretation vs. diplomacy

Two arguments advanced by the Government of Iceland and the Government of Norway against the recognition of EEA State liability are of particular significance. As stated earlier, the Icelandic government submitted in E-7/97 *Sveinbjörnsdóttir* that if due to the absence of State liability in the EFTA pillar homogeneity should be affected, the matter would have to be dealt with politically and through diplomatic channels, and not by the Court[233]. The Court did not accept this argument.

230 See Hans Petter Graver, EEA Supremacy and the Liquidity of Law – does EU Law Trump the Norwegian Constitution?, ARENA Working Papers, 2005, 8 <http://www.arena.uio.no/news/news2005/Arena%20Conference%20Nov05/Graver.pdf> (last visited on 20 November 2009).; Statement of the Government of the Kingdom of Norway in Case E-1/06 Gaming Machines [2007] EFTA Court Report, Report for the Hearing, 28 et seq., at paragraph 63.

231 See Report to the Landtag Nr. 17/2010, www.llv.li/pdf-llv-rk-bua_017_2010-3.pdf (last visited on 16 April 2010).

232 J. Jackson, Brown v Allen, 344 U.S. 443, 540 (1953) (concurring).

233 Supra, lecture 2.

In E-4/01 *Karlsson* the Norwegian government at the oral hearing mentioned the goal laid down in the preamble to the EEA Agreement to establish a dynamic and homogeneous European Economic Area. It then argued that the dynamic development was reserved for the **governments**. This would have meant that the competence of the EFTA Court would have been limited to securing static homogeneity, i.e. homogeneity as it was understood at the time of the signature of the agreement. The EFTA Court did not follow the Norwegian contention[234].

234 Case E-4/01 Karlsson [2002] EFTA Court Report 240, Transcript of the oral hearing, file with the EFTA Court.

Lecture 5
Dialogue with the EU judiciary

A. Introduction

The judicial dialogue between the Court and the EC judiciary is almost always overlooked in the EEA/EFTA capitals. Most EFTA State government officials are not very interested in our interaction with the EC side. They are sitting in Reykjavík and in Oslo and in Vaduz, primarily concerned with questions such as: Are we affected by this, are we affected by that, sometimes even: Can we pick a cherry here or can we pick a cherry there?

The dialogue which we have developed with the ECJ is blossoming. It took us some efforts to get there. As you remember, in Opinion 1/91 the ECJ had serious misgivings concerning the EEA Agreement, it was in particular very critical of another court being established. My approach has always been, let us get close to them, let us be faithful followers, let us take homogeneity and reciprocity seriously and the closer we get to them, the more we will have a chance to have **our own voice heard**. That is exactly how it turned out. At the ECJ, it is now self-evident for Advocates General to do a search of the Court's case law. At the ECJ's chambers we may not yet fully be there, but there are a number of judges and legal secretaries who are not only aware of what we are doing, but are also willing to make it visible in the judgment. That allows us to be referred to. My impression is that in order to gain that reputation, we had to pass some sort of a test. They wanted to see whether we took the homogeneity business serious or not. In particular, they wanted to see if we would use the same tactics as the Swiss Supreme Court and the Austrian Supreme Court under the bilateral Free Trade Agreements (see lecture 3). Once the Court made it clear that it was serious about homogeneity and access to justice, they started to see us as an "*interlocuteur valuable*", a **valuable partner**. A decisive step in this development was clearly the Court's *Sveinbjörnsdóttir* judgment. ECJ President Professor *Vassilios Skouris* called it "[t]he celebrated *Sveinbjörnsdóttir* judgment"[235]. And then CFI President *Bo Vesterdorf* speaks of a "particularly forceful" ruling[236]. Had we not opted for State liability, the Court and

235 Vassilios Skouris, The ECJ and the EFTA Court under the EEA Agreement: A Paradigm for International Cooperation between Judicial Institutions, in: Carl Baudenbacher/Per Tresselt/Thorgeir Örlygsson (eds.), The EFTA Court Ten Years On, Oxford and Portland, Oregon [2005] 123, 124.

236 Bo Vesterdorf, EFTA Court 10th Anniversary, in: Carl Baudenbacher/Per Tresselt/Thorgeir Örlygsson (eds.), The EFTA Court Ten Years On, Oxford and Portland, Oregon [2005], 187.

the EEA Agreement as a whole would most probably have been downgraded. Or, as my predecessor *Thór Vilhjálmsson* used to say: "Without State liability the EEA Agreement and the EFTA Court would never have taken off."

Before I speak about our dialogue with the EC judiciary, let me reach out a bit further because the concept and the **theory of judicial dialogue** go some way beyond what is happening under the EEA Agreement. Interestingly enough, this theory has been developed by Canadian and American authors[237]. They found that in a globalised world there are more and more homogeneous, even identical legal problems, and that it is a most natural thing for supreme courts and international courts to look at each other when deciding on such cases. Among the **homogeneous issues**, you may quote human rights, the protection of the environment, anti-discrimination law, the fight against terrorism. In economic law, antitrust today is a worldwide issue. There is an international competition network, the so-called "ICN", where all the competition authorities take part, not only of the industrialized countries on both sides of the Atlantic Ocean, but also of the African, Asian, and the Latin-American countries[238]. IP law, too, is highly globalised – a patent is defined in more or less the same way nowadays all over the world, and the same holds true for a trade mark.

Then we have legal problems that are even **identical**. This has to do with the fact that multi-national corporations are facing the same problems all over the world. When Harvard University wanted its "*oncomouse*" to be patented they had to go to all the patent offices in the world. In certain jurisdictions they were successful, in others not. Oncoanimals are animals that are genetically engineered and are made especially susceptible to developing cancer. In certain countries the assumption was that this is life and cannot be patented, but the Americans did so[239]. A less controversial question would be whether the color of the *Milka* chocolate can be protected by a trademark. The protection of color was controversial in many countries, but also the trademark protection of the form of the Coca Cola bottle, etc. Cross-border marketing is another example, think of the *Benetton* cases. You may remember that Benetton used shock advertising a couple of years ago. In some jurisdictions the courts found this to constitute unfair competition. In other jurisdictions they said consumers must be considered as informed, not as stupid; the ad's are tasteless but not illegal. Finally, the question of the protection of the *Lego* cube in different jurisdictions would be a further example.

---

237 See in particular Claire L'Heureux-Dubé, The Importance of Dialogue: Globalization and the International Impact of the Rehnquist Court, [1998] 34 Tulsa L.J. 15, 15-16; and Anne-Marie Slaughter, Judicial Globalization, [2000] 40 Va. J. Int'l L., 1103, 1114.

238 www.internationalcompetitionnetwork.org.

239 See, e.g., Rebecca S. Eisenberg, Noncompliance, Nonenforcement, Nonproblem? Rethinking the Anticommons in Biomedical Research Patent Law on Perspective, Institute for Intellectual Property & Information, Houston Law Review Symposium Article, 45 Hous. L. Rev. 1059, 1073 et seq.; Canada Supreme Court Rejects 5-4 Patentability of Harvard 'Oncomouse', 65 Pat. Trademark & Copyright J, 140, 140 [12 December 2002].

B. General levels of inter-court cooperation[240]

1. Prescribed cooperation

The first category of judicial cooperation is **prescribed cooperation**. Historically the position of the Privy Council is to be mentioned here. Today the relationship between the ECJ and the national courts of the Member States is an example of prescribed cooperation, because the national courts are obliged to implement the ECJ's preliminary rulings. But: National courts can still decide whether they want to refer or not. In other words, they are not powerless[241]. *Mutatis mutandis* the same holds true in the EEA and it is my hope that the cooperation between the national courts of the EEA/EFTA States and the EFTA Court will intensify. There is also prescribed cooperation between the European Court of Human Rights in Strasbourg and the national courts in the Member States of the European Human Rights Convention. Finally, the ECJ is the center of gravity when it comes to the application and interpretation of the EEA Agreement and of the bilateral agreements EU – Switzerland[242]. As long as there are homogeneity rules binding other courts to follow, you cannot really speak of dialogue. It is prescribed cooperation.

2. Necessary cooperation

The second level I suggest for distinction would comprise those areas of international law where you have **uniform law** in the Contracting Parties, but no common court. Examples are the Paris Convention for the Protection of Industrial Property, the Berne Convention for the Protection of Literary and Artistic Works, the European Patent Convention, the TRIPs Agreement, the Vienna Sales Convention, and, very importantly, the Convention Relating to the Status of Refugees. The latter is actually one of the few international law tools where even American courts engage in judicial dialogue when it comes, e.g., to the definition of the notion of a refugee[243]. In these cases cooperation is not prescribed but it is **objectively necessary**, because if courts do not cooperate the system cannot function[244]. Professor *Allan Rosas*, the Finnish judge and President of Chamber at the ECJ, also said that the longstanding practice of the ECJ to reference the rulings of the European Court of Human Rights is a case of necessary cooperation and the European Court of Human Rights for its part cites the ECJ.

240 See for the following Carl Baudenbacher, Some Considerations on the Dialogue between High Courts, Second St. Gallen Dispute Resolution Conference 2009, 175, 180 et seq.

241 See Ulrich Haltern, Europarecht. Dogmatik im Kontext, 2. Aufl., Tübingen 2007, at paragraphs 14 et seq., 890 et seq.

242 See Carl Baudenbacher, Wachsende Dynamik im Bilateralismus. Zum Bericht des EU-Rates über die Beziehungen zu den EFTA-Staaten, NZZ International Edition of 14 January 2009.

243 See Eyal Benvenisti, Reclaiming Democracy: The Strategic Uses of Foreign and International Law by National Courts, 102 Am. J. Int'l L. 241, 264 f. [2008].

244 See Joachim Bornkamm, The German Supreme Court: An Actor in the Global Conversation of High Courts, 39 Tex. Int'l L.J. 415, 417–18 [2004].

A similar situation he says exists in the relationship between the ECJ and the WTO Dispute Settlement Mechanism[245].

3. Reception

The third level of cooperation is well known to comparatists, it is **reception**. Most comparative law specialists speak of reception meaning that a certain country takes over a certain piece of legislation from another country. Often this is, however, the wrong focus because in many cases it is not the receiving country voluntarily implementing foreign law, but a foreign power forcing implementation.

4. Cooperation by choice (= dialogue)

Strictly speaking, only **cooperation by choice**, that is what the ECJ does vis-à-vis the EFTA Court – and I have not always taken that view in my earlier publications but then you learn over time – deserves the name of judicial dialogue in the EEA framework. For the sake of completeness, I add that dialogue also takes place between the U.S. Supreme Court and the European Court of Human Rights, the European Court of Human Rights and the Inter-American Court of Human Rights, and the Advocates General of the ECJ and the U.S. Supreme Court, just to name a few examples.

5. Combination of several constellations

Finally you may have a combination of several constellations. An example is again the EEA Agreement, where the EFTA Court is bound to follow or to take into account ECJ case law, whereas the ECJ is not legally bound to follow us, but may do so on a voluntary basis. However, it is fair to say that it would not correspond with the spirit of the Agreement if the ECJ did not do it. ECJ President *Vassilios Skouris* has rightly stated at the symposium held on the occasion of the Court's tenth anniversary on 21 October 2004 in Luxemburg that "ignoring EFTA Court precedents would simply be incompatible with the overriding objective of the EEA agreement which is homogeneity"[246].

---

245 Allan Rosas, Methods of Interpretation – Judicial Dialogue, in: Carl Baudenbacher/Erhard Busek (eds.), The Role of International Courts, [2008] Heidelberg 185 et seq.

246 Vassilios Skouris, The ECJ and the EFTA Court under the EEA Agreement: A Paradigm for International Cooperation between Judicial Institutions, in: Carl Baudenbacher/ Per Tresselt/Thorgeir Örlygsson (eds.), The EFTA Court Ten Years On, Oxford and Portland, Oregon [2005] 123, 125.

C. Dialogue EFTA Court – Union courts

The Court probably tackled fresh legal problems in some 70 cases which led to at least the same number of reactions from the ECJ, the CFI and from Advocates General, occasionally also from the German Supreme Court, the German Supreme Fiscal Court (*Bundesfinanzhof*), the Austrian Supreme Court, the England and Wales Court of Appeal, and from other courts in EC countries. To give an example: When the Supreme Court of Germany did away with the famous real seat theory in international company law vis-à-vis the EEA/EFTA countries in a case involving a Liechtenstein corporation, it made reference to the case law of EFTA Court[247].

1. ECJ and CFI referencing the Court's case law

There is a number of cases in which the ECJ has cited EFTA Court case law as a **main** or as a **leading argument**. The first cases date back to 1997. They dealt with one of the hotly debated issues in the early days of the EEA Agreement: Can you go to another jurisdiction and transmit certain television programs from there to your own Member State because the standards of control are lower in that country than in the country where it is received? Swedish and Norwegian firms went to the United Kingdom and **broadcasted advertisements** to Sweden and Norway, specifically targeting children. The actors in Norway were *Mattel*, the creator of the Barbie doll which has turned fifty now, and *Lego*, the firm which manufactures the famous cubes[248]. In Sweden, there were *De Agostini* and *TV-Shop i Sverige* involved[249]. These cases, too, were essentially about advertising toys. All the proceedings, also *De Agostini* and *TV-Shop i Sverige*, were brought before the Court when Sweden was an EEA/EFTA State. After Sweden joined the European Union, the Swedish Supreme Court withdrew the references in *De Agostini* and *TV-Shop i Sverige* and lodged the cases with the ECJ. The Norwegian cases remained with the Court and were decided first. The Court held that once you have a harmonisation which is the purpose of the "Television Directive" 89/552/EEC, it cannot be that the receiving state is entitled to carry out a second check on the broadcasts. If the broadcasts are lawful under British law, the Norwegian authorities have to accept that. That is nothing else than an emanation of the good old *Cassis de Dijon* principle. What is good in one Member State must be good for other Member States. But the matter was very sensitive. The Court therefore added that if the receiving country's authorities can find a legal basis outside the "Television Directive", namely in the so-called "Misleading Advertising Directive 84/450/EEC", then they can still carry out a second check on these broadcasts. In fact, this was not clear *a priori* because it could be argued that it was not compatible with the purpose of the TV Directive that new barriers were erect-

247 Bundesgerichtshof, Judgment of 19 September 2005, Case II ZR 372/03.

248 Joined Cases E-8/94 and E-9/94 Mattel Scandinavia and Lego Norge [1994–1995] EFTA Court Report 113.

249 Joined Cases C-34/95 to C-36/95 De Agostini and TV-Shop i Sverige [1997] ECR I-3843.

ed. But the ECJ followed the EFTA Court in Joined cases *De Agostini* and *TV-Shop i Sverige*[250].

Another controversial issue in the 1990's was the question of whether the so-called **succession of contracts** constituted a transfer of an undertaking within the meaning of the respective directive. The Transfer of Undertakings Directive 77/187/EEC stated that if you take over another firm or a part of another firm you do not only take over assets but also the working contracts at the same conditions as had existed before the transfer. It was (and is) thus not possible to use the takeover as an opportunity to fire the workers. In the end, this legislation amounted to a job guarantee for the *beati possidentes*, i.e. for those who have a job. The ECJ became more and more expansive in its case law and ruled, e.g., in C-392/92, the famous *Christel Schmidt* case[251], that the following amounted to a transfer of an undertaking: *Christel Schmidt* was a cleaning lady in a savings and loans bank in Northern Germany, employed by the bank. The bank decided to outsource the cleaning to a cleaning firm with the result that *Christel Schmidt* was fired. The cleaning firm offered her a job for the same money, but she was now expected to clean a larger surface. Since this constituted a deterioration of her working conditions, she brought an action and the national court made a reference to the ECJ. No assets were transferred. The ECJ held that this constituted a transfer of an undertaking. The undertaking would consist in the sheer cleaning activity, in the **function itself**. The ECJ's ruling prompted an outcry in many countries, and then German Chancellor *Kohl* proposed to restrict the right to make a reference to the ECJ to the supreme courts of the Member States.

After this, workers tried to go even one step further. Not only should there be a transfer if a sheer activity was outsourced, but also if an activity had been outsourced in the past to an independent service provider and the contract was subsequently awarded to a second service provider. The first cases brought before the EFTA Court concerned Norwegian oil platforms in front of Stavanger[252]. Cleaning and catering on these platforms had been outsourced, and when the respective service contracts ended, new contracts with new providers were concluded. The Court did not give a clear answer to the question whether this constituted a transfer of an undertaking. If I remember correctly, a Norwegian newspaper called our rulings *tungetale* (tongue speaking). In a subsequent case, E-2/96 *Ulstein and Røiseng*, a contract over the provision of ambulance driver services for a hospital had been awarded to a second provider[253]. This time, the EFTA Court held that a mere succession of two contracts for the provision of the same or similar services (ambulance driving) will **not**, as a rule, be sufficient for there to be a **transfer of an undertaking**, business or part of a business within the meaning of the Transfer of Undertakings Directive. Shortly before, Advocate General *La Pergola* in

250 Loc. cit., at paragraph 37.

251 Case C-392/92 Christel Schmidt [1994] ECR I-1311.

252 Cases E-2/95 Eidesund [1995–1996] EFTA Court Report 1 and E-3/95 Langeland [1995–1996] EFTA Court Report 36.

253 Case E-2/96 Ulstein and Røiseng [1995–1996] EFTA Court Report 65.

C-13/95 *Süzen* had invited the ECJ to hold that the termination of a cleaning contract with an undertaking and the subsequent award of that contract to another undertaking did not, in the absence of other factors which may lead to a different classification, fall within the scope of the Directive[254]. The EFTA Court was aware of this opinion, but did not cite it. In C-13/95 *Süzen*, referring to EFTA Court *Ulstein*, the plenum of the ECJ did not qualify the succession of contracts as falling within the scope of the Transfer of Undertakings Directive[255].

Still in the context of the Transfer of Undertakings Directive, the EFTA Court held in three cases that the Transfer of Undertakings Directive was applicable where in the event of succession of contracts the new contract was awarded after a **public tender** had taken place (E-2/95 *Eidesund*, E-2/96 *Ulstein and Røiseng*, and E-3/96 *Ask and Others v ABB and Aker*)[256]. The ECJ (Sixth Chamber) followed this finding in C-172/99 *Oy Liikenne*[257] and held that the circumstance that a transaction came under Directive 92/50/EEC did not of itself rule out the application of Directive 77/187/EEC. The ECJ referred to the EFTA Court's rulings in Cases E-2/95 *Eidesund* and E-3/96 *Ask and Others v ABB and Aker.*

The **most influential** EFTA **Court judgment** has been E-3/00 *Kellogg's*[258]. I gave you the facts and I briefly described the ruling in lecture 4. Let me just add that in *Kellogg's* the Danish government, together with the Dutch and the French government, supported the Norwegians. Denmark acted as an intervener whereas the Netherlands and France submitted written observations. This is explained by the fact that the European Commission had opened proceedings against these three EC States in the late 1990's making similar allegations as ESA in the *Kellogg's* case and that the respective governments assumed that the EFTA Court's ruling could have an impact on the ECJ[259].

In Case C-192/01 *Commission v Denmark*[260] Denmark had blocked the marketing of some fortified foodstuffs. As briefly mentioned before, the plenum of the ECJ rejected the position of the Danish government which had submitted that it was sufficient to show the absence of a nutritional need in order to justify a general prohibition on the sale of foodstuffs enriched with vitamins or minerals. At the same time, the ECJ recognised the **precautionary principle** and formulated essentially the same conditions for its application as the EFTA Court had done in E-3/00 *Kellogg's*. Reference to the

254 Opinion of AG La Pergola delivered on 15 October 1996, C-13/95 Süzen [1997] ECR I-1259.

255 Case C-13/95 Süzen [1997] ECR I-1259.

256 Cases E-2/95 Eidesund [1995–1996] EFTA Court Report 1; E-2/96 Ulstein and Røiseng [1995-1996] EFTA Court Report 65; and E-3/96 Ask and Others v ABB and Aker [1997] EFTA Court Report 1.

257 C-172/99 Oy Liikenne [2001] ECR I-745.

258 Case E-3/00 Kellogg's [2000–2001] EFTA Court Report 73; see with regard to the dialogue between the Court and the Community courts in this field also Alberto Alemanno, Trade in Food – Regulatory and Judicial Approaches in the EC and the WTO, Cameron May [2007], 120 et seq.

259 See Cases C-192/01 Commission v Denmark [2003] ECR I-9693; C-41/02 Commission v The Netherlands [2004] ECR, I-11375; C-24/00 Commission v France [2004] ECR I-1277.

260 Case C-192/01 Commission v Denmark [2003] ECR I-9693.

EFTA Court's *Kellogg's* ruling was made on the following points: (1) A prohibition on the marketing of fortified foodstuffs must be based on a detailed risk assessment. (2) The risk assessment cannot be based on purely hypothetical considerations. (3) It could be appropriate to take into consideration the cumulative effect of the presence on the market of several sources of a particular nutrient and of the possible existence in the future of additional sources. (4) A proper application of the precautionary principle presupposes the identification of the potentially negative consequences for health, and a comprehensive assessment of the risk based on the most reliable scientific data available and the most recent results of international research. (5) Where the existence or extent of the alleged risk can not be determined with certainty, but the likelihood of real harm to public health persists, the precautionary principle justifies restrictive measures. (6) Such measures must be non-discriminatory and objective.

The ECJ did not only follow the Court in C-192/01 *Commission v Denmark*, but also in C-41/02 *Commission v Netherlands* where again the facts were very similar[261]. Moreover, the ECJ relied on EFTA Court *Kellogg's* in C-236/02, a case concerning the release of **genetically modified** *Monsanto* maize, and the CFI did the same in two cases concerning the fortification of animal feedingstuffs with **antibiotics** in T-13/99 *Pfizer Animal Health* and T-70/99 *Alpharma*[262]. Both firms unsuccessfully argued that there was no proof that this would negatively affect human health, but the CFI said that the authorities may invoke the precautionary principle.

The ECJ also followed *Kellogg's* in C-286/02 *Bellio Fratelli* [263], one of the cases which show that access to the ECJ for EFTA actors operating in EC countries is broad[264]. The facts in *Bellio Fratelli* were as follows: A consignment of Norwegian fish flour was exported to Italy. The Italian authorities confiscated it. They had taken samples and had found that the fish flour contained fragments of unidentified animal bones. They suspected that in the container, probably a railway wagon, animal bones had been transported and that it had not been cleaned appropriately. The Italian authorities seized the consignment. They based themselves on two decisions of the EC Council and the EC Commission on certain protection measures against **Mad Cow's Disease**. The Italian court, *the Prefettura di Treviso*, which is near Venice, made a reference to the ECJ. The ECJ held that the provisions on which the seizure had been based were compatible with EEA Article 13, the provision mirroring Article 36 TFEU (ex Article 30 EC). With regard to the precautionary principle and the conditions of its application, the ECJ referred to EFTA Court *Kellogg's* with respect to the following considerations: (1) that in the absence of harmonisation and to the extent that uncertainties continue to exist in the current state of scientific research, it is for the Contracting Parties to decide on the level of protection of human health they wish to ensure,

261 Case C-41/02 Commission v Netherlands [2004] ECR I-11375.

262 Cases C-236/01 Monsanto [2003] ECR I-8105; T-13/99 Pfizer Animal Health [2002] ECR II-3305; and T-70/99 Alpharma [2002] ECR II-3495.

263 Case C-286/02 Bellio Fratelli [2004] ECR I-3465.

264 See supra, lecture 2.

taking account of the fundamental requirements of EEA law and, in particular, the free movement of goods in the EEA, (2) that a risk-management decision rests with each Contracting Party and that a Contracting Party may invoke the precautionary principle with regard to the risk in question if there is relevant scientific uncertainty with regard to the risk in question, but that the respective discretion must be open to judicial review, (3) that measures taken by a Contracting Party must be based on scientific evidence and must be proportionate, non-discriminatory, transparent, and consistent with similar measures already taken; (4) that even if the need to safeguard public health has been recognised as a primary concern, the principle of proportionality must be respected[265].

Next to *Kellogg's*, the most important example of the ECJ referencing the Court's case law as a main or leading argument is the follow on history of the Court's *Paranova v Merck* judgment (E-3/02)[266]. After that ruling, another case was brought by a big pharmaceutical company which ended up before the England and Wales Court of Appeal. Upon a reference from that court, the ECJ entirely followed the approach taken by my Court by stating: … "[T]he condition that packaging be necessary is directed only at the fact of repackaging the product and the choice between a new carton and oversticking – for the purposes of allowing that product to be marketed in the importing State and not at the manner or style in which it has been repackaged." In that respect, the ECJ made reference to paragraphs 41–45 of the Court's *Paranova v Merck* judgment[267].

The ECJ's ruling in C-452/04 *Fidium Finanz*[268] is interesting for several reasons. Firstly, it gives a certain interpretation to the EC Treaty provisions on free movement of capital and the freedom to provide services. Secondly, it is an important example of judicial dialogue with the EFTA Court and thirdly it shows that Switzerland is in a more difficult position vis-à-vis the EC than the EEA/EFTA States when it comes to offering financial services. *Fidium Finanz*, a Swiss financial corporation, not a bank, offered small credits in Germany at interest rates as high as 14 % at a time when normal interests where about three percent, mostly via the internet. The German Financial Market Authority prohibited this activity and told *Fidium Finanz* that if it wanted to carry on this business, it had to establish a subsidiary in Germany, a branch would not suffice. The Swiss corporation took the case to the Administrative Court in Frankfurt. This court made a reference to the ECJ and asked whether the activity in question was covered by the provisions of the EC Treaty on free movement of capital. The provisions of free movement of capital contain a **third country clause** which grants that freedom also to non-Member States, whereas the provisions on the free-

265 References to Case E-3/00 EFTA Surveillance Authority v Norway, EFTA Court Report [2000–2001] 73, paragraphs 25, 26 and 27.

266 Case E-3/02 Paranova v Merck [2003] EFTA Court Report 101.

267 Case C-348/04 Boehringer Ingelheim KG and Others v Swingward Ltd and Others [2007] ECR, I-3391, at paragraph 38; see with regard to this Héctor Armengod/Laura Melusine Baudenbacher, The Repackaging of Pharmaceutical Products and Parallel Trade in the EU, RAJ Pharma December 2009, 783, 784.

268 C-452/04 Fidium Finanz [2006] ECR I-9521.

dom to provide services do not. This is a beautiful case for every class on legal theory. It shows that it is not only dogmatic thought which prompts the ECJ (and any court) to opt for a certain solution, but that also the **judges' pre-understanding** plays a role. The Grand Chamber of the ECJ held that, in principle, both the freedom to provide services within the meaning of Articles 49 et seq. EC (now: Articles 56 et seq. TFEU) and the free movement of capital within the meaning of Articles 56 et seq. EC (now: Articles 63 et seq. TFEU) were affected. In deciding on which freedom prevailed over the other, the ECJ referred to the EFTA Court's judgment in E-1/00 *Íslandsbanki*[269]. In that case, the EFTA Court had applied a center of gravity test and concluded that the "*predominant feature* of the case", which involved a national measure leading to a guarantee for loans from foreign lenders being more expensive than for loans from domestic lenders, constituted movement of capital. The ECJ used the same test, but concluded that "the *predominant consideration*" of the *Fidium Finanz* case was the freedom to provide services. This is the **judicial dialogue aspect** of the case. For the sake of completeness, I may add that in C-42/07 *Liga Portuguesa*, a case concerning a national ban on internet gambling, the Grand Chamber of the ECJ reiterated that where a national measure relates to several fundamental freedoms at the same time, it will in principle examine the measure in relation to only one of those freedoms if it appears, in the circumstances of the case, that the other freedoms are entirely secondary in relation to the first and may be considered together with it. The ECJ referred to its *Fidium Finanz* ruling and to the "case-law cited" there, i.e. also to the EFTA Court's *Íslandsbanki* judgment[270].

The other aspect of *Fidium Finanz* concerns the question of what the ECJ's approach means for **Swiss financial market operators**. In my view, it means that they are excluded from doing business on the territory of the European Union unless they establish a subsidiary there. Whether they are subject to Swiss banking supervision or not is irrelevant. The message is not only directed against Swiss banks, it is also directed against Russian banks, Chinese banks, American banks, Indian banks etc. That shows that the ECJ these days has become aware of its **power**. The judges know that the court is a global player and they use this might in a deliberate and calculated way. There can be no doubt about that. The ECJ sent a message to all the financial centers in the world: If you want to use our market you will have to conclude a **reciprocity agreement** with us guaranteeing that our banks can do the same business in your countries[271].

In C-434/04 *Ahokainen and Leppik*[272] the ECJ, when stating that national legislation under which undenatured ethyl alcohol of an alcoholic strength of more than 80 %

---

269 Case E-1/00 Íslandsbanki [2000-2001] EFTA Court Report 8.

270 Judgment of 8 September 2009, at paragraph 31, nyr.

271 See Carl Baudenbacher, Der Finanzplatz Schweiz im Angesicht der Reziprozitätspolitik der EU, European Law Reporter [2006] 398 et seq.; Christa Tobler, Die Fidium Finanz-Entscheidung des EuGH: ein Vorbote der Luxemburger Rechtsprechung zum bilateralen Recht?, Schweizerische Zeitschrift für internationales und europäisches Recht [2006] 397 et seq.

272 Case C-434/04 Criminal proceedings against Jan-Erik Anders Ahokainen and Mati Leppik [2006] ECR I-9171.

may be imported only by a person who has obtained a licence to do so is in principle contrary to Article 28 EC (now: Article 34 TFEU), made not only reference to its own case law, but also to the EFTA Court's ruling in E-1/94 *Restamark*.

Occasionally, there may be a reference to EFTA Court jurisprudence that has the character of an **additional hint**. That is the best proof that our activity is appreciated by the EC judiciary. The most important citation was the reference to our *Sveinbjörnsdóttir* judgment in C-140/97 *Rechberger*[273]. As I said before, when rejecting the Norwegian government's claim in *Karlsson* that we should overrule *Sveinbjörnsdóttir*, we referenced the ECJ's *Rechberger* judgment[274].

On balance, it appears that the ECJ is willing to refer to EFTA Court rulings in cases concerning the interpretation of EC or EEA law, if the latter has answered a **fresh legal question**, provided the ECJ shares the EFTA Court's position with regard to the outcome and the reasons. Occasionally, the ECJ is also prepared to quote EFTA Court case law as a source of further information.

As far as the dialogue with the CFI (now: General Court) is concerned, it is difficult to draw any conclusions concerning that court's policy in view of the low number of relevant cases. One must not overlook, however, that it was the CFI which opened the dialogue with the EFTA Court in its judgment of 22 January 1997 in Case T-115/94 *Opel Austria*[275]. The CFI has also on other occasions referenced the Court's case law[276].

2. ECJ refraining from referencing the Court's case law

The ECJ will, however, only refer to the EFTA Court's jurisprudence when dealing with the fresh legal issue for the **first time**. In subsequent cases, it will limit itself to citing its own case law (which in substance may be based on EFTA Court jurisprudence). One could say that the EFTA Court's "entitlement" to be quoted seems to be "exhausted" after the first citation. A good example is the ruling in Case C-95/01 *Greenham and Abel* which was about similar facts as C-192/01 *Commission v Denmark* and E-3/00 *ESA v Norway* (*Kellogg's*). Although the ECJ's ruling follows our *Kellogg's* precedent entirely, there is no reference to us, but only to the ECJ's own *Commission*

273 Case C-140/97 Rechberger [1999] ECR I-3499, at paragraph 39.

274 Case E-4/01 Karlsson [2002] EFTA Court Report 240, at paragraph 25 in fine.

275 Case T-115/94 Opel Austria [1997] ECR II-39; see the apt remarks of then CFI President Bo Vesterdorf, EFTA Court 10th Anniversary, in Carl Baudenbacher/Per Tresselt/Thorgeir Örlygsson (eds.), The EFTA Court Ten Years On, Oxford and Portland Oregon [2005], 187, 188. See with regard to CFI Opel Austria supra, lecture 3.

276 Cases T-308/00 Salzgitter AG v Commission, [2004] ECR II-1933: Reference to Case E-6/98 Norway v ESA EFTA Court Report [1999] 74: T-70/90 Alpharma [2002] ECR II-3495 and T-13/99 Pfizer Animal Health [2002] ECR II-3305: References to Case E-3/00 ESA v Norway (Kellogg's) [2000–2001] EFTA Court Report, 73; Joined Cases T-254/00, T-270/00 and T-277/00 Hotel Cipriani, judgment of 28 November 2008, nyr.: References to Joined Cases E-5/04, E-6/04 and E-7/04 Fesil and Finnfjord and Others v EFTA Surveillance Authority [2005] Report of the EFTA Court, 117.

v Denmark judgment[277]. There is occasionally an ECJ judgment which does not follow this narrow approach. At the end it all depends on individuals.

In a number of cases, the ECJ has come to solutions that differ from the ones previously found by the EFTA Court. In such cases, the ECJ will not mention the EFTA Court's judgment. One must therefore conclude that the judicial dialogue between the ECJ and the EFTA Court is essentially **affirmative** in nature. In the following, I will describe the case law of the two courts on the compatibility of State alcohol and tobacco monopolies with the rules on free movement of goods, of State gaming and betting monopolies with the freedom of establishment and of movement of services and of national tax legislation which granted a tax credit to shareholders residing in the country, but denied it to shareholders residing abroad with the rules on free movement of capital.

In all these cases, the Court decided as the first court in the EEA, and it decided as it found them according to legal arguments.

(i)

In Case E-6/96 *Wilhelmsen*,[278] the Court had to rule on whether **Norwegian legislation** according to which the **retail sale** of beer containing more than 4.75 percent alcohol by volume is reserved to the **State alcohol trading monopoly** *Vinmonopolet* was compatible with Articles 11 and 16 EEA. Those provisions correspond to Articles 34 and 37 TFEU (ex Articles 28 and 31 EC). The Court found that certain aspects of the Norwegian system, including the 4.75 percent demarcation, give rise to discrimination between foreign and local beer brands. As far as a possible applicability of an exemption under Article 13 EEA, the provision mirroring Article 36 TFEU (ex Article 30 EC) was concerned, the Court acknowledged combating alcohol abuse to constitute a public health concern. Article 13 EEA would only cease to be applicable if the national court were to find that the measures in question were aimed at protecting domestic production as compared to foreign production or at restricting trade between the Member States in a disguised way. With respect to Article 16 EEA, the Court held that provisions granting an exclusive right for retail sale of beer containing more than 4.75 percent alcohol by volume to *Vinmonopolet* form an inherent part of the regulations designing the system. The Court therefore assessed these provisions in light of Article 16 EEA, but found that since they were, as such, justified under Article 13 EEA, it was not necessary to examine them further. In view of the fact that *Vinmonopolet's* selection of strong beers consisted of ten domestic and seven foreign brands, the Court added that a state retail monopoly retaining an exclusive right to sell products was in practice in a position to discriminate against goods from other countries. It was for the

277 Case C-95/01 [2004] ECR I-1333.
278 Case E-6/96 Wilhelmsen, [1997] EFTA Court Report, 53.

national court to assess whether the selection of products was based only on factors such as higher transport costs for foreign beer and local taste or whether it was a result of a discriminatory application of the retail monopoly. In this context, the EFTA Court held that the national court had to take into account whether the method of selection was able to replace the market mechanism **to the fullest possible extent**[279]. In other words, we used a concept of **"as if competition"**. I may add that Article 16 EEA is very difficult to handle. Economically speaking it is almost impossible to adjust a State monopoly of a commercial character "so as to ensure that no discrimination regarding the conditions under which goods are procured and marketed exists between nationals of Member States", as Articles 16 EEA and 37(1) TFEU state.

Six months later, the ECJ used a different kind of reasoning in its judgment in Case C-189/95 *Criminal proceedings against Harry Franzén* which concerned the **Swedish State monopoly**, *Systembolaget*, on the **retail of alcoholic beverages**[280]. The ECJ held that the existence and operation of the monopoly was to be considered solely under what is now Article 37 TFEU (ex Article 31 EC). Restrictions on trade which are inherent in the existence of a monopoly had to be accepted. This included the limitation of the number of points of sale. The ECJ found, in particular, the criteria and methods of selection used by *Systembolaget* to be non-discriminatory since the monopoly followed a purchase plan which was based on foreseeable changes in consumer demand, the calls for offers were made irrespective of the origin of traders and types of beverage, and the offers were selected on purely commercial or qualitative criteria. The ECJ pointed to the fact that **blind tasting** was used as a selection mechanism and that **consumer panels** were formed. The fact that the system was able to handicap small producers was accepted. Based on these arguments, the ECJ declared the retail monopoly compatible with what is now Article 37 TFEU.

(ii)

In Case 1/06, *Gaming Machines*[281], **Norway** had given the State-owned company *Norsk Tipping* the **exclusive right to operate gaming machines**. Private operators, which so far had been able to operate gaming machines on behalf of charitable organisations, were thereby excluded from the market. The Court held firstly and in accordance with the ECJ's previous case law, that, although the Contracting Parties are free to set the objectives of their policy on gaming and to **define the level of protection** sought, the restrictive measures they impose must nevertheless serve legitimate aims and satisfy the conditions of proportionality. The Court then stated that a limitation in the authorisation of gaming is acceptable only if it reflects a concern to bring about a genuine diminution in gambling opportunities, and if the financing of social activities consti-

279 Loc. cit., at paragraph 107.
280 Case C-189/95 Franzén [1997] ECR I-5909.
281 Case E-1/06, EFTA Surveillance Authority v The Kingdom of Norway, 2007 EFTA Court Report, 8.

tutes only an incidental beneficial consequence and not the real justification for the restrictive policy adopted. With regard to consistency, the Court held that where an EEA State has chosen to fight gambling addiction through the reduction of gambling opportunities by subjecting the operation of gaming machines to a State-owned monopoly, it may **not** endorse or tolerate measures, such as **extensive marketing**, which could lead to an increase of gambling opportunities. A consistent and systematic approach to fighting gambling addiction must also encompass an effective control of the exclusive right holder's activities once the contested legislation has entered into force. With regard to the aim to prevent gambling related crime such as money-laundering and embezzlement, the Court held that Norway had failed to demonstrate that less far-reaching measures will not be equally effective. As regards the aim of fighting gambling addiction, however, the Court found it reasonable to assume that a monopoly operator in the field of gaming machines subject to effective control by the competent public authorities will tend to accommodate that concern better than commercial operators. The effectiveness of **public control and enforcement** of a genuinely restrictive approach to machine gaming was considered the focal point. As the reform of the gaming machine regulation in Norway had not yet taken effect, the Court would not base itself on the general assumption that public control and policy enforcement will not satisfy these requirements. Based on these considerations, the Court dismissed ESA's application for a declaration that Norway had violated the EEA rules on freedom of establishment and on freedom to provide services[282].

In Case E-3/06 *Ladbrokes*[283] the world's largest bookmaker and gaming company had been denied the permission to operate and provide different gaming and betting services in **Norway** and to market these games. The Court accepted the aims of fighting gambling addiction and crime and malpractice as being legitimate aims. In order to be lawfully based on the aim of fighting gambling addiction, legislation must, however, reflect a concern to bring about a genuine diminution in gambling opportunities. The motive of financing benevolent or public-interest activities cannot in itself be regarded as an objective justification for restrictions on free movement. The aim of preventing gambling from being a source of private profit can serve as justification only if the legislation reflects a **moral concern**; if a state-owned monopoly is allowed to offer a range of gambling opportunities, the legislation at issue cannot be said to genuinely pursue this aim. To the extent it would find Norwegian legislation to pursue legitimate aims, the **national court** was told to consider whether it was proportionate. The national court was told that the policy pursued would be inconsistent if the state took, facilitated or tolerated other measures which run counter to the objectives pursued. The **marketing activities** and the development of new games by *Norsk Tipping* were held to be particularly relevant when assessing consistency. The national court was also instructed to examine whether the legislation at issue goes beyond what is necessary to meet the aims pursued.

282 See Eleanor Cashin Ritaine / Eva Lein, La notion de proportionnalité appliquée au droit des jeux de hasard – Les cas Placanica et Autorité de surveillance de l'AELE / Royaume de Norvège, Schweizerisches Jahrbuch für Europarecht = Annuaire suisse de droit européen 2006/2007 [2007] 355.

283 Case E-3/06 Ladbrokes, [2007] EFTA Court Report, 86.

Again, the level of protection chosen by the Norwegian authorities is decisive. Where other, less restrictive measures would have the effect of fully achieving the objectives at the level of protection chosen, an exclusive rights system could not be considered necessary simply because it might offer an even higher level of protection. In order to carry out its assessment, the national court must ascertain whether and to which extent there are genuine risks arising from or connected to the different games of chance.

In its judgment of 8 September 2009 in C-42/07 *Liga Portuguesa*, a case involving a restriction of the freedom to provide services in the form of offering **internet betting on football games**, the ECJ first confirmed its well-established jurisprudence, according to which in the absence of Community harmonization, Member States are free to set the objectives of their gaming policy and to define in detail the level of protection sought. Certain overriding reasons in the public interest were recognised, such as the objectives of consumer protection and the prevention of both fraud and incitement to squander money on gambling, as well as the general need to preserve public order. With regard to the suitability of the restrictive measure, the ECJ **itself** accepted the argument of the monopoly company, *Santa Casa*, and of the Portuguese Government that the main objective pursued by the national legislation was the fight against crime, more specifically the protection of consumers of games of chance against fraud on the part of operators. The ECJ was convinced that the Portuguese system functions in a secure and controlled way because **Santa Casa's long existence**, spanning more than five centuries, was evidence of that body's reliability and the fact that *Santa Casa* operates under the **strict control** of the Portuguese government. With regard to the specific facts of the case, the ECJ added that because of the lack of direct contact between consumer and operator, games of chance accessible via the internet involve different and more substantial risks of fraud by operators against consumers compared with the traditional markets for such games[284].

(iii)

I mentioned before that in Case E-1/04 *Fokus Bank,*[285] the Court rejected the argument put forward by the Norwegian government that a restriction of the right to free movement of capital under Article 40 EEA, consisting in disadvantageous treatment of non-resident shareholders with respect to the granting of an imputation tax credit, could be offset by advantages which shareholders may obtain in their countries of residence by way of invoking provisions of bilateral double taxation agreements. The principle of **legal certainty** would require that the granting of an imputation tax credit to a non-resident shareholder may not depend on whether a tax credit is granted in his or her state of residence in respect of dividend payments. In *Test Claimants in Class IV*,

284 See Simon Planzer, Liga Portuguesa – the ECJ and its Mysterious Ways of Reasoning, [2009] European Law Reporter, 368 et seq.

285 Case E-1/04 Fokus Bank ASA, [2004] EFTA Court Report 11, at paragraph 37.

the ECJ's Grand Chamber acknowledged, in principle, that the effects of double taxation agreements could be taken into account. In *Denkavit*, the ECJ's First Chamber followed that line of argument[286].

(iv)

I will not comment on the ECJ's approach in these cases. You may draw your own conclusions. But I want to add that these cases were not only about enforcing certain public policy goals, but also about securing **important sources of revenue** for the Member States concerned[287].

3. Mutual references – EEA judicial ping pong

In some cases, the dialogue with the Community judiciary has taken place in the form of *ping pong*, so to speak. That way, the courts in both EEA pillars have made significant contributions to **securing a homogeneous development** of the case law. The *Court* has in its very first case, E-1/94 *Restamark*, emphasised the importance of the objective of the Contracting Parties to create a dynamic and homogeneous EEA[288]. The *CFI* in T-115/94 *Opel Austria* stated that the two pillar system underlying the EEA Agreement was reinforced, in addition to the similarity between the terms of the various provisions of the Agreement and the EC Treaty, by specific rules aimed at guaranteeing a homogeneous development of the case law and referred to the judgments of the EFTA Court in E-1/94 *Restamark* and E-2/94 *Scottish Salmon Growers*[289]. In E-9/97 *Sveinbjörnsdóttir*, the Court pointed to the fact that creating a homogeneous EEA is one of the main objectives of the Contracting Parties[290].

Still on homogeneity, in C-452/01 *Ospelt* which involved national restrictions on the free movement of capital, the ECJ saw it as **its task** to ensure that the rules of the EEA Agreement which are identical in substance to those of the EC Treaty are interpreted uniformly [291]. As I said before, *Ospelt* was a case like *Bellio Fratelli*, where an EFTA operator went before a court in an EC Member State and from there to the ECJ, therefore again very relevant from a perspective of **reciprocal access to justice**. In E-1/03 *ESA v Iceland*, when ruling on the compatibility of Icelandic legislation, which imposed a

---

286 Case C-374/04 Test Claimants in Class IV [2006] ECR I-11673; Case C-170/05 Denkavit [2006] ECR I-11949; see with regard to the different approaches of the two EEA Courts Walter Hellerstein/Georg W. Kofler/Ruth Mason, Constitutional Restraints on Corporate Tax Integration, Symposium on Corporate Tax Policy in the European Union, 62 Tax L. Rev. 1, 30 [2008].

287 Concerning the Swedish State retail alcohol monopoly see the Opinion of Advocate General Elmer in Case C-189/95 Franzén [1997] ECR I-5909, at paragraph 108.

288 [1994-1995] EFTA Court Report 15, at paragraphs 32 et seq.

289 [1997] ECR *II-39, at paragraphs 61 and 108.*

290 Case E-9/97 Sveinbjörnsdóttir [1998] EFTA Court Report 95, at paragraphs 49 et seq., in particular 60.

291 C-452/01 Ospelt [2003] ECR I-9743, at paragraph 29.

higher tax per air passenger travelling from Iceland to other EEA States than per passenger travelling on domestic flights, with the freedom to provide services, the Court pointed to the homogeneity objective laid down in EEA law and referred to C-452/01 *Ospelt*[292]. The ECJ took up that ball in C-286/02 *Bellio Fratelli*, a case dealt with under EEA law, by emphasising that, "as Article 6 of the EEA Agreement states, the provisions of the agreement, in so far as they are identical in substance to corresponding rules of the EC Treaty and to acts adopted in application of that Treaty, must, in their implementation and application, be interpreted in conformity with the relevant rulings of the Court given prior to the date of signature of the EEA Agreement. Furthermore, **both the Court and the** EFTA **Court** have recognised the need to ensure that the rules of the EEA Agreement which are identical in substance to those of the Treaty are interpreted uniformly" [293]. On that point, the ECJ referred to C-452/01 *Ospelt* and E-1/03 *EFTA Surveillance Authority v Iceland*. The EFTA Court, for its part, replied eight months later in E-1/04 *Fokus Bank*[294].

The second important series of cases where the two courts acted by way of mutual reference concerns the area of **free movement of capital**. After the conclusion of the EEA Agreement, the Treaty on European Union introduced new provisions on "capital and payments" in the EC Treaty. The provisions of the EEA Agreement remained unchanged.

> *Article 40 EEA provides:*
> *"Within the framework of the provisions of this Agreement, there shall be no restrictions between the Contracting Parties on the movement of capital belonging to persons resident in EC Member States or EFTA States and no discrimination based on the nationality or on the place of residence of the parties or on the place where such capital is invested. Annex XII contains the provisions necessary to implement this Article."*
>
> *Article 56 EC (now: Article 63 TFEU) states:*
> *"1. Within the framework of the provisions set out in this chapter, all restrictions on the movement of capital between Member States and between Member States and third countries shall be prohibited.*
> *2. Within the framework of the provisions set out in this chapter, all restrictions on payments between Member States and between Member States and third countries shall be prohibited."*

---

292 Case E-1/03 EFTA Surveillance Authority v Iceland [2003] EFTA Court Report 143, at paragraph 27.

293 Case C-286/02 Bellio Fratelli [2004] ECR I-3465, at paragraph 34, emphasis added. See in that regard Dirk Buschle, The Free Movement of Capital in the EEA – A Lehrstück in Homogeneity, in: Mario Monti, Prinz Nikolaus von und zu Liechtenstein, Bo Vesterdorf, Jay Westbrook, Luzius Wildhaber (eds.), Economic Law and Justice in Times of Globalisation, Festschrift for Carl Baudenbacher, [2007] Baden-Baden/Berne/Vienna, 75 et seq.

294 Case E-1/04 Fokus Bank [2004] EFTA Court Report 11, at paragraph 22.

The question arose whether the two provisions were still identical in substance which is the precondition for the EEA to function. The courts went step by step. The EFTA Court made the opening in E-1/00 *Íslandsbanki* where it found that Articles 40 EEA and Article 56(1) (now: Article 63[1] TFEU) EC were **similar**[295]. In C-452/01 *Ospelt*, the ECJ held that Article 40 of and Annex XII to the EEA Agreement possessed the same legal scope as that of Article 73b of the Treaty (later: Article 56 EC, now: Article 63 TFEU), which is **identical in substance**. Advocate General *Geelhoed* stated that the EFTA Court had in E-1/00 *Íslandsbanki* concluded that Articles 40 EEA and 56(1) EC (now: Article 63 TFEU) used **comparable** language. In E-1/04 *Fokus Bank*, the Court, referring, *inter alia*, to ECJ *Ospelt* and the AG's opinion in that case, held that the rules governing the free movement of capital in the EEA Agreement were essentially **identical in substance** to those in the EC Treaty. In C-452/04 *Fidium Finanz*, the ECJ did not even discuss the question of substantive identity of EC and EEA law in the field of free movement of capital when referring to the center of gravity test used by the EFTA Court in E-1/00 *Íslandsbanki* in order to demarcate the free movement of capital from the freedom to provide services[296].

4. ECJ reconsidering its case law in light of EFTA Court jurisprudence

Another dialogue feature is that in a couple of cases the ECJ has reconsidered its own case law in the light of EFTA Court jurisprudence. In C-13/95 *Süzen* the ECJ followed the Court's finding in E-2/96 *Ulstein* that the **succession of contracts**, i.e. the replacement of an independent service provider by a second one, does not normally constitute a transfer of an undertaking[297]. The EC Court had previously interpreted the notion of transfer of undertaking in a rather expansive way. This case law had culminated in the famous judgment in C-392/92 *Christel Schmidt*, in which the EC Court held that the succession of functions, i.e. the outsourcing of a mere activity without any assets being transferred (*in casu* the cleaning of a small savings and loans bank) could amount to a transfer of undertaking[298]. In academic literature, *Süzen* has been called a quiet goodbye to *Christel Schmidt*[299]. Seen from that perspective, one is prompted to assume that the ECJ has **reconsidered** its case law in the light of the Court's jurisprudence.

In E-3/00 *Kellogg's* the Court held that a Contracting Party could not limit itself to invoking a **lack of a nutritional need** in the population in order to justify a prohibition to market fortified foodstuffs. Rather, that State had to prove a possible harm to public health even if it could thereby rely on the precautionary principle. The ECJ had found in 174/82 *Sandoz*, when interpreting Articles 28 and 30 EC (now: Articles 34 and 36 TFEU), that the Member States must give marketing permission for fortified

---

295 Case E-1/00 Íslandsbanki [2000-2001] EFTA Court Report 8.
296 C-452/04 Fidium Finanz [2006] ECR I-9521.
297 Case C-13/95 Süzen [1997] ECR I-1259.
298 Case C-392/92 Christel Schmidt [1994] ECR I-1311.
299 Franz Marhold, St.Galler Europarechtsbriefe EU B 1997, 162 et seq.

foodstuffs if the addition of vitamins will satisfy a real need, in particular, of technological or nutritional nature[300]. At the same time the ECJ held that a national regulation according to which the marketing approval for foodstuffs fortified with vitamins which have been lawfully put on the market in other Member States depends on whether the importer shows that there is a need on the market is incompatible with Community law. In C-192/01 *Commission v Denmark*, the ECJ shared the opinion of the Commission which by way of reference to EFTA Court *Kellogg's* had argued that a general ban on the marketing of fortified foodstuffs could not be justified by the mere assertion that there was no respective nutritional need in the Member State concerned. With this, the ECJ has at least **clarified** its *Sandoz* jurisprudence concerning the relevance of the nutritional need argument. Some commentators speak of **overruling**[301].

In one of its *causes célèbres*, E-1/99 *Finanger*, the Court held upon a reference by the Supreme Court of Norway that a provision such as Section 7(3)(b) of the Norwegian Automobile Liability Act, which basically excluded **a passenger of an intoxicated motor vehicle driver** from insurance coverage if he or she knew or must have known that the driver was under the influence of alcohol, was incompatible with the EEA Motor Vehicle Insurance Directives[302]. The Court rejected the argument put forward by the insurance company *Storebrand* and the Governments of Iceland and Norway that the Directives did not deal with rules relating to personal liability but only with insurance law. It made several references to C-129/94 *Ruiz Bernáldez*, where the ECJ had found that a provision of Spanish insurance law which excluded the victim of an intoxicated driver from insurance coverage was incompatible with the Directives[303].

On 14 September 2000, before the oral hearing took place in the Norwegian Supreme Court in *Finanger*, the ECJ (Fifth Chamber) rendered its judgment in Case C-348/98 *Ferreira*[304]. It held, without mentioning EFTA Court *Finanger*, that the Directives did not seek to harmonise the rules of the Member States governing civil liability. Based on this, the ECJ found a provision of the Portuguese Civil Code which stated that, in the case of transport provided free of charge, liability could only be incurred if the passenger proved fault on the part of the driver and that this fault was the cause of the accident to be in line with the Motor Vehicle Insurance Directives. When the Norwegian Supreme Court heard the *Finanger* case, Storebrand pleaded that in *Ferreira* the ECJ had distanced itself from the approach taken by the EFTA Court in *Finanger* and that the Norwegian Supreme Court ought to follow the ECJ's judgment. The Supreme Court **distinguished** the two cases and followed the EFTA Court's *Finanger* ruling.

300 Case 174/82 Sandoz [1983] ECR I-2445.

301 www.pict-pcti.org/research/systemic_issues/news.html; Marco M. Slotboom, Do public health measures receive similar treatment in European Community and World Trade Organization law? [2003] Journal of World Trade 37(3), 553, 585; Marco Bronckers, Exceptions to Liberal Trade in Foodstuffs: The Precautionary Approach and Collective Preferences, in: Carl Baudenbacher, Per Tresselt, Thorgeir Örlygsson (eds.), The EFTA Court Ten Years On, Oxford and Portland, Oregon [2005], 105.

302 Case E-1/99 Finanger [1999] EFTA Court Report 119.

303 Case C-129/94 Ruiz Bernáldez [1996] ECR I-1829.

304 Case C-348/98 Ferreira [2000] ECR I-6711.

In C-537/03 *Candolin*, a Finnish case in which the facts and the law were virtually identical to *Finanger*, the ECJ (First Chamber) eliminated any ambiguities by taking the same position as the EFTA Court. It held that a provision of Finnish automobile liability law (i.e. civil law) which excluded a passenger who took a ride in a car driven by an intoxicated driver was incompatible with the Directives. The Norwegian government did everything to convince the ECJ not to adopt the approach taken by the EFTA Court in *Finanger*. The government wanted the ECJ to **create a judicial conflict**. It argued that the Court's judgment in Finanger was wrong and that the ECJ should not follow it. The ECJ, however, did **concur with the Court**. It did not make reference to our *Finanger* ruling. But it quoted those paragraphs in the Advocate General's conclusions which had made reference to us[305]. It may well be that the ECJ refrained from directly referring to us because the Norwegian government had shown such strong feelings in the case.

5. National courts of EU countries asking the ECJ to clarify its case law in the light of the Court's jurisprudence

As mentioned, in C-348/04, the second *Boehringer* case, the England and Wales Court of Appeal referred the question to the ECJ whether the use by a parallel importer and repackager of pharmaceuticals of its own design elements (referred to as "co-branding") was in line with the Trademark Directive's provisions on the exhaustion principle and the ECJ's case law related thereto, in particular the "necessity test"[306]. The referring court emphasised that whereas the EFTA Court's jurisprudence showed a positive approach towards the parallel importer creating a package design of its own, the Supreme Courts of Austria, Denmark, and Germany, as well as the Svea (Stockholm) Court of Appeal, applied a strict necessity test and tended to prohibit conduct such as Paranova's in the EFTA Court's judgment. In other words, the Court of Appeal (Lord Justice *Jacob*) found that there were two schools of thought in European case law. In this situation it decided to ask the ECJ whether it sided with the Court or with the said national courts. Lord Justice *Jacob* made it clear in his request for a preliminary ruling that his sympathy was with the EFTA Court. He referred, *inter alia*, the question to the ECJ whether the necessity test applied merely to the fact of reboxing or also to the precise **manner and style of the reboxing** carried out by the parallel importer.

Further examples of national courts of EC countries asking the ECJ to clarify its case law in the light of EFTA Court jurisprudence can be found in Cases C-379/05 *Amurta* (request of a preliminary ruling by the Amsterdam Court of Appeal) and C-284/06 *Burda* (request of a preliminary ruling by the German Supreme Fiscal Court)[307]. Both cases dealt with tax matters and the refererring courts pointed to the EFTA Court's *Fokus Bank* ruling.

---

305 Case C-537/03 Candolin [2005] ECR I-5745, at paragraph 22: Reference to paragraph 42 of the Advocate General's Opinion.
306 Case C-348/04 Boehringer Ingelheim II [2007] ECR I-3391.
307 Cases C-379/05 Amurta [2007] ECR I-9569 and C-284/06 Burda [2008] ECR I-4571.

D. Dialogue EFTA Court – Advocates General

1. General

Advocates General have been called *amici curiae* of the ECJ, but as I said, certain Advocates General are also the **friends of the** EFTA **Court**. As already mentioned, there is no Advocate General at the EFTA Court. But we had to decide and we will have to decide important cases in which we would benefit from the existence of an Advocate General, in particular in light of the fact that we also lack a research and documentation department. However, we have an intense exchange with Advocates General of the other side of Avenue Kennedy. The most active man in the early days was Professor *Francis Jacobs*, the longstanding British Advocate General, now Sir *Francis Jacobs*. The late Advocate General *Ad Geelhoed* must also be mentioned. Today, Professors *Miguel Poiares Maduro* from Portugal, *Paolo Mengozzi* from Italy, *Eleanor Sharpston* from the UK and *Verica Trstenjak* from Slovenia are particularly active. For many Advocates General, dealing with the Court's case law has largely become routine. In the early days we counted every single citation and we knew by heart how often we had been quoted. In the meantime, we have lost track.

This development started with the reference of Advocate General *Jacobs* to the Court's ruling in Joined Cases E-8/94 and E-9/94 *Mattel Scandinavia/Lego Norge* in Joined Cases C-34/95 C-35/95 and C-36/95 *De Agostini/TV-Shop i Sverige*, on the questions whether **transfrontier advertising** directed at children fell within the scope of the TV Directive and whether a receiving State may not restrict transmission. Mr *Jacobs* followed the Court's ruling and answered both questions in the affirmative[308]. In C-126/01 *GEMO*, Mr *Jacobs* mentioned the Court's *Husbanken II* judgment as a reference for the so-called "state aid approach" to the issue of whether a **state guarantee** granted by a Member State to an undertaking providing a public service should be regarded as State aid[309]. The question was and partly still is controversial in EC State aid law and has been answered by the ECJ in cases *Ferring* and *Altmark* conversely, i.e. in favour of the so-called "compensation approach"[310]. In the **precautionary principle** cases a number of references were made by Advocates General, in C-192/01 *Commission v Denmark* and in C-95/01 *Greenham and Abel* by AG *Mischo* from Luxemburg[311]. In *Monsanto* the German Advocate General *Alber* referred to EFTA Court *Kellogg's*, in *Commission*

---

308 Opinion of AG Jacobs delivered on 17 September 1996, Joined Cases C-34/95 to C-36/95 De Agostini and TV-Shop i Sverige [1997] ECR I-3843.

309 Opinion of AG Jacobs delivered on 30 April 2002, Case C-126/01 GEMO [2003] ECR I-13769.

310 Cases C-53/00 Ferring [2001] ECR I-9067 and C-280/00 Altmark [2003] ECR I-7747.

311 Opinion of AG Mischo delivered on 12 December 2002, Case C-192/01 Commission v Denmark [2003] ECR I-9693; and Opinion of AG Mischo delivered on 16 May 2002, Case C-95/01 Greenham and Abel [2004] ECR I-1333.

v Netherlands Mr *Poiares Maduro* did it, whereas Advocate General *Geelhoed* did not mention *Kellogg's* in *Bellio Fratelli*[312].

In C-452/01 *Ospelt*, a case on free movement of capital in the EEA, Advocate General *Geelhoed* made reference to EFTA Court case law[313]. I will come back later to the *Ospelt* case. Advocate General *Poiares Maduro* again cited the Court's jurisprudence in Joined Cases C-232/04 and C-233/04 *Güney-Görres and Demir*, transfer of undertaking cases. In C-537/03 *Candolin* Advocate General *Geelhoed* entirely followed our reasoning in the *Finanger* case[314]. Advocate General *Sharpston* found the Court's judgment in *Paranova v Merck* **entirely convincing**. She quoted a whole series of paragraphs verbatim from it and suggested that the ECJ follow on the following points. (1) Permitting parallel imports and repackaging aims at securing free movement of goods. (2) The right to repackage is justified because it contributes to overcoming the partitioning of the EEA market along national boundaries. (3) Where the right to repackage is beyond doubt and the parallel importer has achieved effective access to the market, the necessity requirement cannot be decisive when interpreting the term "legitimate reasons" in Article 7(2) of the Trademark Directive. (4) Imposing the necessity requirement on the parallel importer's strategy of product presentation would constitute a disproportionate restriction on the free movement of goods[315]. Professor *Sharpston* also made ample reference to the Court in another case concerning repackaging of pharmaceuticals and the parallel importer changing the appearance of the packaging, C-276/05 *The Wellcome Foundation*[316].

There were a number of other cases in which Advocates General cited EFTA Court rulings. Important is C-438/05 *Viking Line* where Professor *Poiares Maduro* shared our view that collective agreements enjoy only **limited antitrust immunity** and did not follow the ECJ's approach in *Albany* that had advocated absolute immunity[317]. In C-380/05 *Centro Europa 7*, Advocate General *Poiares Maduro* referred to our *Ladbrokes* judgment where we had been rather critical vis-à-vis the Norwegian state monopoly

312 Opinion of AG Alber delivered on 13 March 2003, Case C-236/01 Monsanto [2003] ECR I-8105; Opinion of AG Poiares Maduro delivered on 14 September 2004, Case C-41/02 Commission v Netherlands [2004] ECR I-11375; Opinion of AG Geelhoed delivered on 29 January 2004, Case C-286/02 Bellio Fratelli [2004] ECR I-3465.

313 Opinion of AG Geelhoed delivered on 10 April 2003, Case C-452/01 Ospelt [2003] ECR I-9743.

314 Opinion of AG Poiares Maduro delivered on 16 June 2005, Joined Cases C-232/04 and C-233/04 Güney-Görres and Demir [2005] ECR I-11237; Opinion of AG Geelhoed delivered on 10 March 2005, Case C-537/03 Candolin [2005] ECR I-5745.

315 Opinion of AG Sharpston delivered on 6 April 2006, Case C-348/04 Boehringer Ingelheim II [2007] ECR I-3391.

316 Opinion of AG Sharpston delivered on 9 October 2008, Case C-276/05 The Wellcome Foundation, nyr, at paragraphs 33-36. The ECJ decided along the same lines as in Boehringer Ingelheim II and cited, inter alia, the paragraph of that ruling which made reference to EFTA Court Paranova v Merck (judgment of 22 December 2008, at paragraph 25); see with regard to the Wellcome Foundation case Héctor Armengod/Laura Melusine Baudenbacher, The Repackaging of Pharmaceutical Products and Parallel Trade in the EU, RAJ Pharma December 2009, 783, 784 et seq.

317 Opinion of AG Poiares Maduro delivered on 23 May 2007, C-438/05 Viking Line [2007] ECR I-10779; see supra, lecture 4.

system in the gaming and betting area with the exception of gaming machines, that means horse race betting, football betting, lotto, scratch cards and the like[318]. Professor *Mengozzi*, the Italian Advocate General, cited the Court's judgment in E-7/01 *Hegelstad v Hydro Texaco*[319] in C-260/07 *Pedro IV Servicios* when discussing whether an exclusive purchasing agreement for motor-vehicle fuels and other fuels has as its object or effect the appreciable restriction of competition within the internal market and may affect trade between Member States[320]. Professor *Trstenjak*, the Advocate General from Slovenia, made reference to E-1/06 *Gaming Machines* and E-3/06 *Ladbrokes*[321] in C-304/08 *Zentrale zur Bekämpfung unlauteren Wettbewerbs e.V. gegen Plus Warenhandelsgesellschaft mbH*[322], to E-1/94 *Restamark*, E-6/96 *Wilhelmsen*, and E-4/04 *Pedicel* in Case C-265/06 *Commission v Portugal* [2008] ECR I-2245[323] and to the above mentioned judgment in Case E-2/98 *Federation of Icelandic Trade* in Joined Cases C-352/07 et seq. *Menarini*[324]. Further examples are the references of Advocate General *Lenz* in C-222/94 *Commission v United Kingdom* to Joined Cases E-8/94 and E-9/94 *Mattel and Lego* [325], of Advocate General *Elmer* in C-189/95 *Franzén* to E-1/94 *Restamark*[326], of Advocate General *Poiares Maduro* in C-319/03 *Briheche* to E-1/02 *University of Oslo*,[327] and of Advocate General *Bot* in C-42/07 *Liga Portuguesa*[328] and in C-203/08 *The Sporting Exchange Ltd* and C-258/08 *Ladbrokes Betting & Gaming Ltd*[329] to E-1/06 *Gaming Machines*[330].

2. Advocates General entering into a substantial discussion with the Court

I mentioned that the ECJ would, as a matter of principle, enter into a dialogue with the EFTA Court if it agreed with the outcome and the reasoning of the latter's judgment.

---

318 Opinion of AG Poiares Maduro delivered on 12 September 2007, C-380/05 Centro Europa 7 [2008] ECR I-349.

319 [2002] EFTA Court Report 310.

320 Opinion of AG Mengozzi of 4 September 2008, C-260/97 Pedro IV Servicios, nyr., footnote 16.

321 Opinion of AG Lenz delivered on 30 April 1996, Case C-222/94 Commission v United Kingdom [1996] ECR I-4025; Opinion of AG Elmer delivered on 4 March 1997, Case C-189/95 Franzén [1997] ECR I-5909; Opinion of AG Poiares Maduro delivered on 29 June 2004, C-319/03 Briheche [2004] ECR I-8807.

322 Opinion of AG Trstenjak of 3 September 2009, Case C-304/08 Zentrale zur Bekämpfung unlauteren Wettbewerbs e. V. v Plus Warenhandelsgesellschaft mbH, at paragraphs 68 and 69.

323 Opinion of AG Trstenjak of 13 December 2007 in Case C-265/06 Commission v Portugal, [2008] ECR I-2245, fn. 10, 13, 44.

324 Opinion of AG Trstenjak of 13 November 2008, Joined Cases C-352/07 to C-356/07, C-365/07 to C-367/07 and C-400/07 Menarini and Others, at paragraphs 79 and 106, nyr.

325 Opinion of AG Lenz of 30 April 1996 in Case C-222/94 Commission v United Kingdom, [1996] ECR I-4025, at paragraph. 3.

326 Opinion of AG Elmer of 4 March 1997 in Case C-189/95 Criminal proceedings against Harry Franzén [1997] ECR I-05909, at paragraph. 3

327 Opinion of AG Poiares Maduro of 29 June 2004 in Case 319/03 Briheche [2004] ECR, I-8807, at paragraphs 34, 36 and 40.

328 Opinion of AG Bot of 14 October 2008, at paragraph 119.

329 Opinion of AG Bot of 17 December 2009, fn. 56.

330 [2007] EFTA Court Report, 7, at paragraph 51.

If this is not the case, it will refrain from making reference.

Certain Advocates General tend to go beyond this narrow concept of dialogue. They would also reference a judgment of the Court if they do not or not fully agree with the outcome or the reasoning. In other words they state that there is a judgment of the Court on a given problem, but for certain reasons they disagree with it. That is a real, substantive, even **dialectic dialogue**. Occasionally the ECJ has followed the Advocate General, occasionally it has preferred to follow us.

In Joined Cases C-34/95 to C-36/95 *De Agostini* and *TV-Shop i Sverige*, Advocate General *Jacobs* advised the ECJ to follow the holding in Jointed Cases E-8/94 and E-9/94 *Mattel Scandinavia/Lego Norge* that the TV Directive prevents receiving States from controlling transfrontier TV broadcasts, but not the *dictum* that such control may be based on the Misleading Advertising Directive[331]. The ECJ followed the EFTA Court's approach. In C-95/01 *Greenham and Abel* and in C-392/01 *Commission v Denmark*, Advocate General *Mischo* advised the ECJ not to follow the EFTA Court's finding that a Member State may not rely on the argument that there was **no nutritional need** in the population when banning the marketing of foodstuff fortified with vitamins and minerals[332]. As already stated, the ECJ did not follow its Advocate General's proposal.

In C-374/04 *Test Claimants in Class IV* and C-170/05 *Denkavit International BV*, Advocate General *Geelhoed* asked the ECJ not to follow the EFTA Court's 2004 *Fokus Bank* ruling which found that a Member State which grants a tax credit to shareholders residing in that State on dividends paid by domestic companies, but **denies** such a favour to shareholders residing in other EEA countries (outbound dividends) violates the free movement of capital and which rejected the idea that such a restriction could be justified based on bilateral **Double Taxation Agreements**[333].

In C-170/04 *Rosengren* Advocate General *Tizzano* found that since the Swedish retail sales State monopoly *Systembolaget* had discretion to refuse orders from private parties that entailed importing products from other Member States, the imposition of the ban on private parties importing those products themselves was contrary to Article 31 EC (now: Article 37 TFEU)[334]. The case was subsequently assigned to the Grand Chamber. Advocate General *Mengozzi* concurred with Mr *Tizzano's* conclusion[335]. He extensively dealt with the Court's judgment in E-4/05 *HOB-vín*. In that case, the Court had ruled, *inter alia*, that the requirements that products of a certain quantity must be delivered

331 Opinion of AG Jacobs of 17 September 1996 in Joined Cases C-34/95 to C-36/95 De Agostini and TV-Shop i Sverige [1997] ECR I-3843.
332 Opinion of AG Mischo of 12 December 2002 in Case C-192/01 Commission v Denmark [2003] ECR I-9693; and Opinion of AG Mischo of 16 May 2002 in Case C-95/01 Greenham and Abel [2004] ECR I-1333.
333 Opinions of AG Geelhoed of 23 February 2006 in Case C-374/04 Test Claimants in Class IV [2006] ECR I-11673; and of 27 April 2006 in Case C-170/05 Denkavit [2006] ECR I-11949.
334 Opinion of AG Tizzano of 30 March 2006 in Case C-170/04 Rosengren [2007] ECR I-4071.
335 Opinion of AG Mengozzi of 30 November 2006 in Case C-170/04 Rosengren [2007] ECR I-4071.

on a pallet and that the price of the pallet must be included in the price of the product relate to the **operation of the monopoly**[336]. Since they exclusively applied to the monopoly, they had to be considered inseparable from its operation. Advocate General *Mengozzi* argued that it could not be deduced from the Court's judgment that national rules which concern other economic actors or private persons are necessarily separable from the operation of the monopoly.

E. Functions of the dialogue EFTA Court – EC judiciary

1. Indicating the origin of the considerations underlying the judgment

It would seem that indicating the origin of the considerations a judgment is based on is simply a matter of intellectual honesty. If you take an idea from another source it is natural that you make it known where it is from. This is the basis of copyright law and I have difficulties to see why judges should not, on principle, be held to the same standards as students and scholars and professors. Moreover, the borrowing court **pays respect** to the lending court.

2. Enhancing the rationality and the quality of judgments

Consulting foreign judgments gives **additional input** to a court. It certainly enhances the rationality of judgments if a court takes into account how another court has gone over a legal problem. Moreover, it improves the quality. EFTA Court judges have time to think particularly thoroughly because their case load is not as high as that of ECJ judges. Input by the EFTA Court may therefore in certain situations be appreciated by the EC judiciary, in particular if the judges in the ECJ are split.

3. Securing influence on the referenced court

On a general level, it has been said that high courts that take part in the modern global judicial dialogue have a better chance to export their own case law to other jurisdictions than courts which prefer to stand aside[337]. *Mutatis mutandis*, this also holds true for the EEA. By paying respect to the Court, the ECJ will make it more inclined to strictly stick to the EEA **homogeneity rules**. That is also my point with regard to the national courts. I mentioned in my fourth lecture that at the Nordic Law Conference here in Reykjavík a couple of years ago, I said that the EFTA Court should start to quote the judgments of the Supreme Court of Iceland, the Supreme Court of Norway, and the

336 Case E-4/05 HOB-vín [2006] EFTA Court Report 3.

337 L'Heureux-Dubé, loc. cit., 37 et seq.

State Court and the Supreme Courts of Liechtenstein[338]. That would make these judges proud and inclined to cooperate with the Court. It has not, however, happened so far.

4. Giving support to the referenced court

Depending on the circumstances, this may constitute a very important function. The EFTA Court is a **small court** which has profited from this kind of backing when the ECJ in C-140/97 *Rechberger* in 1999 made reference to its 1998 *Sveinbjörnsdóttir* ruling[339]. In *Sveinbjörnsdóttir*, the Court had acknowledged, against the opposition of the Governments of Iceland, Norway and Sweden as well as of the European Commission, that State liability is part of EEA law [340]. In Case-4/01 *Karlsson*, which was decided in 2002, the Norwegian government called on the EFTA Court to overrule *Sveinbjörnsdóttir*. The latter confirmed that ruling and explicitly mentioned the fact that the ECJ had cited *Sveinbjörnsdóttir* in *Rechberger*[341]. With this, the Court has, as one commentator stated, in a skillful way taken the ECJ as an ally on board[342]. One will finally have to assume that support by another court may in certain situations also be appreciated by a **big and powerful court** such as the ECJ. This could, for instance, be so in politically sensitive cases. It may also happen that if a big court such as the ECJ is split, a previous judgment of a small court on the same legal question will tip the balance.

G. Conclusion

Let me conclude this last lecture with a quotation from *Allan Rosas* who, together with *Christiaan Timmermans*, is a champion of judicial dialogue at the ECJ. He wrote in a book which I co-edited a year ago:

> *"[F]or me the question as to whether judges should be open to the outside world and be aware of discussions taking place in other relevant jurisdictions, is not any longer a question of opinion. It is a question of whether you are competent or incompetent. If you close your eyes, you belong to the latter category."*[343]

I concur with that view.

338 Det 37. nordiske Juristmøde I Reykjavík, 18.–20. August 2005, Bind II, 79.

339 Case C-140/97 Rechberger [1999] ECR I-3499, at paragraph 39.

340 Case E-9/97 Sveinbjörnsdóttir [1998] EFTA Court Report 115.

341 Case E-4/01 Karlsson [2002] EFTA Court Report 240, 248, at paragraph 25.

342 See Georg Gorton, Bestätigung der Staatshaftungsrechtsprechung des EFTA-Gerichtshofs, 7-8 European Law Reporter, 260, 263 [2002].

343 Allan Rosas, Methods of Interpretation – Judicial Dialogue, in: Carl Baudenbacher/Erhard Busek (eds.), The Role of International Courts, [2008] Heidelberg, 185, 191.

Final remarks

The EFTA Court 16 years on

The EFTA Court is a vulnerable court for a number of reasons. Firstly, it is a **small court**, and the structure of the EFTA pillar resembles a pond with one big fish and two small fishes, one even very small. The Court consists of only three judges which means, *inter alia*, that the judge from the country concerned must also sit in politically sensitive cases. In high profile cases, government representatives have sometimes stated that if the Court would not decide in their favour, this could have negative consequences for the willingness of their country to stay in the EEA. In one case, an agent gave a newspaper interview after the oral hearing and threatened that if the EFTA Court would not rule in favour of his government, the judgment would not be implemented in his country. His minister refused to comment[344]. In the heat of the moment, the agent overlooked that the case, E-3/06 *Ladbrokes*, was a reference from a national court so that the final judgment was to be given by that court. Secondly, appointment and reappointment of the judges lie in the hands of the same governments the Court is called upon to supervise. Thirdly, the Court is being subject to an auditing mechanism which is not fully independent from the governments[345].

On the other hand, the Court received considerable **support** in its work. Approval of the Court's budget by the governments has never been a problem. Certain national courts have from early on made use of the possibility to refer questions on the interpretation of EEA law, and they have loyally implemented the Court's rulings. Important endorsement came (and continues to come) from the ECJ, its Advocates General and the CFI who maintain an ongoing judicial dialogue with their sister court. The same holds true of a number of high courts in EC countries.

Sixteen years after the entry into force of the EEA Agreement, the governments of the EEA/EFTA States appear to have accepted that as far as its legal nature is concerned the agreement is much closer to supranational EU law than to classical international law. And that it has only been possible to maintain the good functioning of the agreement because from the beginning the Court has been committed to the principle of **dynamic homogeneity**. Moreover, the Court has made significant contributions to the

344 See Bergen's Tidende of 2 February 2007.

345 See supra. lecture 1.

development of the case law, but also to the academic debate in EU law. These accomplishments have been recognised in recent publications.

Professor *Horst Krenzler*, the former Director General of External Relations in the European Commission and EC chief negotiator in the EEA negotiations, stated in 2009:

> *"After 15 years of existence of the EEA it must be recognised that this complex decision-making process works highly satisfactorily – in spite of some initial doubts. It was also basically possible to maintain the homogeneity of the law in this large and dynamic European Economic Area thanks to the good functioning of the EFTA Court."*[346]

The former Swedish Judge of the EFTA Court Dr *Sven Norberg* wrote in 2009:

> *"[T]here is no doubt that it is through the EFTA Court that the EEA Agreement is still credible"*[347].

University of Iceland Professor *Elvira Méndez-Pinedo* recently called the effectiveness of EEA law

> *"a silent revolution brought by the EFTA Court"*[348].

Allow me another remark: There is huge interest in the EEA in **Japan**. For the last three years I have participated in workshops in Tokyo and in Kyoto which discussed the possibility of establishing a free trade area comprising, in particular, China, Korea and Japan. Most of the Japanese university professors of international law and of European law are involved in this. One could say that the EEA is more popular in the Far East than in some of our capitals.

The second Icesave Agreement as a sign of trust in the EFTA Court

On 5 June 2009 the Icesave Loan Agreements between the *Icelandic Depositors' and Investors' Guarantee Fund* as borrower, Iceland as guarantor, and the UK Commissioners of Her Majesty's Treasury as lender, and between the *Icelandic Depositors' and Investors' Guarantee Fund* as borrower, Iceland as guarantor and The State of the Netherlands as lender were signed. After the bankruptcy of the *Landsbanki Íslands hf.* in the fall of

346 European Economic Area 1994–2009, EFTA commemorative publication, Brussels, May 2009.

347 Sven Norberg, Disputes in Intergovernmental Economic Relations of a Traditional Character and in those with Supranational Mechanisms, Respectively, in: Carl Baudenbacher (ed.), Dispute Resolution, Stuttgart 2009, 43, 46.

348 EC and EEA Law; A Comparative Study of the Effectiveness of European Law, Groningen 2009, cover.

2008, the *British Financial Services Compensation Scheme Limited* (FSCS) and the Dutch Central Bank paid compensation to *Landsbanki London* and *Landsbanki Amsterdam* depositors in respect of their claims against Landsbanki and the Guarantee Fund. It was agreed that the Guarantee Fund will reimburse the two EC countries the respective amounts. In the case of the UK, the amount was £ 2,350,000,000, in the case of the Netherlands EUR 1,329,242,850. Iceland irrevocably and unconditionally guaranteed to the two countries the due and punctual performance by the Guarantee Fund of the latter's obligations. In case the Guarantee Fund receives any amount in respect of the claims of or formerly of Landsbanki depositors or otherwise in respect of the insolvency of *Landsbanki*, it will pay that amount to the UK and the Netherlands *pro rata* to the amounts of principal the outstanding under the two loan agreements.

In the supplementary **Icesave Loan Agreements** concluded between the same parties on 18 October 2009, there are provisions stating that amounts recovered from the insolvent estate of Icesave's parent company, *Landsbanki Íslands hf.*, shall be divided between the Guarantee Funds of the three countries involved *pro rata* to their claims. However, the two EU countries agreed that if the EFTA Court were to find upon a reference by an Icelandic court that the Icelandic Fund's claims have priority on disbursements from the estate of *Landsbanki Íslands hf.* over other portions of claims for the same deposits, the respective provisions of the Loan Agreements will be automatically null and void. The division will then be in accordance with the Court's verdict[349]. This implies by the way that an Icelandic court which is seized with the matter will basically be obliged to make a reference to the EFTA Court and that the EFTA Court's judgment will be factually binding and have direct effect. It is an open secret that the Dutch and the British wanted to have some sort of a guarantee that there will be a reference if an Icelandic court gets a case. The provisions in question should, beyond the Icesave case, provide ample food for thought to those who believe that national courts in the EEA/EFTA countries are absolutely free in deciding whether to refer a case to the EFTA Court or not and that EEA law and judgments of the EFTA Court have no effect in the legal orders of the EFTA States unless they are being implemented by a special measure. *Liechtensteiner Vaterland*, a daily newspaper, has called this a strong sign of trust in the EFTA Court[350]. In fact, the supplementary Icesave agreements are proof that the EFTA States are benefiting from an independent and credible EFTA Court. In view of certain attempts to undermine the Court's independence, this may even be called an **irony of history**. Thanks to the fact that the Court has been principled, in particular with regard to the concept of dynamic homogeneity, it has acquired the credibility which has now prompted the Governments of the UK and of the Netherlands to accept the Court's competence. Otherwise this door would not have been open[351].

349 www.icenews.is/index.php/2009/10/18/icesave-negotiations-concluded-outcome-presented/, last visited 20 October 2009.

350 www.vaterland.li/page/epaper/pdf_blaettern_gross_frameset.cfm?seite=07_lv_03_2009-10-21, last visited 21 October 2009.

351 See Carl Baudenbacher, Internationale Gerichte als Alternative zur politischen Auseinandersetzung, Neue Zürcher Zeitung Internationale Ausgabe Nr. 285 of 8 December 2009, 13.

Appendix

[1]AGREEMENT ON THE EUROPEAN ECONOMIC AREA

(OJ No L 1, 3.1A.1994, p. 3; and EFTA States' official gazettes)

Amended by:

1. Protocol Adjusting the Agreement on the European Economic Area of 17 March 1993 (OJ No L 1, 3.1.1994, p. 572; and EFTA States' official gazettes).
2. EEA Council Decision No 1/95 of 10 March on the entry into force of the Agreement on the European Economic Area for the Principality of Liechtenstein (OJ No L 86, 20.4.1995, p. 58; EEA Supplement No 14, 20.4.1995, p. 1).
3. Agreement on the participation of the Czech Republic, the Republic of Estonia, the Republic of Cyprus, the Republic of Latvia, the Republic of Lithuania, the Republic of Hungary, the Republic of Malta, the Republic of Poland, the Republic of Slovenia and the Slovak Republic in the European Economic Area of 14 October 2003 (OJ No L 130, 29.4.2004, p. 11; EEA Supplement No 23, 29.4.2004, p. 1).
4. Agreement on the participation of Bulgaria and Romania in the European Economic Area of 25 July 2007 (OJ No L [to be published]).

TABLE OF CONTENTS

1 As amended by the Adjusting Protocol and subsequently by the 2004 EEA Enlargement Agreement (OJ No L 130, 29.4.2004, p. 3 and EEA Supplement No 23, 29.4.2004, p. 1), e.i.f. 1.5.2004, and subsequently by the 2007 EEA Enlargement Agreement (OJ No L [to be published]), provisionally applicable as of 1.8.2007, e.i.f. pending.

[2]THE EUROPEAN COMMUNITY,
THE KINGDOM OF BELGIUM,
THE REPUBLIC OF BULGARIA
THE CZECH REPUBLIC,
THE KINGDOM OF DENMARK,
THE FEDERAL REPUBLIC OF GERMANY,
THE REPUBLIC OF ESTONIA,
IRELAND,
THE HELLENIC REPUBLIC,
THE KINGDOM OF SPAIN,
THE FRENCH REPUBLIC,
THE ITALIAN REPUBLIC,
THE REPUBLIC OF CYPRUS,
THE REPUBLIC OF LATVIA,
THE REPUBLIC OF LITHUANIA,
THE GRAND DUCHY OF LUXEMBOURG,
THE REPUBLIC OF HUNGARY,
MALTA,
THE KINGDOM OF THE NETHERLANDS,
THE REPUBLIC OF AUSTRIA,
THE REPUBLIC OF POLAND,
THE PORTUGUESE REPUBLIC,
ROMANIA,
THE REPUBLIC OF SLOVENIA,
THE SLOVAK REPUBLIC,
THE REPUBLIC OF FINLAND,
THE KINGDOM OF SWEDEN,
THE UNITED KINGDOM OF GREAT BRITAIN AND NORTHERN IRELAND,
AND
[ ][3]
ICELAND,
THE PRINCIPALITY OF LIECHTENSTEIN,
THE KINGDOM OF NORWAY,
[ ][4]
[ ][5]
hereinafter referred to as the CONTRACTING PARTIES;

---

2 As amended by the 2004 EEA Enlargement Agreement (OJ No L 130, 29.4.2004, p. 3 and EEA Supplement No 23, 29.4.2004, p. 1), e.i.f. 1.5.2004, and subsequently by the 2007 EEA Enlargement Agreement (OJ No L [to be published]), provisionally applicable as of 1.8.2007, e.i.f. pending.

3 Austria, Finland and Sweden acceded the European Union on 1 January 1995.

4 Austria, Finland and Sweden acceded the European Union on 1 January 1995.

5 Reference to "the Swiss Confederation" deleted by the Adjusting Protocol.

CONVINCED of the contribution that a European Economic Area will bring to the construction of a Europe based on peace, democracy and human rights;

REAFFIRMING the high priority attached to the privileged relationship between the European Community, its Member States and the EFTA States, which is based on proximity, long-standing common values and European identity;

DETERMINED to contribute, on the basis of market economy, to world-wide trade liberalization and cooperation, in particular in accordance with the provisions of the General Agreement on Tariffs and Trade and the Convention on the Organisation for Economic Cooperation and Development;

CONSIDERING the objective of establishing a dynamic and homogeneous European Economic Area, based on common rules and equal conditions of competition and providing for the adequate means of enforcement including at the judicial level, and achieved on the basis of equality and reciprocity and of an overall balance of benefits, rights and obligations for the Contracting Parties;

DETERMINED to provide for the fullest possible realization of the free movement of goods, persons, services and capital within the whole European Economic Area, as well as for strengthened and broadened cooperation in flanking and horizontal policies;

AIMING to promote a harmonious development of the European Economic Area and convinced of the need to contribute through the application of this Agreement to the reduction of economic and social regional disparities;

DESIROUS of contributing to the strengthening of the cooperation between the members of the European Parliament and of the Parliaments of the EFTA States, as well as between the social partners in the European Community and in the EFTA States;

CONVINCED of the important role that individuals will play in the European Economic Area through the exercise of the rights conferred on them by this Agreement and through the judicial defence of these rights;

DETERMINED to preserve, protect and improve the quality of the environment and to ensure a prudent and rational utilization of natural resources on the basis, in particular, of the principle of sustainable development, as well as the principle that precautionary and preventive action should be taken;

DETERMINED to take, in the further development of rules, a high level of protection concerning health, safety and the environment as a basis;

NOTING the importance of the development of the social dimension, including equal treatment of men and women, in the European Economic Area and wishing to ensure economic and social progress and to promote conditions for full employment, an improved standard of living and improved working conditions within the European Economic Area;

DETERMINED to promote the interests of consumers and to strengthen their position in the market place, aiming at a high level of consumer protection;

ATTACHED to the common objectives of strengthening the scientific and technological basis of European industry and of encouraging it to become more competitive at the international level;

CONSIDERING that the conclusion of this Agreement shall not prejudge in any way the possibility of any EFTA State to accede to the European Communities;

WHEREAS, in full deference to the independence of the courts, the objective of the Contracting Parties is to arrive at, and maintain, a uniform interpretation and application of this Agreement and those provisions of Community legislation which are substantially reproduced in this Agreement and to arrive at an equal treatment of individuals and economic operators as regards the four freedoms and the conditions of competition;

WHEREAS this Agreement does not restrict the decision-making autonomy or the treaty-making power of the Contracting Parties, subject to the provisions of this Agreement and the limitations set by public international law;

HAVE DECIDED to conclude the following Agreement:

PART I
OBJECTIVES AND PRINCIPLES

Article 1

1. The aim of this Agreement of association is to promote a continuous and balanced strengthening of trade and economic relations between the Contracting Parties with equal conditions of competition, and the respect of the same rules, with a view to creating a homogeneous European Economic Area, hereinafter referred to as the EEA.
2. In order to attain the objectives set out in paragraph 1, the association shall entail, in accordance with the provisions of this Agreement:
   (a) the free movement of goods;
   (b) the free movement of persons;
   (c) the free movement of services;

(d) the free movement of capital;
(e) the setting up of a system ensuring that competition is not distorted and that the rules thereon are equally respected; as well as
(f) closer cooperation in other fields, such as research and development, the environment, education and social policy.

Article 2

For the purposes of this Agreement:

(a) the term "Agreement" means the main Agreement, its Protocols and Annexes as well as the acts referred to therein;
(b)[6] the term "EFTA States" means the [7] Iceland, the Principality of Liechtenstein and the Kingdom of Norway;
(c) the term "Contracting Parties" means, concerning the Community and the EC Member States, the Community and the EC Member States, or the Community, or the EC Member States. The meaning to be attributed to this expression in each case is to be deduced from the relevant provisions of this Agreement and from the respective competences of the Community and the EC Member States as they follow from the Treaty establishing the European Economic Community [8];
(d)[9] the term "Act of Accession of 16 April 2003" shall mean the Act concerning the conditions of Accession of the Czech Republic, the Republic of Estonia, the Republic of Cyprus, the Republic of Latvia, the Republic of Lithuania, the Republic of Hungary, the Republic of Malta, the Republic of Poland, the Republic of Slovenia and the Slovak Republic and the adjustments to the Treaties on which the European Union is founded, adopted in Athens on 16 April 2003;
(e)[10] the term "Act of Accession of 25 April 2005" shall mean the Act concerning the conditions of accession of the Republic of Bulgaria and Romania and the adjustments to the Treaties on which the European Union is founded, adopted in Luxembourg on 25 April 2005;
(f)[11] the term "Protocol of Accession of 25 April 2005" shall mean the Protocol concerning the conditions and arrangements for admission of the Republic of Bulgaria and Romania to the European Union, adopted in Luxembourg on 25 April 2005.

---

6 As replaced by the Adjusting Protocol and subsequently by the 2004 EEA Enlargement Agreement (OJ No L 130, 29.4.2004, p. 3 and EEA Supplement No 23, 29.4.2004, p. 1), e.i.f. 1.5.2004.

7 Words "Republic of" deleted by the 2007 EEA Enlargement Agreement (OJ No L [to be published]), provisionally applicable as of 1.8.2007, e.i.f. pending.

8 Words "and the Treaty establishing the European Coal and Steel Community" deleted by the 2004 EEA Enlargement Agreement (OJ No L 130, 29.4.2004, p. 3 and EEA Supplement No 23, 29.4.2004, p. 1), e.i.f. 1.5.2004.

9 Paragraph added by the 2004 EEA Enlargement Agreement (OJ No L 130, 29.4.2004, p. 3 and EEA Supplement No 23, 29.4.2004, p. 1), e.i.f. 1.5.2004.

10 Paragraph added by the 2007 EEA Enlargement Agreement (OJ No L [to be published]), provisionally applicable as of 1.8.2007, e.i.f. pending.

11 Paragraph added by the 2007 EEA Enlargement Agreement (OJ No L [to be published]), provisionally applicable as of 1.8.2007, e.i.f. pending.

Article 3

The Contracting Parties shall take all appropriate measures, whether general or particular, to ensure fulfilment of the obligations arising out of this Agreement.
They shall abstain from any measure which could jeopardize the attainment of the objectives of this Agreement.
Moreover, they shall facilitate cooperation within the framework of this Agreement.

Article 4

Within the scope of application of this Agreement, and without prejudice to any special provisions contained therein, any discrimination on grounds of nationality shall be prohibited.

Article 5

A Contracting Party may at any time raise a matter of concern at the level of the EEA Joint Committee or the EEA Council according to the modalities laid down in Articles 92 (2) and 89 (2), respectively.

Article 6

Without prejudice to future developments of case law, the provisions of this Agreement, in so far as they are identical in substance to corresponding rules of the Treaty establishing the European Economic Community and the Treaty establishing the European Coal and Steel Community and to acts adopted in application of these two Treaties, shall, in their implementation and application, be interpreted in conformity with the relevant rulings of the Court of Justice of the European Communities given prior to the date of signature of this Agreement.

Article 7

Acts referred to or contained in the Annexes to this Agreement or in decisions of the EEA Joint Committee shall be binding upon the Contracting Parties and be, or be made, part of their internal legal order as follows:

(a) an act corresponding to an EEC regulation shall as such be made part of the internal legal order of the Contracting Parties;
(b) an act corresponding to an EEC directive shall leave to the authorities of the Contracting Parties the choice of form and method of implementation.

PART II
FREE MOVEMENT OF GOODS

CHAPTER 1
BASIC PRINCIPLES

Article 8

1. Free movement of goods between the Contracting Parties shall be established in conformity with the provisions of this Agreement.
2. Unless otherwise specified, Articles 10 to 15, 19, 20 and 25 to 27 shall apply only to products originating in the Contracting Parties.
3. Unless otherwise specified, the provisions of this Agreement shall apply only to:
   (a) products falling within Chapters 25 to 97 of the Harmonized Commodity Description and Coding System, excluding the products listed in Protocol 2;
   (b) products specified in Protocol 3, subject to the specific arrangements set out in that Protocol.

Article 9

1. The rules of origin are set out in Protocol 4. They are without prejudice to any international obligations which have been, or may be, subscribed to by the Contracting Parties under the General Agreement on Tariffs and Trade.
2. With a view to developing the results achieved in this Agreement, the Contracting Parties will continue their efforts in order further to improve and simplify all aspects of rules of origin and to increase cooperation in customs matters.
3. A first review will take place before the end of 1993. Subsequent reviews will take place at two-yearly intervals. On the basis of these reviews, the Contracting Parties undertake to decide on the appropriate measures to be included in this Agreement.

Article 10

Customs duties on imports and exports, and any charges having equivalent effect, shall be prohibited between the Contracting Parties. Without prejudice to the arrangements set out in Protocol 5, this shall also apply to customs duties of a fiscal nature.

Article 11

Quantitative restrictions on imports and all measures having equivalent effect shall be prohibited between the Contracting Parties.

Article 12

Quantitative restrictions on exports and all measures having equivalent effect shall be prohibited between the Contracting Parties.

Article 13
The provisions of Articles 11 and 12 shall not preclude prohibitions or restrictions on imports, exports or goods in transit justified on grounds of public morality, public policy or public security; the protection of health and life of humans, animals or plants; the protection of national treasures possessing artistic, historic or archaeological value; or the protection of industrial and commercial property. Such prohibitions or restrictions shall not, however, constitute a means of arbitrary discrimination or a disguised restriction on trade between the Contracting Parties.

Article 14
No Contracting Party shall impose, directly or indirectly, on the products of other Contracting Parties any internal taxation of any kind in excess of that imposed directly or indirectly on similar domestic products.
Furthermore, no Contracting Party shall impose on the products of other Contracting Parties any internal taxation of such a nature as to afford indirect protection to other products.

Article 15
Where products are exported to the territory of any Contracting Party, any repayment of internal taxation shall not exceed the internal taxation imposed on them whether directly or indirectly.

Article 16
1. The Contracting Parties shall ensure that any State monopoly of a commercial character be adjusted so that no discrimination regarding the conditions under which goods are procured and marketed will exist between nationals of EC Member States and EFTA States.
2. The provisions of this Article shall apply to any body through which the competent authorities of the Contracting Parties, in law or in fact, either directly or indirectly supervise, determine or appreciably influence imports or exports between Contracting Parties. These provisions shall likewise apply to monopolies delegated by the State to others.

CHAPTER 2
AGRICULTURAL AND FISHERY PRODUCTS

Article 17
Annex I contains specific provisions and arrangements concerning veterinary and phytosanitary matters.

Article 18
Without prejudice to the specific arrangements governing trade in agricultural products, the Contracting Parties shall ensure that the arrangements provided for in Articles 17

and 23 (a) and (b), as they apply to products other than those covered by Article 8(3), are not compromised by other technical barriers to trade. Article 13 shall apply.

Article 19

1. The Contracting Parties shall examine any difficulties that might arise in their trade in agricultural products and shall endeavour to seek appropriate solutions.
2. The Contracting Parties undertake to continue their efforts with a view to achieving progressive liberalization of agricultural trade.
3. To this end, the Contracting Parties will carry out, before the end of 1993 and subsequently at two-yearly intervals, reviews of the conditions of trade in agricultural products.
4. In the light of the results of these reviews, within the framework of their respective agricultural policies and taking into account the results of the Uruguay Round, the Contracting Parties will decide, within the framework of this Agreement, on a preferential, bilateral or multilateral, reciprocal and mutually beneficial basis, on further reductions of any type of barriers to trade in the agricultural sector, including those resulting from State monopolies of a commercial character in the agricultural field.

Article 20

Provisions and arrangements that apply to fish and other marine products are set out in Protocol 9.

CHAPTER 3
COOPERATION IN CUSTOMS-RELATED MATTERS AND TRADE FACILITATION

Article 21

1. In order to facilitate trade between them, the Contracting Parties shall simplify border controls and formalities. Arrangements for this purpose are set out in Protocol 10.
2. The Contracting Parties shall assist each other in customs matters in order to ensure that customs legislation is correctly applied. Arrangements for this purpose are set out in Protocol 11.
3. The Contracting Parties shall strengthen and broaden cooperation with the aim of simplifying the procedures for trade in goods, in particular in the context of Community programmes, projects and actions aimed at trade facilitation, in accordance with the rules set out in Part VI.
4. Notwithstanding Article 8 (3), this Article shall apply to all products.

Article 22

A Contracting Party which is considering the reduction of the effective level of its duties or charges having equivalent effect applicable to third countries benefiting from most-favoured-nation treatment, or which is considering the suspension of their application, shall, as far as may be practicable, notify the EEA Joint Committee not later than thirty days before such reduction or suspension comes into effect. It shall take note of any representations by other Contracting Parties regarding any distortions which might result there from.

CHAPTER 4
OTHER RULES RELATING TO THE FREE MOVEMENT OF GOODS

Article 23

Specific provisions and arrangements are laid down in:

(a) Protocol 12 and Annex II in relation to technical regulations, standards, testing and certification;

(b) Protocol 47 in relation to the abolition of technical barriers to trade in wine;

(c) Annex III in relation to product liability.

They shall apply to all products unless otherwise specified.

Article 24

Annex IV contains specific provisions and arrangements concerning energy.

Article 25

Where compliance with the provisions of Articles 10 and 12 leads to:

(a) re-export towards a third country against which the exporting Contracting Party maintains, for the product concerned, quantitative export restrictions, export duties or measures or charges having equivalent effect; or

(b) a serious shortage, or threat thereof, of a product essential to the exporting Contracting Party;

and where the situations referred to above give rise, or are likely to give rise, to major difficulties for the exporting Contracting Party, that Contracting Party may take appropriate measures in accordance with the procedures set out in Article 113.

Article 26

Anti-dumping measures, countervailing duties and measures against illicit commercial practices attributable to third countries shall not be applied in relations between the Contracting Parties, unless otherwise specified in this Agreement.

CHAPTER 5
COAL AND STEEL PRODUCTS

Article 27

Provisions and arrangements concerning coal and steel products are set out in Protocols 14 and 25.

PART III
FREE MOVEMENT OF PERSONS, SERVICES AND CAPITAL

CHAPTER 1
WORKERS AND SELF-EMPLOYED PERSONS

Article 28

1. Freedom of movement for workers shall be secured among EC Member States and EFTA States.
2. Such freedom of movement shall entail the abolition of any discrimination based on nationality between workers of EC Member States and EFTA States as regards employment, remuneration and other conditions of work and employment.
3. It shall entail the right, subject to limitations justified on grounds of public policy, public security or public health:
   (a) to accept offers of employment actually made;
   (b) to move freely within the territory of EC Member States and EFTA States for this purpose;
   (c) to stay in the territory of an EC Member State or an EFTA State for the purpose of employment in accordance with the provisions governing the employment of nationals of that State laid down by law, regulation or administrative action;
   (d) to remain in the territory of an EC Member State or an EFTA State after having been employed there.
4. The provisions of this Article shall not apply to employment in the public service.
5. Annex V contains specific provisions on the free movement of workers.

Article 29

In order to provide freedom of movement for workers and self-employed persons, the Contracting Parties shall, in the field of social security, secure, as provided for in Annex VI, for workers and self-employed persons and their dependants, in particular:

(a) aggregation, for the purpose of acquiring and retaining the right to benefit and of calculating the amount of benefit, of all periods taken into account under the laws of the several countries;

(b) payment of benefits to persons resident in the territories of Contracting Parties.

Article 30

In order to make it easier for persons to take up and pursue activities as workers and self-employed persons, the Contracting Parties shall take the necessary measures, as contained in Annex VII, concerning the mutual recognition of diplomas, certificates and other evidence of formal qualifications, and the coordination of the provisions laid down by law, regulation or administrative action in the Contracting Parties concerning the taking up and pursuit of activities by workers and self-employed persons.

CHAPTER 2
RIGHT OF ESTABLISHMENT

Article 31

1. Within the framework of the provisions of this Agreement, there shall be no restrictions on the freedom of establishment of nationals of an EC Member State or an EFTA State in the territory of any other of these States. This shall also apply to the setting up of agencies, branches or subsidiaries by nationals of any EC Member State or EFTA State established in the territory of any of these States.
   Freedom of establishment shall include the right to take up and pursue activities as self-employed persons and to set up and manage undertakings, in particular companies or firms within the meaning of Article 34, second paragraph, under the conditions laid down for its own nationals by the law of the country where such establishment is effected, subject to the provisions of Chapter 4.
2. Annexes VIII to XI contain specific provisions on the right of establishment.

Article 32

The provisions of this Chapter shall not apply, so far as any given Contracting Party is concerned, to activities which in that Contracting Party are connected, even occasionally, with the exercise of official authority.

Article 33

The provisions of this Chapter and measures taken in pursuance thereof shall not prejudice the applicability of provisions laid down by law, regulation or administrative action providing for special treatment for foreign nationals on grounds of public policy, public security or public health.

Article 34

Companies or firms formed in accordance with the law of an EC Member State or an EFTA State and having their registered office, central administration or principal place of business within the territory of the Contracting Parties shall, for the purposes of this Chapter, be treated in the same way as natural persons who are nationals of EC Member States or EFTA States.
'Companics or firms' means companies or firms constituted under civil or commercial law, including cooperative societies, and other legal persons governed by public or private law, save for those which are non-profit-making.

Article 35

The provisions of Article 30 shall apply to the matters covered by this Chapter.

CHAPTER 3
SERVICES

Article 36

1. Within the framework of the provisions of this Agreement, there shall be no restrictions on freedom to provide services within the territory of the Contracting Parties in respect of nationals of EC Member States and EFTA States who are established in an EC Member State or an EFTA State other than that of the person for whom the services are intended.
2. Annexes IX to XI contain specific provisions on the freedom to provide services.

Article 37

Services shall be considered to be 'services' within the meaning of this Agreement where they are normally provided for remuneration, in so far as they are not governed by the provisions relating to freedom of movement for goods, capital and persons.
'Services' shall in particular include:
(a) activities of an industrial character;
(b) activities of a commercial character;
(c) activities of craftsmen;
(d) activities of the professions.
Without prejudice to the provisions of Chapter 2, the person providing a service may, in order to do so, temporarily pursue his activity in the State where the service is provided, under the same conditions as are imposed by that State on its own nationals.

Article 38

Freedom to provide services in the field of transport shall be governed by the provisions of Chapter 6.

Article 39

The provisions of Articles 30 and 32 to 34 shall apply to the matters covered by this Chapter.

CHAPTER 4
CAPITAL

Article 40

Within the framework of the provisions of this Agreement, there shall be no restrictions between the Contracting Parties on the movement of capital belonging to persons resident in EC Member States or EFTA States and no discrimination based on the nationality or on the place of residence of the parties or on the place where such capital is invested. Annex XII contains the provisions necessary to implement this Article.

Article 41
Current payments connected with the movement of goods, persons, services or capital between Contracting Parties within the framework of the provisions of this Agreement shall be free of all restrictions.

Article 42
1. Where domestic rules governing the capital market and the credit system are applied to the movements of capital liberalized in accordance with the provisions of this Agreement, this shall be done in a non-discriminatory manner.
2. Loans for the direct or indirect financing of an EC Member State or an EFTA State or its regional or local authorities shall not be issued or placed in other EC Member States or EFTA States unless the States concerned have reached agreement thereon.

Article 43
1. Where differences between the exchange rules of EC Member States and EFTA States could lead persons resident in one of these States to use the freer transfer facilities within the territory of the Contracting Parties which are provided for in Article 40 in order to evade the rules of one of these States concerning the movement of capital to or from third countries, the Contracting Party concerned may take appropriate measures to overcome these difficulties.
2. If movements of capital lead to disturbances in the functioning of the capital market in any EC Member State or EFTA State, the Contracting Party concerned may take protective measures in the field of capital movements.
3. If the competent authorities of a Contracting Party make an alteration in the rate of exchange which seriously distorts conditions of competition, the other Contracting Parties may take, for a strictly limited period, the necessary measures in order to counter the consequences of such alteration.
4. Where an EC Member State or an EFTA State is in difficulties, or is seriously threatened with difficulties, as regards its balance of payments either as a result of an overall disequilibrium in its balance of payments, or as a result of the type of currency at its disposal, and where such difficulties are liable in particular to jeopardize the functioning of this Agreement, the Contracting Party concerned may take protective measures.

Article 44
The Community, on the one hand, and the EFTA States, on the other, shall apply their internal procedures, as provided for in Protocol 18, to implement the provisions of Article 43.

Article 45
1. Decisions, opinions and recommendations related to the measures laid down in Article 43 shall be notified to the EEA Joint Committee.
2. All measures shall be the subject of prior consultations and exchange of information within the EEA Joint Committee.

3. In the situation referred to in Article 43 (2), the Contracting Party concerned may, however, on the grounds of secrecy and urgency take the measures, where this proves necessary, without prior consultations and exchange of information.
4. In the situation referred to in Article 43 (4), where a sudden crisis in the balance of payments occurs and the procedures set out in paragraph 2 cannot be followed, the Contracting Party concerned may, as a precaution, take the necessary protective measures. Such measures must cause the least possible disturbance in the functioning of this Agreement and must not be wider in scope than is strictly necessary to remedy the sudden difficulties which have arisen.
5. When measures are taken in accordance with paragraphs 3 and 4, notice thereof shall be given at the latest by the date of their entry into force, and the exchange of information and consultations as well as the notifications referred to in paragraph 1 shall take place as soon as possible thereafter.

CHAPTER 5
ECONOMIC AND MONETARY POLICY COOPERATION

Article 46

The Contracting Parties shall exchange views and information concerning the implementation of this Agreement and the impact of the integration on economic activities and on the conduct of economic and monetary policies. Furthermore, they may discuss macro-economic situations, policies and prospects. This exchange of views and information shall take place on a non-binding basis.

CHAPTER 6
TRANSPORT

Article 47

1. Articles 48 to 52 shall apply to transport by rail, road and inland waterway.
2. Annex XIII contains specific provisions on all modes of transport.

Article 48

1. The provisions of an EC Member State or an EFTA State, relative to transport by rail, road and inland waterway and not covered by Annex XIII, shall not be made less favourable in their direct or indirect effect on carriers of other States as compared with carriers who are nationals of that State.
2. Any Contracting Party deviating from the principle laid down in paragraph 1 shall notify the EEA Joint Committee thereof. The other Contracting Parties which do not accept the deviation may take corresponding countermeasures.

Article 49
Aid shall be compatible with this Agreement if it meets the needs of coordination of transport or if it represents reimbursement for the discharge of certain obligations inherent in the concept of a public service.

Article 50
1. In the case of transport within the territory of the Contracting Parties, there shall be no discrimination which takes the form of carriers charging different rates and imposing different conditions for the carriage of the same goods over the same transport links on grounds of the country of origin or of destination of the goods in question.
2. The competent authority according to Part VII shall, acting on its own initiative or on application by an EC Member State or an EFTA State, investigate any cases of discrimination falling within this Article and take the necessary decisions within the framework of its internal rules.

Article 51
1. The imposition, in respect of transport operations carried out within the territory of the Contracting Parties, of rates and conditions involving any element of support or protection in the interest of one or more particular undertakings or industries, shall be prohibited unless authorized by the competent authority referred to in Article 50(2).
2. The competent authority shall, acting on its own initiative or on application by an EC Member State or an EFTA State, examine the rates and conditions referred to in paragraph 1, taking account in particular of the requirements of an appropriate regional economic policy, the needs of underdeveloped areas and the problems of areas seriously affected by political circumstances, on the one hand, and of the effects of such rates and conditions on competition between the different modes of transport, on the other.
   The competent authority shall take the necessary decisions within the framework of its internal rules.
3. The prohibition provided for in paragraph 1 shall not apply to tariffs fixed to meet competition.

Article 52
Charges or dues in respect of the crossing of frontiers which are charged by a carrier in addition to transport rates shall not exceed a reasonable level after taking the costs actually incurred thereby into account. The Contracting Parties shall endeavour to reduce these costs progressively.

PART IV
COMPETITION AND OTHER COMMON RULES

CHAPTER 1
RULES APPLICABLE TO UNDERTAKINGS

Article 53

1. The following shall be prohibited as incompatible with the functioning of this Agreement: all agreements between undertakings, decisions by associations of undertakings and concerted practices which may affect trade between Contracting Parties and which have as their object or effect the prevention, restriction or distortion of competition within the territory covered by this Agreement, and in particular those which:
   (a) directly or indirectly fix purchase or selling prices or any other trading conditions;
   (b) limit or control production, markets, technical development, or investment;
   (c) share markets or sources of supply;
   (d) apply dissimilar conditions to equivalent transactions with other trading parties, thereby placing them at a competitive disadvantage;
   (e) make the conclusion of contracts subject to acceptance by the other parties of supplementary obligations which, by their nature or according to commercial usage, have no connection with the subject of such contracts.
2. Any agreements or decisions prohibited pursuant to this Article shall be automatically void.
3. The provisions of paragraph 1 may, however, be declared inapplicable in the case of:
   – any agreement or category of agreements between undertakings;
   – any decision or category of decisions by associations of undertakings;
   – any concerted practice or category of concerted practices;

   which contributes to improving the production or distribution of goods or to promoting technical or economic progress, while allowing consumers a fair share of the resulting benefit, and which does not:
   (a) impose on the undertakings concerned restrictions which are not indispensable to the attainment of these objectives;
   (b) afford such undertakings the possibility of eliminating competition in respect of a substantial part of the products in question.

Article 54

Any abuse by one or more undertakings of a dominant position within the territory covered by this Agreement or in a substantial part of it shall be prohibited as incompatible with the functioning of this Agreement in so far as it may affect trade between Contracting Parties.

Such abuse may, in particular, consist in:
(a) directly or indirectly imposing unfair purchase or selling prices or other unfair trading conditions;
(b) limiting production, markets or technical development to the prejudice of consumers;
(c) applying dissimilar conditions to equivalent transactions with other trading parties, thereby placing them at a competitive disadvantage;
(d) making the conclusion of contracts subject to acceptance by the other parties of supplementary obligations which, by their nature or according to commercial usage, have no connection with the subject of such contracts.

Article 55

1. Without prejudice to the provisions giving effect to Articles 53 and 54 as contained in Protocol 21 and Annex XIV of this Agreement, the EC Commission and the EFTA Surveillance Authority provided for in Article 108(1) shall ensure the application of the principles laid down in Articles 53 and 54.
   The competent surveillance authority, as provided for in Article 56, shall investigate cases of suspected infringement of these principles, on its own initiative, or on application by a State within the respective territory or by the other surveillance authority. The competent surveillance authority shall carry out these investigations in cooperation with the competent national authorities in the respective territory and in cooperation with the other surveillance authority, which shall give it its assistance in accordance with its internal rules.
   If it finds that there has been an infringement, it shall propose appropriate measures to bring it to an end.
2. If the infringement is not brought to an end, the competent surveillance authority shall record such infringement of the principles in a reasoned decision.
   The competent surveillance authority may publish its decision and authorize States within the respective territory to take the measures, the conditions and details of which it shall determine, needed to remedy the situation. It may also request the other surveillance authority to authorize States within the respective territory to take such measures.

Article 56

1. Individual cases falling under Article 53 shall be decided upon by the surveillance authorities in accordance with the following provisions:
   (a) individual cases where only trade between EFTA States is affected shall be decided upon by the EFTA Surveillance Authority;
   (b) without prejudice to subparagraph (c), the EFTA Surveillance Authority decides, as provided for in the provisions set out in Article 58, Protocol 21 and the rules adopted for its implementation, Protocol 23 and Annex XIV, on cases where the turnover of the undertakings concerned in the territory of the EFTA States equals 33 per cent or more of their turnover in the territory covered by this Agreement;

(c) the EC Commission decides on the other cases as well as on cases under (b) where trade between EC Member States is affected, taking into account the provisions set out in Article 58, Protocol 21, Protocol 23 and Annex XIV.
2. Individual cases falling under Article 54 shall be decided upon by the surveillance authority in the territory of which a dominant position is found to exist. The rules set out in paragraph 1(b) and (c) shall apply only if dominance exists within the territories of both surveillance authorities.
3. Individual cases falling under subparagraph (c) of paragraph 1, whose effects on trade between EC Member States or on competition within the Community are not appreciable, shall be decided upon by the EFTA Surveillance Authority.
4. The terms 'undertaking' and 'turnover' are, for the purposes of this Article, defined in Protocol 22.

Article 57

1. Concentrations the control of which is provided for in paragraph 2 and which create or strengthen a dominant position as a result of which effective competition would be significantly impeded within the territory covered by this Agreement or a substantial part of it, shall be declared incompatible with this Agreement.
2. The control of concentrations falling under paragraph 1 shall be carried out by:
   (a) the EC Commission in cases falling under Regulation (EEC) No 4064/89 in accordance with that Regulation and in accordance with Protocols 21 and 24 and Annex XIV to this Agreement. The EC Commission shall, subject to the review of the EC Court of Justice, have sole competence to take decisions on these cases;
   (b) the EFTA Surveillance Authority in cases not falling under subparagraph (a) where the relevant thresholds set out in Annex XIV are fulfilled in the territory of the EFTA States in accordance with Protocols 21 and 24 and Annex XIV. This is without prejudice to the competence of EC Member States.

Article 58

With a view to developing and maintaining a uniform surveillance throughout the European Economic Area in the field of competition and to promoting a homogeneous implementation, application and interpretation of the provisions of this Agreement to this end, the competent authorities shall cooperate in accordance with the provisions set out in Protocols 23 and 24.

Article 59

1. In the case of public undertakings and undertakings to which EC Member States or EFTA States grant special or exclusive rights, the Contracting Parties shall ensure that there is neither enacted nor maintained in force any measure contrary to the rules contained in this Agreement, in particular to those rules provided for in Articles 4 and 53 to 63.

2. Undertakings entrusted with the operation of services of general economic interest or having the character of a revenue-producing monopoly shall be subject to the rules contained in this Agreement, in particular to the rules on competition, in so far as the application of such rules does not obstruct the performance, in law or in fact, of the particular tasks assigned to them. The development of trade must not be affected to such an extent as would be contrary to the interests of the Contracting Parties.
3. The EC Commission as well as the EFTA Surveillance Authority shall ensure within their respective competence the application of the provisions of this Article and shall, where necessary, address appropriate measures to the States falling within their respective territory.

Article 60

Annex XIV contains specific provisions giving effect to the principles set out in Articles 53, 54, 57 and 59.

CHAPTER 2
STATE AID

Article 61

1. Save as otherwise provided in this Agreement, any aid granted by EC Member States, EFTA States or through State resources in any form whatsoever which distorts or threatens to distort competition by favouring certain undertakings or the production of certain goods shall, in so far as it affects trade between Contracting Parties, be incompatible with the functioning of this Agreement.
2. The following shall be compatible with the functioning of this Agreement:
   (a) aid having a social character, granted to individual consumers, provided that such aid is granted without discrimination related to the origin of the products concerned;
   (b) aid to make good the damage caused by natural disasters or exceptional occurrences;
   (c) aid granted to the economy of certain areas of the Federal Republic of Germany affected by the division of Germany, in so far as such aid is required in order to compensate for the economic disadvantages caused by that division.
3. The following may be considered to be compatible with the functioning of this Agreement:
   (a) aid to promote the economic development of areas where the standard of living is abnormally low or where there is serious underemployment;
   (b) aid to promote the execution of an important project of common European interest or to remedy a serious disturbance in the economy of an EC Member State or an EFTA State;

(c) aid to facilitate the development of certain economic activities or of certain economic areas, where such aid does not adversely affect trading conditions to an extent contrary to the common interest;
(d) such other categories of aid as may be specified by the EEA Joint Committee in accordance with Part VII.

Article 62

1. All existing systems of State aid in the territory of the Contracting Parties, as well as any plans to grant or alter State aid, shall be subject to constant review as to their compatibility with Article 61. This review shall be carried out:
   (a) as regards the EC Member States, by the EC Commission according to the rules laid down in Article 93 of the Treaty establishing the European Economic Community;
   (b) as regards the EFTA States, by the EFTA Surveillance Authority according to the rules set out in an agreement between the EFTA States establishing the EFTA Surveillance Authority which is entrusted with the powers and functions laid down in Protocol 26.
2. With a view to ensuring a uniform surveillance in the field of State aid throughout the territory covered by this Agreement, the EC Commission and the EFTA Surveillance Authority shall cooperate in accordance with the provisions set out in Protocol 27.

Article 63

Annex XV contains specific provisions on State aid.

Article 64

1. If one of the surveillance authorities considers that the implementation by the other surveillance authority of Articles 61 and 62 of this Agreement and Article 5 of Protocol 14 is not in conformity with the maintenance of equal conditions of competition within the territory covered by this Agreement, exchange of views shall be held within two weeks according to the procedure of Protocol 27, paragraph (f).

   If a commonly agreed solution has not been found by the end of this two-week period, the competent authority of the affected Contracting Party may immediately adopt appropriate interim measures in order to remedy the resulting distortion of competition.

   Consultations shall then be held in the EEA Joint Committee with a view to finding a commonly acceptable solution.

   If within three months the EEA Joint Committee has not been able to find such a solution, and if the practice in question causes, or threatens to cause, distortion of competition affecting trade between the Contracting Parties, the interim measures may be replaced by definitive measures, strictly necessary to offset the effect of such distortion. Priority shall be given to such measures that will least disturb the functioning of the EEA.

2. The provisions of this Article will also apply to State monopolies, which are established after the date of signature of the Agreement.

CHAPTER 3
OTHER COMMON RULES

Article 65

1. Annex XVI contains specific provisions and arrangements concerning procurement which, unless otherwise specified, shall apply to all products and to services as specified.
2. Protocol 28 and Annex XVII contain specific provisions and arrangements concerning intellectual, industrial and commercial property, which, unless otherwise specified, shall apply to all products and services.

PART V
HORIZONTAL PROVISIONS RELEVANT TO THE FOUR FREEDOMS

CHAPTER 1
SOCIAL POLICY

Article 66

The Contracting Parties agree upon the need to promote improved working conditions and an improved standard of living for workers.

Article 67

1. The Contracting Parties shall pay particular attention to encouraging improvements, especially in the working environment, as regards the health and safety of workers. In order to help achieve this objective, minimum requirements shall be applied for gradual implementation, having regard to the conditions and technical rules obtaining in each of the Contracting Parties. Such minimum requirements shall not prevent any Contracting Party from maintaining or introducing more stringent measures for the protection of working conditions compatible with this Agreement.
2. Annex XVIII specifies the provisions to be implemented as the minimum requirements referred to in paragraph 1.

Article 68

In the field of labour law, the Contracting Parties shall introduce the measures necessary to ensure the good functioning of this Agreement. These measures are specified in Annex XVIII.

Article 69

1. Each Contracting Party shall ensure and maintain the application of the principle that men and women should receive equal pay for equal work.
   For the purposes of this Article, 'pay' means the ordinary basic or minimum wage or salary and any other consideration, whether in cash or in kind, which the worker receives, directly or indirectly, in respect of his employment from his employer.

Equal pay without discrimination based on sex means:

   (a) that pay for the same work at piece rates shall be calculated on the basis of the same unit of measurement;
   (b) that pay for work at time rates shall be the same for the same job.

2. Annex XVIII contains specific provisions for the implementation of paragraph 1.

Article 70

The Contracting Parties shall promote the principle of equal treatment for men and women by implementing the provisions specified in Annex XVIII.

Article 71

The Contracting Parties shall endeavour to promote the dialogue between management and labour at European level.

CHAPTER 2
CONSUMER PROTECTION

Article 72

Annex XIX contains provisions on consumer protection.

CHAPTER 3
ENVIRONMENT

Article 73

1. Action by the Contracting Parties relating to the environment shall have the following objectives:
   (a) to preserve, protect and improve the quality of the environment;
   (b) to contribute towards protecting human health;
   (c) to ensure a prudent and rational utilization of natural resources.
2. Action by the Contracting Parties relating to the environment shall be based on the principles that preventive action should be taken, that environmental damage

should as a priority be rectified at source, and that the polluter should pay. Environmental protection requirements shall be a component of the Contracting Parties' other policies.

Article 74
Annex XX contains the specific provisions on protective measures which shall apply pursuant to Article 73.

Article 75
The protective measures referred to in Article 74 shall not prevent any Contracting Party from maintaining or introducing more stringent protective measures compatible with this Agreement.

CHAPTER 4
STATISTICS

Article 76

1. The Contracting Parties shall ensure the production and dissemination of coherent and comparable statistical information for describing and monitoring all relevant economic, social and environmental aspects of the EEA.
2. To this end the Contracting Parties shall develop and use harmonized methods, definitions and classifications as well as common programmes and procedures organizing statistical work at appropriate administrative levels and duly observing the need for statistical confidentiality.
3. Annex XXI contains specific provisions on statistics.
4. Protocol 30 contains specific provisions on the organization of cooperation in the field of statistics.

CHAPTER 5
COMPANY LAW

Article 77
Annex XXII contains specific provisions on company law.
PART VI

Part VI
COOPERATION OUTSIDE THE FOUR FREEDOMS

Article 78

The Contracting Parties shall strengthen and broaden cooperation in the framework of the Community's activities in the fields of:

- research and technological development,
- information services,
- the environment,
- education, training and youth,
- social policy,
- consumer protection,
- small and medium-sized enterprises,
- tourism,
- the audiovisual sector, and
- civil protection,

in so far as these matters are not regulated under the provisions of other Parts of this Agreement.

Article 79

1. The Contracting Parties shall strengthen the dialogue between them by all appropriate means, in particular through the procedures provided for in Part VII, with a view to identifying areas and activities where closer cooperation could contribute to the attainment of their common objectives in the fields referred to in Article 78.
2. They shall, in particular, exchange information and, at the request of a Contracting Party, hold consultations within the EEA Joint Committee in respect of plans or proposals for the establishment or amendment of framework programmes, specific programmes, actions and projects in the fields referred to in Article 78.
3. Part VII shall apply mutatis mutandis with regard to this Part whenever the latter or Protocol 31 specifically provides therefore.

Article 80

The cooperation provided for in Article 78 shall normally take one of the following forms:

- participation by EFTA States in EC framework programmes, specific programmes, projects or other actions;
- establishment of joint activities in specific areas, which may include concertation or coordination of activities, fusion of existing activities and establishment of ad hoc joint activities;
- the formal and informal exchange or provision of information;
- common efforts to encourage certain activities throughout the territory of the Contracting Parties;
- parallel legislation, where appropriate, of identical or similar content;

– coordination, where this is of mutual interest, of efforts and activities via, or in the context of, international organizations, and of cooperation with third countries.

Article 81

Where cooperation takes the form of participation by EFTA States in an EC framework programme, specific programme, project or other action, the following principles shall apply:

(a) The EFTA States shall have access to all parts of a programme.

(b) The status of the EFTA States in the committees which assist the EC Commission in the management or development of a Community activity to which EFTA States may be contributing financially by virtue of their participation shall take full account of that contribution.

(c) Decisions by the Community, other than those relating to the general budget of the Community, which affect directly or indirectly a framework programme, specific programme, project or other action, in which EFTA States participate by a decision under this Agreement, shall be subject to the provisions of Article 79(3). The terms and conditions of the continued participation in the activity in question may be reviewed by the EEA Joint Committee in accordance with Article 86.

(d) At the project level, institutions, undertakings, organizations and nationals of EFTA States shall have the same rights and obligations in the Community programme or other action in question as those applicable to partner institutions, undertakings, organizations and nationals of EC Member States. The same shall apply mutatis mutandis to participants in exchanges between EC Member States and EFTA States, under the activity in question.

(e) EFTA States, their institutions, undertakings, organizations and nationals shall have the same rights and obligations with regard to dissemination, evaluation and exploitation of results as those applicable to EC Member States, their institutions, undertakings, organizations and nationals.

(f) The Contracting Parties undertake, in accordance with their respective rules and regulations, to facilitate the movement of participants in the programme and other action to the extent necessary.

Article 82

1. When the cooperation envisaged under the present Part involves a financial participation of the EFTA States, this participation shall take one of the following forms:
   (a) The contribution of the EFTA States, arising from their participation in Community activities, shall be calculated proportionally:
      – to the commitment appropriations; and
      – to the payment appropriations;

   entered each year for the Community in the general budget of the Community for each budgetary line corresponding to the activities in question.

   The 'proportionality factor' determining the participation of the EFTA States shall be the sum of the ratios between, on the one hand, the gross domestic product at market prices of each of the EFTA States and, on the other hand, the sum of the gross domestic products at market prices of the EC Member States and of that EFTA State. This factor shall be calculated, for each budgetary year, on the basis of the most recent statistical data.

The amount of the contribution of the EFTA States shall be additional, both in commitment appropriations and in payment appropriations, to the amounts entered for the Community in the general budget on each line corresponding to the activities concerned.

The contributions to be paid each year by the EFTA States shall be determined on the basis of the payment appropriations.

Commitments entered into by the Community prior to the entry into force, on the basis of this Agreement, of the participation of the EFTA States in the activities in question – as well as the payments which result from this – shall give rise to no contribution on the part of the EFTA States.

(b) The financial contribution of EFTA States deriving from their participation in certain projects or other activities shall be based on the principle that each Contracting Party shall cover its own costs, with an appropriate contribution which shall be fixed by the EEA Joint Committee to the Community's overhead costs.

(c) The EEA Joint Committee shall take the necessary decisions concerning the contribution of the Contracting Parties to the costs of the activity in question.

2. The detailed provisions for the implementation of this Article are set out in Protocol 32.

Article 83

Where cooperation takes the form of an exchange of information between public authorities, the EFTA States shall have the same rights to receive, and obligations to provide, information as EC Member States, subject to the requirements of confidentiality, which shall be fixed by the EEA Joint Committee.

Article 84

Provisions governing cooperation in specific fields are set out in Protocol 31.

Article 85

Unless otherwise provided for in Protocol 31, cooperation already established between the Community and individual EFTA States in the fields referred to in Article 78 on the date of entry into force of this Agreement shall thereafter be governed by the relevant provisions of this Part and of Protocol 31.

Article 86

The EEA Joint Committee shall, in accordance with Part VII, take all decisions necessary for the implementation of Articles 78 to 85 and measures derived therefrom, which may include, inter alia, supplementing and amending the provisions of Protocol 31, as well as adopting any transitional arrangements required by way of implementation of Article 85.

Article 87
The Contracting Parties shall take the necessary steps to develop, strengthen or broaden cooperation in the framework of the Community's activities in fields not listed in Article 78, where such cooperation is considered likely to contribute to the attainment of the objectives of this Agreement, or is otherwise deemed by the Contracting Parties to be of mutual interest. Such steps may include the amendment of Article 78 by the addition of new fields to those listed therein.

Article 88
Without prejudice to provisions of other Parts of this Agreement, the provisions of this Part shall not preclude the possibility for any Contracting Party to prepare, adopt and implement measures independently.

PART VII
INSTITUTIONAL PROVISIONS

CHAPTER 1
THE STRUCTURE OF THE ASSOCIATION

Section 1
The EEA Council

Article 89
1. An EEA Council is hereby established. It shall, in particular, be responsible for giving the political impetus in the implementation of this Agreement and laying down the general guidelines for the EEA Joint Committee.
   To this end, the EEA Council shall assess the overall functioning and the development of the Agreement. It shall take the political decisions leading to amendments of the Agreement.
2. The Contracting Parties, as to the Community and the EC Member States in their respective fields of competence, may, after having discussed it in the EEA Joint Committee, or directly in exceptionally urgent cases, raise in the EEA Council any issue giving rise to a difficulty.
3. The EEA Council shall by decision adopt its rules of procedure.

Article 90

1. The EEA Council shall consist of the members of the Council of the European Communities and members of the EC Commission, and of one member of the Government of each of the EFTA States.
   Members of the EEA Council may be represented in accordance with the conditions to be laid down in its rules of procedure.
2. Decisions by the EEA Council shall be taken by agreement between the Community, on the one hand, and the EFTA States, on the other.

Article 91

1. The office of President of the EEA Council shall be held alternately, for a period of six months, by a member of the Council of the European Communities and a member of the Government of an EFTA State.
2. The EEA Council shall be convened twice a year by its President. The EEA Council shall also meet whenever circumstances so require, in accordance with its rules of procedure.

Section 2
The EEA Joint Committee

Article 92

1. An EEA Joint Committee is hereby established. It shall ensure the effective implementation and operation of this Agreement. To this end, it shall carry out exchanges of views and information and take decisions in the cases provided for in this Agreement.
2. The Contracting Parties, as to the Community and the EC Member States in their respective fields of competence, shall hold consultations in the EEA Joint Committee on any point of relevance to the Agreement giving rise to a difficulty and raised by one of them.
3. The EEA Joint Committee shall by decision adopt its rules of procedure.

Article 93

1. The EEA Joint Committee shall consist of representatives of the Contracting Parties.
2. The EEA Joint Committee shall take decisions by agreement between the Community, on the one hand, and the EFTA States speaking with one voice, on the other.

Article 94

1. The office of President of the EEA Joint Committee shall be held alternately, for a period of six months, by the representative of the Community, i.e. the EC Commission, and the representative of one of the EFTA States.
2. In order to fulfil its functions, the EEA Joint Committee shall meet, in principle, at least once a month. It shall also meet on the initiative of its President or at the re-

quest of one of the Contracting Parties in accordance with its rules of procedure.

3. The EEA Joint Committee may decide to establish any subcommittee or working group to assist it in carrying out its tasks. The EEA Joint Committee shall in its rules of procedure lay down the composition and mode of operation of such subcommittees and working groups. Their tasks shall be determined by the EEA Joint Committee in each individual case.
4. The EEA Joint Committee shall issue an annual report on the functioning and the development of this Agreement.

Section 3
Parliamentary cooperation

Article 95

1. An EEA Joint Parliamentary Committee is hereby established. It shall be composed of equal numbers of, on the one hand, members of the European Parliament and, on the other, members of Parliaments of the EFTA States. The total number of members of the Committee is laid down in the Statute in Protocol 36.
2. The EEA Joint Parliamentary Committee shall alternately hold sessions in the Community and in an EFTA State in accordance with the provisions laid down in Protocol 36.
3. The EEA Joint Parliamentary Committee shall contribute, through dialogue and debate, to a better understanding between the Community and the EFTA States in the fields covered by this Agreement.
4. The EEA Joint Parliamentary Committee may express its views in the form of reports or resolutions, as appropriate. It shall, in particular, examine the annual report of the EEA Joint Committee, issued in accordance with Article 94 (4), on the functioning and the development of this Agreement.
5. The President of the EEA Council may appear before the EEA Joint Parliamentary Committee in order to be heard by it.
6. The EEA Joint Parliamentary Committee shall adopt its rules of procedure.

Section 4
Cooperation between economic and social partners

Article 96

1. Members of the Economic and Social Committee and other bodies representing the social partners in the Community and the corresponding bodies in the EFTA States shall work to strengthen contacts between them and to cooperate in an organized and regular manner in order to enhance the awareness of the economic and social aspects of the growing interdependence of the economies of the Contracting Parties and of their interests within the context of the EEA.
2. To this end, an EEA Consultative Committee is hereby established. It shall be composed of equal numbers of, on the one hand, members of the Economic and Social Committee of the Community and, on the other, members of the EFTA

Consultative Committee. The EEA Consultative Committee may express its views in the form of reports or resolutions, as appropriate.

3. The EEA Consultative Committee shall adopt its rules of procedure.

CHAPTER 2
THE DECISION-MAKING PROCEDURE

Article 97

This Agreement does not prejudge the right for each Contracting Party to amend, without prejudice to the principle of non-discrimination and after having informed the other Contracting Parties, its internal legislation in the areas covered by this Agreement:

- if the EEA Joint Committee concludes that the legislation as amended does not affect the good functioning of this Agreement; or
- if the procedures referred to in Article 98 have been completed.

Article 98

The Annexes to this Agreement and Protocols 1 to 7, 9 to 11, 19 to 27, 30 to 32, 37, 39, 41 and 47, as appropriate, may be amended by a decision of the EEA Joint Committee in accordance with Articles 93 (2), 99, 100, 102 and 103.

Article 99

1. As soon as new legislation is being drawn up by the EC Commission in a field which is governed by this Agreement, the EC Commission shall informally seek advice from experts of the EFTA States in the same way as it seeks advice from experts of the EC Member States for the elaboration of its proposals.
2. When transmitting its proposal to the Council of the European Communities, the EC Commission shall transmit copies thereof to the EFTA States.
   At the request of one of the Contracting Parties, a preliminary exchange of views takes place in the EEA Joint Committee.
3. During the phase preceding the decision of the Council of the European Communities, in a continuous information and consultation process, the Contracting Parties consult each other again in the EEA Joint Committee at the significant moments at the request of one of them.
4. The Contracting Parties shall cooperate in good faith during the information and consultation phase with a view to facilitating, at the end of the process, the decision-taking in the EEA Joint Committee.

Article 100

The EC Commission shall ensure experts of the EFTA States as wide a participation as possible according to the areas concerned, in the preparatory stage of draft measures to be submitted subsequently to the committees which assist the EC Commission in the exercise of its executive powers. In this regard, when drawing up draft measures the EC

Commission shall refer to experts of the EFTA States on the same basis as it refers to experts of the EC Member States.
In the cases where the Council of the European Communities is seized in accordance with the procedure applicable to the type of committee involved, the EC Commission shall transmit to the Council of the European Communities the views of the experts of the EFTA States.

Article 101

1. In respect of committees which are covered neither by Article 81 nor by Article 100 experts from EFTA States shall be associated with the work when this is called for by the good functioning of this Agreement.
   These committees are listed in Protocol 37. The modalities of such an association are set out in the relevant sectoral Protocols and Annexes dealing with the matter concerned.
2. If it appears to the Contracting Parties that such an association should be extended to other committees which present similar characteristics, the EEA Joint Committee may amend Protocol 37.

Article 102

1. In order to guarantee the legal security and the homogeneity of the EEA, the EEA Joint Committee shall take a decision concerning an amendment of an Annex to this Agreement as closely as possible to the adoption by the Community of the corresponding new Community legislation with a view to permitting a simultaneous application of the latter as well as of the amendments of the Annexes to the Agreement. To this end, the Community shall, whenever adopting a legislative act on an issue which is governed by this Agreement, as soon as possible inform the other Contracting Parties in the EEA Joint Committee.
2. The part of an Annex to this Agreement which would be directly affected by the new legislation is assessed in the EEA Joint Committee.
3. The Contracting Parties shall make all efforts to arrive at an agreement on matters relevant to this Agreement.
   The EEA Joint Committee shall, in particular, make every effort to find a mutually acceptable solution where a serious problem arises in any area which, in the EFTA States, falls within the competence of the legislator.
4. If, notwithstanding the application of the preceding paragraph, an agreement on an amendment of an Annex to this Agreement cannot be reached, the EEA Joint Committee shall examine all further possibilities to maintain the good functioning of this Agreement and take any decision necessary to this effect, including the possibility to take notice of the equivalence of legislation. Such a decision shall be taken at the latest at the expiry of a period of six months from the date of referral to the EEA Joint Committee or, if that date is later, on the date of entry into force of the corresponding Community legislation.
5. If, at the end of the time limit set out in paragraph 4, the EEA Joint Committee has not taken a decision on an amendment of an Annex to this Agreement, the

affected part thereof, as determined in accordance with paragraph 2, is regarded as provisionally suspended, subject to a decision to the contrary by the EEA Joint Committee. Such a suspension shall take effect six months after the end of the period referred to in paragraph 4, but in no event earlier than the date on which the corresponding EC act is implemented in the Community. The EEA Joint Committee shall pursue its efforts to agree on a mutually acceptable solution in order for the suspension to be terminated as soon as possible.

6. The practical consequences of the suspension referred to in paragraph 5 shall be discussed in the EEA Joint Committee. The rights and obligations which individuals and economic operators have already acquired under this Agreement shall remain. The Contracting Parties shall, as appropriate, decide on the adjustments necessary due to the suspension.

Article 103

1. If a decision of the EEA Joint Committee can be binding on a Contracting Party only after the fulfilment of constitutional requirements, the decision shall, if a date is contained therein, enter into force on that date, provided that the Contracting Party concerned has notified the other Contracting Parties by that date that the constitutional requirements have been fulfilled.
   In the absence of such a notification by that date, the decision shall enter into force on the first day of the second month following the last notification.
2. If upon the expiry of a period of six months after the decision of the EEA Joint Committee such a notification has not taken place, the decision of the EEA Joint Committee shall be applied provisionally pending the fulfilment of the constitutional requirements unless a Contracting Party notifies that such a provisional application cannot take place. In the latter case, or if a Contracting Party notifies the non-ratification of a decision of the EEA Joint Committee, the suspension provided for in Article 102 (5) shall take effect one month after such a notification but in no event earlier than the date on which the corresponding EC act is implemented in the Community.

Article 104

Decisions taken by the EEA Joint Committee in the cases provided for in this Agreement shall, unless otherwise provided for therein, upon their entry into force be binding on the Contracting Parties which shall take the necessary steps to ensure their implementation and application.

CHAPTER 3
HOMOGENEITY, SURVEILLANCE PROCEDURE AND SETTLEMENT OF DISPUTES

Section 1
Homogeneity

Article 105

1. In order to achieve the objective of the Contracting Parties to arrive at as uniform an interpretation as possible of the provisions of the Agreement and those provisions of Community legislation which are substantially reproduced in the Agreement, the EEA Joint Committee shall act in accordance with this Article.
2. The EEA Joint Committee shall keep under constant review the development of the case law of the Court of Justice of the European Communities and the EFTA Court. To this end judgments of these Courts shall be transmitted to the EEA Joint Committee which shall act so as to preserve the homogeneous interpretation of the Agreement.
3. If the EEA Joint Committee within two months after a difference in the case law of the two Courts has been brought before it, has not succeeded to preserve the homogeneous interpretation of the Agreement, the procedures laid down in Article 111 may be applied.

Article 106

In order to ensure as uniform an interpretation as possible of this Agreement, in full deference to the independence of courts, a system of exchange of information concerning judgments by the EFTA Court, the Court of Justice of the European Communities and the Court of First Instance of the European Communities and the Courts of last instance of the EFTA States shall be set up by the EEA Joint Committee. This system shall comprise:

(a) transmission to the Registrar of the Court of Justice of the European Communities of judgments delivered by such courts on the interpretation and application of, on the one hand, this Agreement or, on the other hand, the Treaty establishing the European Economic Community and the Treaty establishing the European Coal and Steel Community, as amended or supplemented, as well as the acts adopted in pursuance thereof in so far as they concern provisions which are identical in substance to those of this Agreement;

(b) classification of these judgments by the Registrar of the Court of Justice of the European Communities including, as far as necessary, the drawing up and publication of translations and abstracts;

(c) communications by the Registrar of the Court of Justice of the European Communities of the relevant documents to the competent national authorities, to be designated by each Contracting Party.

Article 107

Provisions on the possibility for an EFTA State to allow a court or tribunal to ask the Court of Justice of the European Communities to decide on the interpretation of an EEA rule are laid down in Protocol 34.

Section 2
Surveillance procedure

Article 108

1. The EFTA States shall establish an independent surveillance authority (EFTA Surveillance Authority) as well as procedures similar to those existing in the Community including procedures for ensuring the fulfilment of obligations under this Agreement and for control of the legality of acts of the EFTA Surveillance Authority regarding competition.
2. The EFTA States shall establish a court of justice (EFTA Court).

The EFTA Court shall, in accordance with a separate agreement between the EFTA States, with regard to the application of this Agreement be competent, in particular, for:

(a) actions concerning the surveillance procedure regarding the EFTA States;
(b) appeals concerning decisions in the field of competition taken by the EFTA Surveillance Authority;
(c) the settlement of disputes between two or more EFTA States.

Article 109

1. The fulfilment of the obligations under this Agreement shall be monitored by, on the one hand, the EFTA Surveillance Authority and, on the other, the EC Commission acting in conformity with the Treaty establishing the European Economic Community[12].
2. In order to ensure a uniform surveillance throughout the EEA, the EFTA Surveillance Authority and the EC Commission shall cooperate, exchange information and consult each other on surveillance policy issues and individual cases.
3. The EC Commission and the EFTA Surveillance Authority shall receive any complaints concerning the application of this Agreement. They shall inform each other of complaints received.
4. Each of these bodies shall examine all complaints falling within its competence and shall pass to the other body any complaints which fall within the competence of that body.
5. In case of disagreement between these two bodies with regard to the action to be taken in relation to a complaint or with regard to the result of the examination,

12 Words "and the Treaty establishing the European Coal and Steel Community" deleted by the 2004 EEA Enlargement Agreement (OJ No L 130, 29.4.2004, p. 3 and EEA Supplement No 23, 29.4.2004, p. 1), e.i.f. 1.5.2004.

either of the bodies may refer the matter to the EEA Joint Committee which shall deal with it in accordance with Article 111.

Article 110

Decisions under this Agreement by the EFTA Surveillance Authority and the EC Commission which impose a pecuniary obligation on persons other than States, shall be enforceable. The same shall apply to such judgments under this Agreement by the Court of Justice of the European Communities, the Court of First Instance of the European Communities and the EFTA Court.

Enforcement shall be governed by the rules of civil procedure in force in the State in the territory of which it is carried out. The order for its enforcement shall be appended to the decision, without other formality than verification of the authenticity of the decision, by the authority which each Contracting Party shall designate for this purpose and shall make known to the other Contracting Parties, the EFTA Surveillance Authority, the EC Commission, the Court of Justice of the European Communities, the Court of First Instance of the European Communities and the EFTA Court.

When these formalities have been completed on application by the party concerned, the latter may proceed to enforcement, in accordance with the law of the State in the territory of which enforcement is to be carried out, by bringing the matter directly before the competent authority.

Enforcement may be suspended only by a decision of the Court of Justice of the European Communities, as far as decisions by the EC Commission, the Court of First Instance of the European Communities or the Court of Justice of the European Communities are concerned, or by a decision of the EFTA Court as far as decisions by the EFTA Surveillance Authority or the EFTA Court are concerned. However, the courts of the States concerned shall have jurisdiction over complaints that enforcement is being carried out in an irregular manner.

Section 3
Settlement of disputes

Article 111

1. The Community or an EFTA State may bring a matter under dispute which concerns the interpretation or application of this Agreement before the EEA Joint Committee in accordance with the following provisions.
2. The EEA Joint Committee may settle the dispute. It shall be provided with all information which might be of use in making possible an indepth examination of the situation, with a view to finding an acceptable solution. To this end, the EEA Joint Committee shall examine all possibilities to maintain the good functioning of the Agreement.
3. If a dispute concerns the interpretation of provisions of this Agreement, which are identical in substance to corresponding rules of the Treaty establishing the European Economic Community and the Treaty establishing the European Coal and Steel Community and to acts adopted in application of these two Treaties and

if the dispute has not been settled within three months after it has been brought before the EEA Joint Committee, the Contracting Parties to the dispute may agree to request the Court of Justice of the European Communities to give a ruling on the interpretation of the relevant rules.

If the EEA Joint Committee in such a dispute has not reached an agreement on a solution within six months from the date on which this procedure was initiated or if, by then, the Contracting Parties to the dispute have not decided to ask for a ruling by the Court of Justice of the European Communities, a Contracting Party may, in order to remedy possible imbalances,

- either take a safeguard measure in accordance with Article 112(2) and following the procedure of Article 113;
- or apply Article 102 mutatis mutandis.

4. If a dispute concerns the scope or duration of safeguard measures taken in accordance with Article 111(3) or Article 112, or the proportionality of rebalancing measures taken in accordance with Article 114, and if the EEA Joint Committee after three months from the date when the matter has been brought before it has not succeeded to resolve the dispute, any Contracting Party may refer the dispute to arbitration under the procedures laid down in Protocol 33. No question of interpretation of the provisions of this Agreement referred to in paragraph 3 may be dealt with in such procedures. The arbitration award shall be binding on the parties to the dispute.

CHAPTER 4
SAFEGUARD MEASURES

Article 112

1. If serious economic, societal or environmental difficulties of a sectorial or regional nature liable to persist are arising, a Contracting Party may unilaterally take appropriate measures under the conditions and procedures laid down in Article 113.
2. Such safeguard measures shall be restricted with regard to their scope and duration to what is strictly necessary in order to remedy the situation. Priority shall be given to such measures as will least disturb the functioning of this Agreement.
3. The safeguard measures shall apply with regard to all Contracting Parties.

Article 113

1. A Contracting Party which is considering taking safeguard measures under Article 112 shall, without delay, notify the other Contracting Parties through the EEA Joint Committee and shall provide all relevant information.
2. The Contracting Parties shall immediately enter into consultations in the EEA Joint Committee with a view to finding a commonly acceptable solution.
3. The Contracting Party concerned may not take safeguard measures until one month has elapsed after the date of notification under paragraph 1, unless the consultation

procedure under paragraph 2 has been concluded before the expiration of the stated time limit. When exceptional circumstances requiring immediate action exclude prior examination, the Contracting Party concerned may apply forthwith the protective measures strictly necessary to remedy the situation.

For the Community, the safeguard measures shall be taken by the EC Commission.

4. The Contracting Party concerned shall, without delay, notify the measures taken to the EEA Joint Committee and shall provide all relevant information.
5. The safeguard measures taken shall be the subject of consultations in the EEA Joint Committee every three months from the date of their adoption with a view to their abolition before the date of expiry envisaged, or to the limitation of their scope of application.

   Each Contracting Party may at any time request the EEA Joint Committee to review such measures.

Article 114

1. If a safeguard measure taken by a Contracting Party creates an imbalance between the rights and obligations under this Agreement, any other Contracting Party may towards that Contracting Party take such proportionate rebalancing measures as are strictly necessary to remedy the imbalance. Priority shall be given to such measures as will least disturb the functioning of the EEA.
2. The procedure under Article 113 shall apply.

PART VIII
FINANCIAL MECHANISM

Article 115

With a view to promoting a continuous and balanced strengthening of trade and economic relations between the Contracting Parties, as provided for in Article 1, the Contracting Parties agree on the need to reduce the economic and social disparities between their regions. They note in this regard the relevant provisions set out elsewhere in this Agreement and its related Protocols, including certain of the arrangements regarding agriculture and fisheries.

Article 116

A Financial Mechanism shall be established by the EFTA States to contribute, in the context of the EEA and in addition to the efforts already deployed by the Community in this regard, to the objectives laid down in Article 115.

Article 117

[13]Provisions governing the Financial Mechanisms are set out in Protocol 38, Protocol 38a and Addendum to Protocol 38a.

PART IX
GENERAL AND FINAL PROVISIONS

Article 118

1. Where a Contracting Party considers that it would be useful in the interests of all the Contracting Parties to develop the relations established by this Agreement by extending them to fields not covered thereby, it shall submit a reasoned request to the other Contracting Parties within the EEA Council. The latter may instruct the EEA Joint Committee to examine all the aspects of this request and to issue a report.
   The EEA Council may, where appropriate, take the political decisions with a view to opening negotiations between the Contracting Parties.
2. The agreements resulting from the negotiations referred to in paragraph 1 will be subject to ratification or approval by the Contracting Parties in accordance with their own procedures.

Article 119

The Annexes and the acts referred to therein as adapted for the purposes of this Agreement as well as the Protocols shall form an integral part of this Agreement.

Article 120

[14]Unless otherwise provided in this Agreement and in particular in Protocols 41 and 43, the application of the provisions of this Agreement shall prevail over provisions in existing bilateral or multilateral agreements binding the European Economic Community, on the one hand, and one or more EFTA States, on the other, to the extent that the same subject matter is governed by this Agreement.

Article 121

The provisions of this Agreement shall not preclude cooperation:

(a) within the framework of the Nordic cooperation to the extent that such cooperation does not impair the good functioning of this Agreement;

(b) within the framework of the regional union between Switzerland and Liechtenstein to the extent that the objectives of this union are not attained by the ap-

---

13 Article replaced by the 2004 EEA Enlargement Agreement (OJ No L 130, 29.4.2004, p. 3 and EEA Supplement No 23, 29.4.2004, p. 1), e.i.f. 1.5.2004, and subsequently replaced by the 2007 EEA Enlargement Agreement (OJ No L [to be published]), provisionally applicable as of 1.8.2007, e.i.f. pending.

14 The words "Protocols 41, 43 and 44" replaced by the words "Protocols 41 and 43".

plication of this Agreement and the good functioning of this Agreement is not impaired;

(c) [ ][15]

Article 122

The representatives, delegates and experts of the Contracting Parties, as well as officials and other servants acting under this Agreement shall be required, even after their duties have ceased, not to disclose information of the kind covered by the obligation of professional secrecy, in particular information about undertakings, their business relations or their cost components.

Article 123

Nothing in this Agreement shall prevent a Contracting Party from taking any measures:

(a) which it considers necessary to prevent the disclosure of information contrary to its essential security interests;

(b) which relate to the production of, or trade in, arms, munitions and war materials or other products indispensable for defence purposes or to research, development or production indispensable for defence purposes, provided that such measures do not impair the conditions of competition in respect of products not intended for specifically military purposes;

(c) which it considers essential to its own security in the event of serious internal disturbances affecting the maintenance of law and order, in time of war or serious international tension constituting threat of war or in order to carry out obligations it has accepted for the purpose of maintaining peace and international security.

Article 124

The Contracting Parties shall accord nationals of EC Member States and EFTA States the same treatment as their own nationals as regards participation in the capital of companies or firms within the meaning of Article 34, without prejudice to the application of the other provisions of this Agreement.

Article 125

This Agreement shall in no way prejudice the rules of the Contracting Parties governing the system of property ownership.

15 Paragraph (c) deleted by the 2004 EEA Enlargement Agreement (OJ No L 130, 29.4.2004, p. 3 and EEA Supplement No 23, 29.4.2004, p. 1), e.i.f. 1.5.2004.

Article 126

1.[16] The Agreement shall apply to the territories to which the Treaty establishing the European Economic Community[17] is applied and under the conditions laid down in that Treaty[18], and to the territories of Iceland[19], the Principality of Liechtenstein and the Kingdom of Norway[20].

2. Notwithstanding paragraph 1, this Agreement shall not apply to the Åland Islands. The Government of Finland may, however, give notice, by a declaration deposited when ratifying this Agreement with the Depositary, which shall transmit a certified copy thereof to the Contracting Parties, that the Agreement shall apply to those Islands under the same conditions as it applies to other parts of Finland subject to the following provisions:
   (a) The provisions of this Agreement shall not preclude the application of the provisions in force at any given time on the Åland Islands on:
      (i) restrictions on the right for natural persons who do not enjoy regional citizenship in Åland, and for legal persons, to acquire and hold real property on the Åland Islands without permission by the competent authorities of the Islands;
      (ii) restrictions on the right of establishment and the right to provide services by natural persons who do not enjoy regional citizenship in Åland, or by any legal person, without permission by the competent authorities of the Åland Islands.
   (b) The rights enjoyed by Ålanders in Finland shall not be affected by this Agreement.
   (c) The authorities of the Åland Islands shall apply the same treatment to all natural and legal persons of the Contracting Parties.

Article 127

Each Contracting Party may withdraw from this Agreement provided it gives at least twelve months' notice in writing to the other Contracting Parties.

Immediately after the notification of the intended withdrawal, the other Contracting Parties shall convene a diplomatic conference in order to envisage the necessary modifications to bring to the Agreement.

---

16 The words "the Kingdom of Norway, the Kingdom of Sweden and the Swiss Confederation" shall be replaced by the words "the Kingdom of Norway and the Kingdom of Sweden".

17 Words " and the Treaty establishing the European Coal and Steel Community" deleted by the 2004 EEA Enlargement Agreement (OJ No L 130, 29.4.2004, p. 3 and EEA Supplement No 23, 29.4.2004, p. 1), e.i.f. 1.5.2004.

18 Words "those Treaties" replaced by the words "that Treaty" by the 2004 EEA Enlargement Agreement (OJ No L 130, 29.4.2004, p. 3 and EEA Supplement No 23, 29.4.2004, p. 1), e.i.f. 1.5.2004.

19 Words "Republic of" deleted by the 2007 EEA Enlargement Agreement (OJ No L [to be published]), provisionally applicable as of 1.8.2007, e.i.f. pending.

20 Words "the Republic of Austria, the Republic of Finland, the Republic of Iceland, the Principality of Liechtenstein, the Kingdom of Norway and the Kingdom of Sweden" replaced by the words "the Republic of Iceland, the Principality of Liechtenstein and the Kingdom of Norway" by the 2004 EEA Enlargement Agreement (OJ No L 130, 29.4.2004, p. 3 and EEA Supplement No 23, 29.4.2004, p. 1), e.i.f. 1.5.2004.

Article 128

1.[21] Any European State becoming a member of the Community shall, and the Swiss Confederation or any European State becoming a member of EFTA may, apply to become a party to this Agreement. It shall address its application to the EEA Council.

2. The terms and conditions for such participation shall be the subject of an agreement between the Contracting Parties and the applicant State. That agreement shall be submitted for ratification or approval by all Contracting Parties in accordance with their own procedures.

Article 129

1. This Agreement is drawn up in a single original in the Danish, Dutch, English, Finnish, French, German, Greek, Icelandic, Italian, Norwegian, Portuguese, Spanish and Swedish languages, each of these texts being equally authentic.

   [22] Pursuant to the enlargements of the European Economic Area the versions of this Agreement in the Bulgarian, Czech, Estonian, Hungarian, Latvian, Lithuanian, Maltese, Polish, Romanian, Slovak and Slovenian languages shall be equally authentic.

   [23] The texts of the acts referred to in the Annexes are equally authentic in the Bulgarian, Czech, Danish, Dutch, English, Estonian, Finnish, French, German, Greek, Hungarian, Italian, Latvian, Lithuanian, Maltese, Polish, Portuguese, Romanian, Slovak, Slovenian, Spanish and Swedish languages as published in the Official Journal of the European Union and shall for the authentication thereof be drawn up in the Icelandic and Norwegian languages and published in the EEA Supplement to the Official Journal of the European Union.

2. This Agreement shall be ratified or approved by the Contracting Parties in accordance with their respective constitutional requirements.

   It shall be deposited with the General Secretariat of the Council of the European Communities by which certified copies shall be transmitted to all other Contracting Parties.

   The instruments of ratification or approval shall be deposited with the General Secretariat of the Council of the European Communities which shall notify all other Contracting Parties.

---

21 Subparagraph introduced by the Adjusting Protocol replaces former text.

22 Subparagraph inserted by the 2004 EEA Enlargement Agreement (OJ No L 130, 29.4.2004, p. 3 and EEA Supplement No 23, 29.4.2004, p. 1), e.i.f. 1.5.2004, and subsequently replaced by the 2007 EEA Enlargement Agreement (OJ No L [to be published]), provisionally applicable as of 1.8.2007, e.i.f. pending.

23 Subparagraph replaced by the 2004 EEA Enlargement Agreement (OJ No L 130, 29.4.2004, p. 3 and EEA Supplement No 23, 29.4.2004, p. 1), e.i.f. 1.5.2004, and subsequently replaced by 2007 EEA Enlargement Agreement (OJ No L [to be published]), provisionally applicable as of 1.8.2007, e.i.f. pending.

3.[24] This Agreement shall enter into force on the date and under the conditions provided for in the Protocol Adjusting the Agreement on the European Economic Area.

IN WITNESS WHEREOF the undersigned plenipotentiaries, being duly authorised thereto, have signed this Protocol.

DONE at Brussels, this seventeenth day of March in the year one thousand nine hundred and ninety-three.

24 Subparagraph introduced by the Adjusting Protocol replaces former text.

AGREEMENT BETWEEN THE EFTA STATES ON THE ESTABLISHMENT OF A SURVEILLANCE AUTHORITY AND A COURT OF JUSTICE

(OJ L 344, 31.1.1994, p. 3; and EFTA States' official gazettes)

Amended by:

1. Protocol Adjusting the Agreement between the EFTA States on the Establishment of a Surveillance Authority and a Court of Justice of 17 March 1993 (EFTA States' official gazettes).
2. Protocol amending Protocol 4 to the Agreement between the EFTA States on the Establishment of a Surveillance Authority and a Court of Justice of 24 November 1993 (EFTA States' official gazettes).
3. Agreement amending Protocol 4 to the Agreement between the EFTA States on the Establishment of a Surveillance Authority and a Court of Justice of 7 March 1994 (EFTA States' official gazettes).
4. Agreement amending Protocols 2 and 3 to the Agreement between the EFTA States on the Establishment of a Surveillance Authority and a Court of Justice of 21 March 1994 (EFTA States' official gazettes).
5. Agreement Adjusting certain Agreements between the EFTA States of 29 December 1994 (EFTA States' official gazettes).
6. Protocol Regarding the Application to Liechtenstein of Decisions and Other Measures taken under certain Agreements between the EFTA States of 18 May 1995 (EFTA States' official gazettes)
7. Decision of the Committee of Representatives of the Contracting Parties to the ESA/Court Agreement of 10 August 1996 amending Protocol 5 to the Agreement between the EFTA States on the Establishment of a Surveillance Authority and a Court of Justice (EFTA States' official gazette).
8. Agreement amending Protocol 4 to the Agreement between the EFTA States on the Establishment of a Surveillance Authority and a Court of Justice of 14 March 1997 (EFTA States' official gazettes).
9. Agreement amending Protocol 3 to the Agreement between the EFTA States on the Establishment of a Surveillance Authority and a Court of Justice of 6 March 1998 (EFTA States' official gazettes).

10. Agreement amending Protocol 4 to the Agreement between the EFTA States on the Establishment of a Surveillance Authority and a Court of Justice of 27 March 1998 (EFTA States' official gazettes).
11. Agreement amending Protocol 4 to the Agreement between the EFTA States on the Establishment of a Surveillance Authority and a Court of Justice of 17 July 1998 (EFTA States' official gazettes).
12. Decision amending Protocol 5 to the Agreement between the EFTA States on the Establishment of a Surveillance Authority and a Court of Justice of 25 March 1999 (EFTA States' official gazettes).
13. Agreement amending Protocol 4 to the Agreement between the EFTA States on the Establishment of a Surveillance Authority and a Court of Justice of 15 July 1999 (EFTA States' official gazettes).
14. Agreement amending Protocol 4 to the Agreement between the EFTA States on the Establishment of a Surveillance Authority and a Court of Justice of 11 May 2000 (EFTA States' official gazettes).
15. Agreement amending Protocol 3 on the Agreement between the EFTA States on the Establishment of a Surveillance Authority and a Court of Justice of 10 December 2001 (EFTA States' official gazettes).
16. Agreement amending Protocol 4 to the Agreement between the EFTA States on the Establishment of a Surveillance Authority and a Court of Justice of 4 June 2004 (EFTA States' official gazettes).
17. Agreement amending Protocol 4 to the Agreement between the EFTA States on the Establishment of a Surveillance Authority and a Court of Justice of 4 June 2004 – Inserting new article 13 and 22 in chapter XII of part III (EFTA States' official gazettes).
18. Agreement amending Protocol 4 to the Agreement between the EFTA states on the establishment of a surveillance authority and a court of justice of 24 September 2004 (EFTA States' official gazettes).
19. Agreement amending Protocol 4 to the Agreement between the EFTA states on the establishment of a surveillance authority and a court of justice of 3 December 2004 (EFTA States' official gazettes).
20. Agreement amending Protocol 4 to the Agreement between the EFTA states on the establishment of a surveillance authority and a court of justice of 11 March 2005 (EFTA States' official gazettes).
21. Agreement amending Protocol 4 to the Agreement between the EFTA states on the establishment of a surveillance authority and a court of justice of 10 March 2006 (EFTA States' official gazettes).
22. Agreement amending Protocol 4 to the Agreement between the EFTA states on the establishment of a surveillance authority and a court of justice of 1 February 2007 (EFTA States' official gazettes).

THE REPUBLIC OF ICELAND,
THE PRINCIPALITY OF LIECHTENSTEIN,
THE KINGDOM OF NORWAY,
[...] [1]
[...] [2]
HAVING REGARD to the EEA Agreement;

CONSIDERING that, in accordance with Article 108(1) of the EEA Agreement, the EFTA States shall establish an independent surveillance authority (EFTA Surveillance Authority) as well as create procedures similar to those existing in the European Community including procedures for ensuring the fulfilment of the obligations under the EEA Agreement and for control of the legality of acts of the EFTA Surveillance Authority regarding competition;

FURTHER CONSIDERING that, in accordance with Article 108(2) of the EEA Agreement, the EFTA States shall establish a court of justice of the EFTA States;

RECALLING the objective of the Contracting Parties to the EEA Agreement, in full deference to the independence of the courts, to arrive at and maintain a uniform interpretation and application of the EEA Agreement and those provisions of the Community legislation which are substantially reproduced in that Agreement and to arrive at an equal treatment of individuals and economic operators as regards the four freedoms and the conditions of competition;

REITERATING that the EFTA Surveillance Authority and the Commission of the European Communities shall cooperate, exchange information and consult each other on surveillance policy issues and individual cases;

CONSIDERING that the preambles to acts adopted in application of the Treaties establishing the European Economic Community and the European Coal and Steel Community shall, in so far as those acts correspond to the provisions of Protocols 1 to 4 and to the provisions of the acts corresponding to those listed in Annexes I and II to this Agreement, be relevant to the extent necessary for the proper interpretation and application of the provisions of these Protocols and Annexes;

WHEREAS in the application of Protocols 1 to 4 to this Agreement due account shall be paid to the legal and administrative practices of the Commission of the European Communities prior to the entry into force of this Agreement;

HAVE DECIDED to conclude the following Agreement:

---

1 Reference to "the Swiss Confederation" deleted by the Surveillance and Court Adjusting Protocol.
2 References to "the Republic of Austria, the Republic of Finland and the Kingdom of Sweden" deleted by the Adjusting Agreement.

PART I

Article 1

For the purposes of this Agreement:

(a) the term 'EEA Agreement' means the main part of the EEA Agreement, its Protocols and Annexes as well as the acts referred to therein;

(b) the term 'EFTA States' means the Republic of Iceland and the Kingdom of Norway and, under the conditions laid down by Article 1(2) of the Protocol Adjusting the Agreement between the EFTA States on the Establishment of a Surveillance Authority and a Court of Justice, the Principality of Liechtenstein.[3]

Article 2

The EFTA States shall take all appropriate measures, whether general or particular, to ensure fulfilment of the obligations arising out of this Agreement.

They shall abstain from any measure which could jeopardize the attainment of the objectives of this Agreement.

Article 3

1. Without prejudice to future developments of case law, the provisions of Protocols 1 to 4 and the provisions of the acts corresponding to those listed in Annexes I and II to this Agreement, in so far as they are identical in substance to corresponding rules of the Treaty establishing the European Economic Community and the Treaty establishing the European Coal and Steel Community and to acts adopted in application of these two Treaties, shall in their implementation and application be interpreted in conformity with the relevant rulings of the Court of Justice of the European Communities given prior to the date of signature of the EEA Agreement.
2. In the interpretation and application of the EEA Agreement and this Agreement, the EFTA Surveillance Authority and the EFTA Court shall pay due account to the principles laid down by the relevant rulings by the Court of Justice of the European Communities given after the date of signature of the EEA Agreement and which concern the interpretation of that Agreement or of such rules of the Treaty establishing the European Economic Community and the Treaty establishing the European Coal and Steel Community in so far as they are identical in substance to the provisions of the EEA Agreement or to the provisions of Protocols 1 to 4 and the provisions of the acts corresponding to those listed in Annexes I and II to the present Agreement.

3 Paragraph replaced by the Surveillance and Court Adjusting Protocol and subsequently replaced by the Adjusting Agreement.

PART II
THE EFTA SURVEILLANCE AUTHORITY

Article 4

An independent surveillance authority among the EFTA States, the EFTA Surveillance Authority, is hereby established.

Article 5

1. The EFTA Surveillance Authority shall, in accordance with the provisions of this Agreement and the provisions of the EEA Agreement and in order to ensure the proper functioning of the EEA Agreement:
   (a) ensure the fulfilment by the EFTA States of their obligations under the EEA Agreement and this Agreement;
   (b) ensure the application of the rules of the EEA Agreement on competition;
   (c) monitor the application of the EEA Agreement by the other Contracting Parties to that Agreement.
2. To this end, the EFTA Surveillance Authority shall:
   (a) take decisions and other measures in cases provided for in this Agreement and in the EEA Agreement;
   (b) formulate recommendations, deliver opinions and issue notices or guidelines on matters dealt with in the EEA Agreement, if that Agreement or the present Agreement expressly so provides or if the EFTA Surveillance Authority considers it necessary;
   (c) carry out cooperation, exchange of information and consultations with the Commission of the European Communities as provided for in this Agreement and the EEA Agreement;
   (d) carry out the functions which, through the application of Protocol 1 to the EEA Agreement, follow from the acts referred to in the Annexes to that Agreement, as specified in Protocol 1 to the present Agreement.

Article 6

In accordance with the provisions of this Agreement and the EEA Agreement, the EFTA Surveillance Authority may, in carrying out the duties assigned to it, request all the necessary information from the Governments and competent authorities of the EFTA States and from undertakings and associations of undertakings.

Article 7

The EFTA Surveillance Authority shall consist of three members, who shall be chosen on the grounds of their general competence and whose independence is beyond doubt.[4]

---

4 Paragraph replaced by the Surveillance and Court Adjusting Protocol and subsequently replaced by the Adjusting Agreement.

Save as in the circumstances set out in the third paragraph of Article 9 at least two of the three members shall be nationals of the EFTA States.[5]

Article 8

The members of the EFTA Surveillance Authority shall be completely independent in the performance of their duties. They shall neither seek nor take instructions from any Government or other body. They shall refrain from any action incompatible with their duties. Each EFTA State undertakes to respect this principle and not to seek to influence the members of the EFTA Surveillance Authority in the performance of their tasks.

The members of the EFTA Surveillance Authority shall not, during their term of office, engage in any other occupation, whether gainful or not.

When entering upon their duties they shall give a solemn undertaking that, both during and after their term of office, they will respect the obligations arising therefrom and in particular their duty to behave with integrity and discretion as regards the acceptance, after they have ceased to hold office, of certain appointments or benefits. In the event of any breach of these obligations, the EFTA Court may, on application by the EFTA Surveillance Authority, rule that the member concerned be, according to the circumstances, either compulsorily retired or deprived of his right to a pension or other benefits in its stead.

Article 9

The members of the EFTA Surveillance Authority shall be appointed by common accord of the Governments of the EFTA States.

Their term of office shall be four years. It shall be renewable.

[6]In case one of the members, in the opinion of the two other members, is disqualified from acting in a particular case, the two other members shall agree on a person to replace him chosen from the list established by common accord by the Governments of the EFTA States. If they cannot agree that person shall be chosen from the list by lot by the President of the EFTA Court. With regard to a member chosen in this way the rules applicable to regular members shall apply mutatis mutandis. In any case Article 8, second paragraph, and Article 10 shall not apply.

Article 10

Apart from normal replacement, or death, the duties of a member of the EFTA Surveillance Authority shall end when he resigns or is compulsorily retired. The vacancy thus caused shall be filled for the remainder of the member's term of office.

Article 11

If a member of the EFTA Surveillance Authority no longer fulfils the conditions required for the performance of his duties or if he has been guilty of serious misconduct,

---

5 Paragraph replaced by the Adjusting Agreement.

6 Paragraph added by the Adjusting Agreement.

the EFTA Court may, on application by the EFTA Surveillance Authority, compulsorily retire him.

Article 12
The President of the EFTA Surveillance Authority shall be appointed from among its members for a period of two years by common accord of the Governments of the EFTA States.

Article 13
The EFTA Surveillance Authority shall adopt its own rules of procedure.

Article 14
The EFTA Surveillance Authority shall appoint officials and other servants to enable it to function.
The EFTA Surveillance Authority may consult experts or decide to set up such committees and other bodies as it considers necessary to assist it in accomplishing its tasks.
In the performance of their duties, officials and other servants of the EFTA Surveillance Authority shall neither seek nor accept instructions from any Government or from any body external to the EFTA Surveillance Authority.
Members of the EFTA Surveillance Authority, officials and other servants thereof as well as members of committees shall be required, even after their duties have ceased, not to disclose information of the kind covered by the obligation of professional secrecy, in particular information about undertakings, their business relations or their cost components.

Article 15
The EFTA Surveillance Authority shall act by majority of its Members. [...] [7]
The rules of procedure shall determine the quorum.

Article 16
Decisions of the EFTA Surveillance Authority shall state the reasons on which they are based.

Article 17
Save as otherwise provided in this Agreement or in the EEA Agreement, decisions of the EFTA Surveillance Authority shall be notified to those to whom they are addressed and shall take effect upon such notification.

Article 18
Decisions of the EFTA Surveillance Authority shall be published in accordance with the provisions of this Agreement and of the EEA Agreement.

---

7 Second sentence deleted by the Adjusting Agreement.

Article 19
Decisions of the EFTA Surveillance Authority which impose a pecuniary obligation on persons other than States, shall be enforceable in accordance with Article 110 of the EEA Agreement.

Article 20
Individuals and economic operators shall be entitled to address and be addressed by the EFTA Surveillance Authority in any official language of the EFTA States and the European Communities as regards notifications, applications and complaints. This shall also cover all instances of a proceeding, whether it be opened on notification, application or complaint or ex officio by the EFTA Surveillance Authority.

Article 21
The EFTA Surveillance Authority shall annually publish a general report on its activities.

PART III
THE EFTA STATES' FULFILMENT OF THEIR OBLIGATIONS UNDER THE EEA AGREEMENT AND THE PRESENT AGREEMENT

Article 22
In order to ensure the proper application of the EEA Agreement, the EFTA Surveillance Authority shall monitor the application of the provisions of the EEA Agreement and of the present Agreement by the EFTA States.

Article 23
The EFTA Surveillance Authority shall, in accordance with Articles 22 and 37 of this Agreement and Articles 65(1) and 109 of, and Annex XVI to, the EEA Agreement as well as subject to the provisions contained in Protocol 2 to the present Agreement, ensure that the provisions of the EEA Agreement concerning procurement are applied by the EFTA States.

Article 24
The EFTA Surveillance Authority shall, in accordance with Articles 49, 61 to 64 and 109 of, and Protocols 14, 26, 27, and Annexes XIII, section I(iv), and XV to, the EEA Agreement, as well as subject to the provisions contained in Protocol 3 to the present Agreement, give effect to the provisions of the EEA Agreement concerning State aid as well as ensure that those provisions are applied by the EFTA States.
In application of Article 5(2)(b), the EFTA Surveillance Authority shall, in particular, upon the entry into force of this Agreement, adopt acts corresponding to those listed in Annex I.

Article 25
The EFTA Surveillance Authority shall, in accordance with Articles 53 to 60 and 109 of, and Protocols 21 to 25 and Annex XIV to, the EEA Agreement, as well as subject to the provisions contained in Protocol 4 to the present Agreement, give effect to the provisions of the EEA Agreement relating to the implementation of the competition rules applicable to undertakings as well as ensure that those provisions are applied.
In application of Article 5(2)(b), the EFTA Surveillance Authority shall, in particular, upon the entry into force of this Agreement, adopt acts corresponding to those listed in Annex II.

Article 26
Provisions governing the cooperation, exchange of information and consultation between the EFTA Surveillance Authority and the Commission of the European Communities concerning the application of the EEA Agreement are laid down in Article 109 as well as in Articles 58 and 62(2) of, and Protocols 1, 23, 24, and 27 to, the EEA Agreement.

PART IV
THE EFTA COURT

Article 27
A court of justice of the EFTA States, hereinafter referred to as the EFTA Court, is hereby established. It shall function in accordance with the provisions of this Agreement and of the EEA Agreement.

Article 28
The EFTA Court shall consist of three judges.[8]

Article 29
Decisions of the Court shall be valid only when all its members are sitting in the deliberations.[9]

Article 30
The Judges shall be chosen from persons whose independence is beyond doubt and who possess the qualifications required for appointment to the highest judicial offices in their respective countries or who are jurisconsults of recognized competence. They shall be appointed by common accord of the Governments of the EFTA States for a term of six years.

8 Text replaced by the Surveillance and Court Adjusting Protocol and subsequently replaced by the Adjusting Agreement.
9 Text replaced by the Surveillance and Court Adjusting Protocol and subsequently replaced by the Adjusting Agreement.

Retiring Judges shall be eligible for reappointment.[10]
The Judges shall elect the President of the EFTA Court from among their number for a term of three years. He may be re-elected.[11]
In case one of the Judges, in the opinion of the two other Judges, is disqualified from acting in a particular case, the two other Judges shall agree on a person to replace him chosen from a list established by common accord by the Governments of the EFTA States. If they cannot agree that person shall be chosen from the list by lot by the President. With regard to a Judge chosen in this way the rules applicable to regular Judges shall apply mutatis mutandis. In any case Article 4, second paragraph, and Article 13, of Protocol 5 shall not apply.[12]

Article 31
If the EFTA Surveillance Authority considers that an EFTA State has failed to fulfil an obligation under the EEA Agreement or of this Agreement, it shall, unless otherwise provided for in this Agreement, deliver a reasoned opinion on the matter after giving the State concerned the opportunity to submit its observations.
If the State concerned does not comply with the opinion within the period laid down by the EFTA Surveillance Authority, the latter may bring the matter before the EFTA Court.

Article 32
The EFTA Court shall have jurisdiction in actions concerning the settlement of disputes between two or more EFTA States regarding the interpretation or application of the EEA Agreement, the Agreement on a Standing Committee of the EFTA States or the present Agreement.

Article 33
The EFTA States concerned shall take the necessary measures to comply with the judgments of the EFTA Court.

Article 34
The EFTA Court shall have jurisdiction to give advisory opinions on the interpretation of the EEA Agreement.
Where such a question is raised before any court or tribunal in an EFTA State, that court or tribunal may, if it considers it necessary to enable it to give judgment, request the EFTA Court to give such an opinion.
An EFTA State may in its internal legislation limit the right to request such an advisory opinion to courts and tribunals against whose decisions there is no judicial remedy under national law.

---

10 Paragraph replaced by the Surveillance and Court Adjusting Protocol and subsequently replaced by the Adjusting Agreement.
11 Paragraph replaced by the Adjusting Agreement.
12 Paragraph replaced by the Adjusting Agreement.

Article 35

The EFTA Court shall have unlimited jurisdiction in regard to penalties imposed by the EFTA Surveillance Authority.

Article 36

The EFTA Court shall have jurisdiction in actions brought by an EFTA State against a decision of the EFTA Surveillance Authority on grounds of lack of competence, infringement of an essential procedural requirement, or infringement of this Agreement, of the EEA Agreement or of any rule of law relating to their application, or misuse of powers.

Any natural or legal person may, under the same conditions, institute proceedings before the EFTA Court against a decision of the EFTA Surveillance Authority addressed to that person or against a decision addressed to another person, if it is of direct and individual concern to the former.

The proceedings provided for in this Article shall be instituted within two months of the publication of the measure, or of its notification to the plaintiff, or, in the absence thereof, of the day on which it came to the knowledge of the latter, as the case may be.

If the action is well founded the decision of the EFTA Surveillance Authority shall be declared void.

Article 37

Should the EFTA Surveillance Authority, in infringement of this Agreement or the provisions of the EEA Agreement, fail to act, an EFTA State may bring an action before the EFTA Court to have the infringement established.

The action shall be admissible only if the EFTA Surveillance Authority has first been called upon to act. If, within two months of being so called upon, the EFTA Surveillance Authority has not defined its position, the action may be brought within a further period of two months.

Any natural or legal person may, under the conditions laid down in the preceding paragraphs, complain to the EFTA Court that the EFTA Surveillance Authority has failed to address to that person any decision.

Article 38

If a decision of the EFTA Surveillance Authority has been declared void or if it has been established that the EFTA Surveillance Authority, in infringement of this Agreement or of the provisions of the EEA Agreement, has failed to act, the EFTA Surveillance Authority shall take the necessary measures to comply with the judgment.

This obligation shall not affect any obligation which may result from the application of Article 46, second paragraph.

Article 39

Save as otherwise provided for in Protocol 7 to this Agreement, the EFTA Court shall have jurisdiction in actions against the EFTA Surveillance Authority relating to compensation for damage provided for in Article 46, second paragraph.

Article 40
Actions brought before the EFTA Court shall not have suspensory effect. The EFTA Court may, however, if it considers that circumstances so require, order that application of the contested act be suspended.

Article 41
The EFTA Court may in any case before it prescribe any necessary interim measures.

PART V
GENERAL AND FINAL PROVISIONS

Article 42
The Protocols and Annexes to this Agreement shall form an integral part thereof.

Article 43
1. The Statute of the EFTA Court is laid down in Protocol 5 to this Agreement.
2. The EFTA Court shall adopt its rules of procedure to be approved by the Governments of the EFTA States by common accord.

Article 44
1. The legal capacity, privileges and immunities to be recognized and granted by the EFTA States in connection with the EFTA Surveillance Authority and the EFTA Court are laid down in Protocols 6 and 7 to this Agreement, respectively.
2. The EFTA Surveillance Authority and the EFTA Court, respectively, may conclude with the Government of the States in whose territory their seats are situated an agreement relating to the privileges and immunities to be recognized and granted in connection with it.

Article 45
The seat of the EFTA Surveillance Authority and the EFTA Court, respectively, shall be determined by common accord of the Governments of the EFTA States.

Article 46
The contractual liability of the EFTA Surveillance Authority shall be governed by the law applicable to the contract in question.
In the case of non-contractual liability, the EFTA Surveillance Authority shall, in accordance with the general principles of law, make good any damage caused by it, or by its servants, in the performance of its duties.

Article 47
The Governments of the EFTA States shall, on a proposal from the EFTA Surveillance Authority and after consulting a committee consisting of the members of Parliament

of the EFTA States who are members of the EEA Joint Parliamentary Committee, each year before 1 January by common accord establish a budget for the coming year and the apportionment of those expenses between the EFTA States.
The EFTA Surveillance Authority shall be consulted before a decision modifying or amending its proposal for a budget is adopted.

Article 48
The Governments of the EFTA States shall, on a proposal from the EFTA Court, each year before 1 January by common accord establish a budget for the EFTA Court for the coming year and the apportionment of those expenses between them.

Article 49
The Governments of the EFTA States may, unless otherwise provided in this Agreement, on a proposal from or after hearing the EFTA Surveillance Authority, by common accord amend the main Agreement as well as Protocols 1 to 4 and 6 and 7. Such an amendment shall be submitted to the EFTA States for acceptance and shall enter into force provided it is approved by all EFTA States. Instruments of acceptance shall be deposited with the Government of Sweden which shall notify all other EFTA States.

Article 50
1. Any EFTA State which withdraws from the EEA Agreement shall ipso facto cease to be a Party to the present Agreement on the same day as that withdrawal takes effect.
2. Any EFTA State which accedes to the European Community shall ipso facto cease to be a Party to the present Agreement on the same day as that accession takes effect.
3. The Governments of the remaining EFTA States shall, by common accord, decide on the necessary amendments to be made to the present Agreement.

Article 51
Any EFTA State acceding to the EEA Agreement shall accede to the present Agreement on such terms and conditions as may be laid down by common accord by the EFTA States. The instrument of accession shall be deposited with the Government of Sweden which shall notify the other EFTA States.

Article 52
The EFTA States shall communicate to the EFTA Surveillance Authority the measures taken for the implementation of this Agreement.

Article 53
1. This Agreement, drawn up in a single copy and authentic in the English language, shall be ratified by the Contracting Parties in accordance with their respective constitutional requirements.

Before the entry into force of this Agreement, it shall also be drawn up and authenticated in Finnish, French, German, Icelandic, Italian, Norwegian and Swedish.

2. This Agreement shall be deposited with the Government of Sweden which shall transmit a certified copy to each EFTA State.
   The instruments of ratification shall be deposited with the Government of Sweden which shall notify all other EFTA States.
3. This Agreement shall enter into force on the date and under the conditions provided for in the Protocol Adjusting the Agreement between the EFTA States on the Establishment of a Surveillance Authority and a Court of Justice.[13]

IN WITNESS WHEREOF the undersigned plenipotentiaries, being duly authorized thereto, have signed the present Agreement.

DONE at Oporto, this 2nd day of May 1992, in a single authentic copy in the English language which shall be deposited with the Government of Sweden. The Depositary shall transmit certified copies to all Signatory States and States acceding to this Agreement.

13 Paragraph replaced by the Surveillance and Court Adjusting Protocol.

Table of Abbreviations

A

AG	Advocate General
Am. J. Int'l L.	American Journal of International Law
ATF	Recueil des Arrêts du Tribunal Fédéral Suisse

C

Cal. L. Rev.	California Law Review
cf.	confer
CFI	Court of First Instance
Chi. J. Int'l L.	Chicago Journal of International Law
CJEL	Columbia Journal of European Law
CML Rev.	Common Market Law Review

D

dec.	decision
doc.	document

E

E.B.L.Rev.	European Business Law Review
EBOA	EFTA Board of Auditors
EC	European Community, Treaty establishing the European Community
ECHR	European Court of Human Rights
ECJ	European Court of Justice, Court of Justice of the European Union
ECR	European Court Reports
ed(s).	editor(s)/edition(s)
EEA	European Economic Area, European Economic Area Agreement
EEC	European Economic Community
EFTA	European Free Trade Association
e.g.	exempli gratia
ELR	European Law Reporter
ESA	EFTA Surveillance Authority
Eur. L. Rev.	European Law Review
etc.	et cetera
et seq.	et sequens
EU	European Union
EWR	Europäischer Wirtschaftsraum
EWS	Europäisches Wirtschafts- und Steuerrecht

F

FIDE	Fédération Internationale pour le Droit Européen
FSCS	Financial Services Compensation Scheme
FTA	Free Trade Agreement

G

GLE	Group of Legal Experts
GRUR Int.	Gewerblicher Rechtsschutz und Urheberrecht, Internationaler Teil

I

ICJ	International Court of Justice
ICN	International Competition Network
i.e.	id est
IP	Intellectual Property

J

J. Transnat'l L. & Pol.	Journal of Transnational Law and Policy

L

LES	Amtliche Liechtensteinische Entscheidungssammlung
loc. cit.	loco citato

N

No	number
NJA	Nytt Juridiskt Arkiv
nyr.	not yet reported
N.Y.U. J. Int'l L. & Pol.	New York University Journal of International Law and Policy
NZZ	Neue Zürcher Zeitung

R

RAJ	Regulatory Affair Journal (Pharma)
Rt.	(Norsk) Retstidende

S

SCA	Surveillance and Court Agreement
sc.	Scilicet
StGH	Staatsgerichtshof (Liechtenstein)
St. John's L. Rev.	St. John's Law Review
SPC	Summary of Product Characteristics

T

Tax L. Rev.	Tax Law Review
w	Treaty on European Union
Tex. Int'l L.J.	Texas International Law Journal
TFEU	Treaty on the Functioning of the European Union
TRIPS	Agreement on Trade-Related Aspects of Intellectual Property Rights
Tulsa L.J	Tulsa Law Journal

U

U.K.	United Kingdom
U.S.	United States

V

v / vs	versus
Va. J. Int'l L.	Virginia Journal of International Law
VAT	value added tax
VGH	Verwaltungsgerichtshof (Liechtenstein)
Vol.	volume

W

WTO	World Trade Organization

Z

ZBl	Schweizerisches Zentralblatt für Staats- und Verwaltungsrecht

Selected Bibliography

Alberto Alemanno, Trade in Food. Regulatory and Judicial Approaches in the EC and the WTO, London 2007.

Knut Almestad, The duties of co-operation of national authorities and the Community institutions under Article 10 (ex Article 5) of the Treaty of Rome: the EEA variant, FIDE: XIX congress. Vol. I [2000], 427.

Chittharanjan F. Amerasinghe, Judges of the International Court of Justice – Election and Qualifications, [2001] 14 Leiden Journal of International Law, 335.

Héctor Armengod/Laura Melusine Baudenbacher, The Repackaging of Pharmaceutical Products and Parallel Trade in the EU, RAJ Pharma December 2009, 783.

Mariano J. Aznar-Gómez, Article 2, in: Andreas Zimmermann/Christian Tomuschat/Karin Oellers-Frahm (eds.), The Statute of the International Court of Justice. A Commentary, Oxford 2006.

Andreas Batliner, Die Anwendung des EWR-Rechts durch liechtensteinische Gerichte – Erfahrungen eines Richters, Liechtensteinische Juristen-Zeitung 4/04, 139.

Carl Baudenbacher, Between Homogeneity and Independence: The Legal Position of the EFTA Court in the European Economic Area, [1997] 3 CJEL, 169.

Carl Baudenbacher, Der EFTA-Gerichtshof, das EWR-Abkommen und die Fortentwicklung des EG-Vertrags, Festschrift für Herbert Batliner, Vaduz 2004, 97.

Carl Baudenbacher, Der Finanzplatz Schweiz im Angesicht der Reziprozitätspolitik der EU, European Law Reporter [2006] 398 et seq.

Carl Baudenbacher, EFTA Court – Legal framework and case law, 3rd ed., Luxembourg 2008.

Carl Baudenbacher, Erla María: Viðurkennd réttarsköpun dómstóla, [2007] Tímariti lögfræðinga, 147.

Carl Baudenbacher, Governments before the EFTA Court, in: Festskrift til Claus Gulmann, Kopenhagen 2006, 23.

Carl Baudenbacher, If Not State Liability, Then What? Reflections Ten Years After the EFTA Court's Sveinbjörnsdóttir Ruling, [2009] 10 Chi. J. Int'l L. 333.

Carl Baudenbacher, Some Considerations on the Dialogue between High Courts, in: Baudenbacher (ed.), Dispute Resolution, Stuttgart 2009, 175.

Carl Baudenbacher, Wirtschafts-, schuld- und verfahrensrechtliche Grundprobleme der Allgemeinen Geschäftsbedingungen, Zurich 1983.

Eyal Benvenisti, Reclaiming Democracy: The Strategic Uses of Foreign and International Law by National Courts, 102 Am. J. Int'l L. 241, 264 f. [2008].

Ulf Bernitz, European Law in Sweden, Stockholm 2002.

Ulf Bernitz, The Application of EEA Law in Sweden, in: Mario Monti, Prinz Nikolaus von und zu Liechtenstein, Bo Vesterdorf, Jay Westbrook (eds.), Economic Law and Justice in Times of Globalisation, Festschrift for Carl Baudenbacher, Baden-Baden/Berne/Vienna 2007, 29.

Ulf Bernitz, The EEC-EFTA Free Trade Agreements with Special Reference to the Position of Sweden and the other Scandinavian EFTA Countries, [1986] CMLR, 567.

Davíð Þór Björgvinsson, EES-réttur og landsréttur [Reykjavík, Bókaútgáfan Codex, 2006].

Joachim Bornkamm, The German Supreme Court: An Actor in the Global Conversation of High Courts, 39 Tex. Int'l L.J. 415 (2004).

Marco Bronckers, Exceptions to Liberal Trade in Foodstuffs: The Precautionary Approach and Collective Preferences, in: Carl Baudenbacher/Per Tresselt/Thorgeir Örlygsson (eds.), The EFTA Court Ten Years On, Oxford and Portland, Oregon 2005, 105.

L. Neville Brown/Tom Kennedy, The Court of Justice of the European Communities, 5th ed., London 2000.

Thomas Bruha, Is the EEA an Internal Market?, in: Peter-Christian Müller-Graff and Erling Selvig (eds.), EEA-EU Relations, Berlin 1999, 97.

Henrik Bull, European Law and Norwegian Courts, in: Mueller-Graff/Selvig (eds.), The Approach to European Law in Germany and Norway, Berlin 2004, 95.

Henrik Bull, The EEA Agreement and Norwegian Law, E.B.L.Rev. 1994, 291.

Dirk Buschle, The Free Movement of Capital in the EEA – A *Lehrstück* in Homogeneity, in: Mario Monti, Prinz Nikolaus von und zu Liechtenstein, Bo Vesterdorf/Jay Westbrook/Luzius Wildhaber (eds.), Economic Law and Justice in Times of Globalisation, Festschrift for Carl Baudenbacher, Baden-Baden/Berne/Vienna 2007, 75.

Eleanor Cashin Ritaine / Eva Lein, La notion de proportionnalité appliquée au droit des jeux de hasard – Les cas Placanica et Autorité de surveillance de l'AELE / Royaume de Norvège, Schweizerisches Jahrbuch für Europarecht = Annuaire suisse de droit européen 2006 / 2007 [2007] 355.

Per Christiansen, The EFTA Court, [1997] 22 European Law Review, 539.

Rebecca S. Eisenberg, Noncompliance, Nonenforcement, Nonproblem? Rethinking the Anticommons in Biomedical Research Patent Law on Perspective, Institute for Intellectual Property & Information, Houston Law Review Symposium Article, 45 Hous. L. Rev. 1059 [2008].

John Forman, The EEA Agreement Five Years On: Dynamic Homogeneity in Practice and Its Implementation by the Two EEA Courts, [1999] CML Rev. 751, 753.

Walter van Gerven, The Genesis of EEA Law and the Principles of Primacy and Direct Effect, [1992–93] 16 Fordham International Law Journal, 955.

Georg Gorton, Bestätigung der Staatshaftungsrechtsprechung des EFTA-Gerichtshofs, 7-8 European Law Reporter, 260, 263 [2002].

Claire L'Heureux-Dubé, The Importance of Dialogue: Globalization and the International Impact of the Rehnquist Court, [1998] 34 Tulsa L.J. 15.

Peter-Christian Müller-Graff, The Impact of Climate, Geography and Other Non-Legal Factors on EC law and EEA law, in: Carl Baudenbacher / Per Tresselt / Thorgeir Örlygsson, (eds.), The EFTA Court Ten Years On, Oxford and Portland, Oregon, [2005] 55.

Olivier Jacot-Guillarmod, Federal Tribunal (Switzerland), Decision of 25 January 1979, *Bosshard Partners Intertrading AG v Sunlight AG*. AFT 105 II 49, [1981] CMLRev., 427.

Ulrich Haltern, Europarecht. Dogmatik im Kontext, 2. Aufl., Tübingen 2007.

Kurt Herndl, Der EFTA-Gerichtshof und Österreich – ein Beispiel für nützliche Zusammenarbeit?, Afmælisrit Thor Vilhjálmsson, Reykjavík 2000, 247.

Walter Hellerstein / Georg W. Kofler / Ruth Mason, Constitutional Restraints on Corporate Tax Integration, Symposium on Corporate Tax Policy in the European Union, 62 Tax L. Rev. 1 [2008].

Bernhard Hofstötter, Rechtsfehlerhafte Abweisung einer EWR-Staatshaftungsklage als judikatives Unrecht?: (Urteil des Obersten Gerichtshofs vom 7. Dezember 2006 [CO.2004.2-25]), Jus & News Jan 2007, 33.

Keenan D. Kmiec, The Origin and Current Meanings of "Judicial Activism", 92 California Law Review, 1441 (2004).

Pieter Jan Kuijper/Marco Bronckers, WTO Law in the European Court of Justice, [2005] CML Rev., 1313, 1317 et seq.

Brian Leitner, American Legal Realism, The University of Texas School of Law, Public Law and Legal Theory Research Paper No. 042, October 2002.

Skúli Magnússon, Málskot ákvarðana um að leita ráðgefandi álits EFTA-dómstólsins frá sjónarhóli EES-réttar, Úlfljótur, 1. ed. [2009], 5.

Franz Marhold, St.Galler Europarechtsbriefe EU B 1997, 162.

Elvira Méndez-Pinedo, EC and EEA Law; A Comparative Study of the Effectiveness of European Law, [2009] Groningen.

Laura Molinari, The Effect of the Kalanke Decision on the European Union: A Decision With Teeth, But Little Bite, 71 St. John's L. Rev. 591.

Jonas Myhre, Parallel imports and "co-branding" of pharmaceuticals – analysis and comments, [2008] Nordiskt Immateriellt Rättsskydd, 388.

Sven Norberg, Disputes in Intergovernmental Economic Relations of a Traditional Character and in those with Supranational Mechanisms, Respectively, in: Carl Baudenbacher, (ed.), Dispute Resolution, Stuttgart 2009, 43.

Sven Norberg, Perspectives on the Future Development of the EEA Agreement, in: Afmaelisrit Thór Vilhjálmsson, Reykjavík 2000, 367.

Thorgeir Örlygsson, Iceland and the EFTA Court, Twelve Years of Experience, in: Mario Monti, Prinz Nikolaus von und zu Liechtenstein, Bo Vesterdorf, Jay Westbrook, (eds.), Economic Law and Justice in Times of Globalisation, Festschrift for Carl Baudenbacher, Baden-Baden/Berne/Vienna 2007, 225.

Vlad Perju, Reason and Authority in the European Court of Justice, [2009] 49 Va. J. Int'l L. 307.

Louis-Edmond Pettiti, Independence of International Judges, in: Shimon Shetreet/Jules Dechênes, (eds.), Judicial Independence, Dordrecht/Boston/Lancaster 1985, 496.

Simon Planzer, Liga Portuguesa – the ECJ and its Mysterious Ways of Reasoning, [2009] European Law Reporter, 368 et seq.

Hjalte Rasmussen, On Law and Policy in the European Court of Justice, Dordrecht 1986.

Cesare P. Romano, The Proliferation of International Judicial Bodies: The Pieces of the Puzzle, 31 N.Y.U. J. Int'l L. & Pol. 709 (1999).

Allan Rosas, Methods of Interpretation – Judicial Dialogue, in: Carl Baudenbacher/Erhard Busek (eds.), The Role of International Courts, Heidelberg 2008, 185.

Henry G. Schermers, The Direct Application of Treaties with Third States: Note Concerning the Polydor and Pabst Cases, [1982] CMLRev. 563.

Henry G. Schermers, The International Court of Justice in Relation to Other Courts, in: Sam Muller/David Raič/Hanna Thuránszky (eds.), The International Court of Justice: its Future Role After Fifty Years, Editorial Introduction, The Hague Boston London 1997, 261.

Walter R. Schluep, Was ist Wirtschaftsrecht?, Festschrift für Walter Hug, Berne 1968, 25.

Fredrik Sejersted, Between sovereignty and supranationalism in the EEA context, in: Peter-Christian Müller-Graff and Erling Selvig (eds.), The European Economic Area: Norway's basic status in the legal construction of Europe, Berlin 1997.

Constanze Semmelmann, Staatshaftung in Liechtenstein – ein Sonderweg im EWR?: (Fürstlicher Oberster Gerichtshof Liechtenstein, Urteil vom 7. Dezember 2006, CO.2004.2-25.), [1997] 4 European Law Reporter, 131.

Leif Sevón, Primacy and Direct Effect in the EEA. Some Reflections, in: Liber Amicorum Ole Due, Copenhagen 1994, 339.

Leif Sevón and *Martin Johansson*, The protection of the rights of individuals under the EEA Agreement, [1999] 24 European Law Review, 380.

Vassilios Skouris, The ECJ and the EFTA Court under the EEA Agreement: A Paradigm for International Cooperation between Judicial Institutions, in: Carl Baudenbacher/Per Tresselt/Thorgeir Örlygsson (eds.), The EFTA Court Ten Years On, Oxford and Portland, Oregon, [2005] 123 et seq.

Anne-Marie Slaughter, Judicial Globalization, [2000] 40 Va. J. Int'l L. 1103.

Marco M. Slotboom, Do public health measures receive similar treatment in European Community and World Trade Organization law?, [2003] Journal of World Trade 37(3), 553.

Ole Spiermann, The Other Side of the Story: An Unpopular Essay on the Making of the European Community Legal Order, [1999] European Journal of International Law Vol. 10 No. 4, 763.

Stefán Már Stefánsson, State Liability in Community Law and EEA Law, in: Carl Baudenbacher/Per Tresselt/Thorgeir Örlygsson (eds.), The EFTA Court Ten Years On, Oxford and Portland, Oregon, [2005], 145.

Ernst Steindorff, Politik des Gesetzes als Auslegungsmaßstab im Wirtschaftsrecht, Festschrift for Karl Larenz, Munich 1973, 217.

John Temple Lang, The Duties of National Courts Under Community Constitutional Law, [1997] 22 Eur. L. Rev. 3.

John Temple Lang, The Importance of the EFTA Court, in: Porritt, J. (ed.), European Current Law, March 2006, xi–xiv.

Christiaan Timmermans, Creative Homogeneity, in: Martin Johansson/Nils Wahl/Ulf Bernitz (eds.), A European for all seasons: Liber Amicorum in Honour of Sven Norberg, Brussels 2006, 471.

Christa Tobler, Die Fidium Finanz-Entscheidung des EuGH: ein Vorbote der Luxemburger Rechtsprechung zum bilateralen Recht?, Schweizerische Zeitschrift für internationales und europäisches Recht [2006], 397 et seq.

Bo Vesterdorf, EFTA Court 10th Anniversary, in: Carl Baudenbacher/Per Tresselt/Thorgeir Örlygsson (eds.), The EFTA Court Ten Years On, Oxford and Portland, Oregon [2005], 187.

Author

Prof. Dr. Carl Baudenbacher has been a Judge of the EFTA Court since 1995. In 2003 he was elected President of the Court. Since 1990 he has also been a Director of the University of St. Gallen's Institute of European and International Law. In the latter capacity, he is the Chairman of the St. Gallen International Competition Law Forum ICF and of the St. Gallen International Dispute Resolution Conference. Apart for his ample research in business and economic law, President Baudenbacher has always taken a keen interest in the relation between law and politics in international justice, a curiosity he further developed during his years as a permanent Visiting Professor at the University of Texas School of Law. The present book is based on lectures the author gave at the University of Iceland School of Law in 2009. Its aim is to explain the working and the case law of the EFTA Court in view of its embeddedness in the institutional framework of the Agreement on the European Economic Area. Although Europe is a special case with regard to the judicialisation of law, Baudenbacher's insight and his conclusions may contribute to a better understanding of the functioning of international courts in general.